Man in Perspective:
An Introduction to
Cultural Anthropology

Consulting Editor:

John Fischer

Tulane University

Cara E. Richards

Transylvania University

Man in Perspective:

An Introduction
to Cultural
Anthropology

 Random House · New York

Library of Congress Cataloging in Publication Data
Richards, Cara Elizabeth, 1927–
    Man in perspective.
    Bibliography: p.
    1. Ethnology. I. Title.
GN315.R46   301.2   79–37632
ISBN 0–394–31061–6

Manufactured in the United States of America by
The Kingsport Press, Inc., Kingsport, Tenn.

Typography by Andrea Clark
Cover design by Hermann Strohbach

First Edition
987654321

To Elmer Lawson
who is responsible for
my writing this book

Acknowledgments

Many teachers, colleagues, friends, relatives, and casual acquaintances have influenced the contents of this book both directly and indirectly. Since it is impossible to list them all, I can only acknowledge grateful awareness of their contributions.

Specifically, I want to thank Ray Ware, Professor of Economics at Transylvania University, who patiently read each chapter and made invaluable suggestions. I also want to thank Gregory Russell who chased down elusive references and did the initial preparation of the bibliography, glossary, and index. Marilyn Murphey typed the manuscript and Anne Sullivan assisted with proofreading.

I also want to thank John Fischer whose thoughtful criticism forced me to rethink some passages and expand others. Of course, nothing could have been accomplished without the editors, Susan Gilbert and Hugh Treadwell, of Random House, who have been very patient with me.

Finally, I want to express my gratitude to Richard Honey of Transylvania University, Robert J. Smith of Cornell University, and the students who read portions of the manuscript and gave support, encouragement, and suggestions.

C. E. R.

Lexington, Kentucky
December 1971

Foreword

This is a new kind of introduction to cultural anthropology. It combines the advantages of a unified text and a collection of readings. Each chapter begins with a substantial excerpt describing some particular human culture, giving the reader a series of vivid and concrete images that are used to illustrate the author's conceptual and theoretical discussion. The introduction of excerpts from a variety of authors and cultures holds the reader's attention and adds meaning to the theoretical writings, which at a more abstract level reflect a single, unified point of view for the entire book.

Many scholars who write textbooks succumb to the temptation of trying to dazzle their colleagues with their erudition and originality. They are likely to spend too much time in passing judgment on controversies of the moment or in piling up obscure documentation of minor points when they should be setting forth basic concepts and theories that are taken for granted by the specialist but that remain to be absorbed by the outsider. Professor Richards, however, has written a textbook primarily for beginning students and their teachers. She has carefully selected her material to present fundamental concepts and she has expressed herself clearly and consistently. Technical terms have been chosen for their importance and clearly defined on first use. The excerpts have been chosen for their inherent interest as well as for their theoretical relevance. All this material has been rigorously pruned to fit into a book that is of a size easily mastered during a semester's or quarter's course in introductory cultural anthropology.

The selective judgment that Professor Richards exhibits is possible only from a thoroughly informed, critical scholar and experienced teacher. The reader venturing into anthropology for the first time may be assured that this book is as sound and mature an introduction to the field as it is readable.

Laymen often think of anthropology as being concerned only with strange, faraway, and unimportant cultures. Yet the reader will discover that some of Professor Richards' descriptive excerpts are written by members of American culture about themselves and their own society. Certainly most cultural anthropologists intend that their concepts and generalizations should hold for all known cultures, modern as well as ancient, their own as well as foreign. The following writings on American culture help demonstrate this universality of anthropology's sphere of interest. They also demonstrate to today's urban and suburban students how American culture has changed from its largely rural backgrounds of a few generations ago. And the use of these "different" American materials can serve as a bridge for the student to the understanding and appreciation of the more alien cultures that are still the subject of much anthropological research, which we all need to understand more deeply in these days of growing international and intercultural communication.

J. L. FISCHER

New Orleans
December 1971

Contents

Introduction

In speaking of "culture" we have reference to the conventional understandings, manifest in act and artifact, that characterize societies. . . . Still more concretely we speak of culture, as did Tylor, as knowledge, belief, art, law, and custom. . . . the quality of organization among the conveniently separable elements of the whole of a culture is probably a universal feature of culture and may be added to the definition: culture is an organization of conventional understandings manifest in act and artifact (Redfield 1941:132–133).

This quotation from Redfield sets forth the main characteristics of the primary and basic concept of the field of cultural anthropology —the concept of culture. Culture consists of ideas, organized into a pattern, learned primarily from other people, and shared with other people. Culture cannot be studied directly, since it is ideational, but has to be inferred from the observable data. The description of a culture, therefore, is a construct of the analyzer, based on his observations of behavior (both physical and verbal) and of the material results of behavior—the artifacts of a society.

As we look at human groups the world over we see that . . . all the activities in which they engage can be shown to function in the final analysis (1) to maintain the biologic functioning of the group members; (2) to reproduce new members of the group; (3) to socialize new members into functioning adults; (4) to produce and distribute goods and services necessary to life; (5) to maintain order within the group, and between itself and outsiders; and (6) to define the "meaning of life" and maintain the motivation to survive and engage in the activities necessary for survival. . . .

With regard to the activities so described, we can offer a hypothesis . . . that these six classes of activities represent not only what various groups the world over actually do but, additionally, what these groups have to do if they are to survive and continue as human groups (Bennett and Tumin 1964:9).

These functional prerequisites of continuous social life form the basis for the structure of this book. In each of the first seven chapters there is at least one first-hand account that illustrates how a particular society provided for one of the functional prerequisites. The excerpt is then analyzed and the topic discussed in more detail. The last chapter of the book deals with some trends in anthropology and some of the conceptual tools of anthropologists.

Man in Perspective:
An Introduction to
Cultural Anthropology

1 Survival: Hunters and Gatherers

A functional prerequisite to the survival of a society is the survival of its individual members. To ensure individual survival, a society must see to it that each person receives adequate air, water, food, clothing, and shelter. Societies have solved these survival problems in various ways. Hunting and gathering wild food products from the environment was one of the earliest ways human societies ensured the adequate nutrition of their members. Products of the environment were also used to make clothing and shelter in climates where these were necessary. Until recently, societies have not concerned themselves with the problem of providing clean air, and the only societies that considered adequate water to be a survival problem were those in environments where it was scarce.

Since air and water are still minor problems (except to industrial nations), and clothing and shelter are not equally essential in all environments, we will concentrate in this chapter on the search for food, which must be available in quantity every day for long-term survival. Even though it is possible for individuals to exist without food for a day or so now and then, if deprivation is a regular thing, the individual will be weakened and will probably succumb to disease more readily than someone who is adequately fed every day.

In the following excerpt, pay particular attention to the kinds of food consumed, the sources of clothing and shelter, how these things were obtained, and how they were prepared for eventual use. Also note who is responsible for the various tasks in this system.

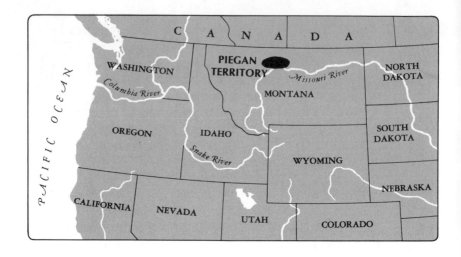

Survival and the Piegan Hunter

Winter came that year in the early part of November.* The lakes and streams froze over, there were several falls of snow, which the northwest winds gathered up and piled in coulées ° and on the lee side of the hills. It was not long before the buffalo began to keep away from the river, where the big camps were. A few, of course, were always straggling in, but the great herds stayed out on the plains to the north and south of us. Since the buffalo did not approach the stream the Indians were obliged to go out on a two or three days' camping trip in order to get what meat and skins they needed, and several times during the season I went with them, accompanying my friends, Weasel Tail and Talks-with-the-buffalo. On these short hunts few lodges ° were taken, fifteen or twenty people arranging to camp together, so we were somewhat crowded for room. Only enough women to do the cooking accompanied the outfit.

As a rule, the hunters started out together every morning, and sighting a large herd of buffalo, approached as cautiously as possible, until finally the animals became alarmed and started to run, and then a grand

*Abridged from *My Life as an Indian* by James Willard Schultz, pp. 39–40, 42–46, 108–110, 174, 177–179. Copyright MCMVII, Forest and Stream Publishing Co. Copyright © 1935 James Willard Schultz. By permission of the author's estate and Fawcett Publications, Inc. Schultz was a "squaw man" with the Piegan Blackfoot Indians during the latter part of the nineteenth century. He experienced their life both while they were an autonomous people and after they were settled on a reservation in a dependent relationship to the United States government. The book consists of his recollections.
° This gloss mark indicates a word to be found in the Glossary at the end of the book.

chase took place, and if everything was favorable many fat cows were killed. Nearly all the Piegans had guns of one kind or another; either flintlock ° or percussion-cap,° smooth-bore ° or rifle; but in the chase many of them, especially if riding swift, trained horses, preferred to use the bow and arrow, as two or three arrows could be discharged at as many different animals while one was reloading a gun. Some of the hunters killed twenty and more buffalo on a single run, but I think the average number to the man was not more than three.

When on these short hunts a medicine man always accompanied a party, and the evenings were passed in praying to the Sun for success in the hunt, and in singing songs, especially the song of the wolf, the most successful of hunters. Everyone retired early, for there was little cheer in a fire of buffalo chips.

By the latter end of November the trade for robes was in full swing, thousands of buffalo had been killed, and the women were busily engaged in tanning the hides, a task of no little labor. I have often heard and read that Indian women received no consideration from their husbands, and led a life of exceedingly hard and thankless work. That is very wide of the truth so far as the natives of the northern plains were concerned. It is true that the women gathered fuel for the lodge—bundles of dry willow, or limbs from a fallen cottonwood. They also did the cooking, and besides tanning robes, converted the skins of deer, elk, antelope, and mountain sheep into soft buckskin ° for family use. But when they felt like it they rested; they realized that there were other days coming, and they took their time about anything they had to do. Their husbands never interfered with them, any more than they did with him in his task of providing the hides and skins and meat, the staff of life. The majority—nearly all of them—were naturally industrious and took pride in their work, in putting away parfleche ° after parfleche of choice dried meats and pemmican,° in tanning soft robes and buckskins for home use or sale, in embroidering wonderful patterns of beads or colored porcupine quills upon moccasin tops, dresses, leggings, and saddle trappings. When robes were to be traded they got their share of the proceeds; if the husband chose to buy liquor, well and good—they bought blankets and red and blue trade cloth, vermilion,° beads, bright prints, and various other articles of use and adornment.

. . .

One evening in the latter part of January there was much excitement in the three great camps. Some Piegan hunters, just returned from a few days' buffalo chase out on the plain to the north of the river, had seen a white buffalo. The news quickly spread, and from all quarters Indians came in to the post for powder and balls, flints, percussion caps, tobacco, and various other articles. There was to be an exodus of hunting parties from the three villages in the morning and men were betting with each other as to which of the tribes would secure the skin of the white animal; each one, of course, betting on his own tribe. By nearly all of the tribes of the plains an albino buffalo was considered a sacred thing, the especial property of the Sun. When one was killed the hide was always beautifully tanned, and at the next medicine lodge was given to the Sun with great ceremony, hung above all the other offerings on the center post of the structure, and there left to shrivel gradually and fall to pieces. War parties of other tribes, passing the deserted place, would not touch it for fear of calling down upon themselves the wrath of the Sun. The man who killed such an animal was thought to have received the special favor of the Sun, and not only he, but his whole tribe.

. . .

I joined one of the hunting parties the next morning, going, as usual, with my friends, Talks-with-the-buffalo and Weasel Tail. . . .

. . .

We started early . . . and never stopped until we arrived at a willow-bordered stream running out from the west butte of the Sweetgrass Hills and eventually disappearing in the dry plain. It was an ideal camping place—plenty of shelter, plenty of wood and water. The big herd with the albino buffalo had been last seen some fifteen miles southeast of our camp, and had run westward when pursued. Our party thought that we had selected the best location possible in order to scour the country in

search of it. Those who had seen it reported that it was a fair-sized animal, and so swift that it had run up to the head of the herd at once and remained there—so far from their horses' best speed, that they never could determine whether it was bull or cow.

Other parties, Piegans, Blackfeet, and Bloods, were encamped east of us along the hills, and southeast of us out on the plain. We had agreed to do no running, to frighten the buffalo as little as possible until the albino had been found, or it became time to return to the river. Then, of course, a big run or two would be made in order to load the pack animals with meat and hides.

The weather was unfavorable, to say nothing of the intense cold; a thick haze of glittering frost flakes filled the air, through which the sun shone dimly. We were almost at the foot of the west butte, but it and its pine forest had vanished in the shining frost fog. Nevertheless, we rode out daily on our quest, toward the Little River. . . .

I cannot remember how many days that cold time lasted, during which we vainly hunted for the albino buffalo. The change came about ten o'clock one morning as we were riding slowly around the west side of the butte. We felt suddenly an intermittent tremor of warm air in our faces; the frost haze vanished instantly and we could see the Rockies, partially enveloped in dense, dark clouds. "Hah!" exclaimed a medicine-pipe man. "Did I not pray for a black wind last night? And see, here it is; my Sun power is strong."

Even as he spoke the chinook ° came on in strong, warm gusts and settled into a roaring, snapping blast. The thin coat of snow on the grass disappeared. One felt as if summer had come.

We were several hundred feet above the plain, on the lower slope of the butte, and in every direction, as far as we could see, there were buffalo, buffalo, and still more buffalo. They were a grand sight. . . .

It seemed about as useless as looking for the proverbial needle to attempt to locate a single white animal among all those dark ones. We all dismounted, and, adjusting my long telescope, I searched herd after herd until my vision became blinded, and then I passed the instrument to someone beside me. Nearly all of the party tried it, but the result was the same; no white buffalo. We smoked and talked about the animal we were after; each one had his opinion as to where it was at that moment, and they varied in locality from the Missouri River to the Saskatchewan, from the Rockies to the Bear's Paw Mountains. While we were talking there appeared a commotion among the buffalo southeast of us. I got the telescope to bear upon the place and saw that a number of Indians

FACING PAGE: A Piegan Indian camp as depicted by Maximilian Bodmer. *Courtesy of the American Museum of Natural History*

were chasing a herd of a hundred or more due westward. They were far behind them, more than a mile, and the buffalo were widening that distance rapidly, but still the riders kept on in a long, straggling line. I passed the glass to Weasel Tail and told what I had seen. Everyone sprang to his feet.

"It must be," said my friend, "that they have found the white one, or they would give up the chase. They are far behind and their horses are tired. Yes, it is the white one they follow. I see it! I see it!"

We were mounted in a moment and riding out to intercept the herd; riding at a trot, occasionally broken by a short lope, for the horses must be kept fresh for the final run. In less than half an hour we arrived at a low, long, mound-like elevation, near which the herd should pass. We could see them coming straight toward it. So we got behind it and waited, my companions, as usual, removing their saddles and piling them in a heap. We realized, of course, that the buffalo might get wind of us and turn long before they were near enough for us to make a dash at them, but we had to take that chance. After a long time, our leader, peering over the top of the mound, told us to be ready; we all mounted. Then he called out for us to come on, and we dashed over the rise; the herd was yet over 500 yards distant, had winded us, and turned south. Whips were plied; short-handled quirts ° of rawhide which stung and maddened the horses. At first we gained rapidly on the herd, then for a time kept at about their speed, and finally began to lose distance. Still we kept on, for we could all see the coveted prize, the albino, running at the head of the herd. I felt sure that none of us could overtake it, but because the others did, I kept my horse going, too, shamefully quirting him when he was doing his best.

Then out from a coulée right in front of the flying herd dashed a lone horseman, right in among them, scattering the animals in all directions. In much less time than it takes to tell it, he rode up beside the albino. We could see him lean over and sink arrow after arrow into its ribs, and presently it stopped, wobbled, and fell over on its side. When we rode up to the place the hunter was standing over it, hands raised, fervently praying, promising the Sun the robe and the tongue of the animal. It was a three-year-old cow, yellowish-white in color, but with normal-colored eyes. The successful hunter was a Piegan, Medicine Weasel by name. He was so excited, he trembled so, that he could not use his knife, and some of our party took off the hide for him, and cut out the tongue, he standing over them all the time and begging them to be careful, to make no gashes, for they were doing the work for the Sun. None of the meat was taken. It was considered a sacrilege to eat it; the tongue was to be dried and given to the Sun with the robe. While the animal was being skinned, the party we had seen chasing the herd came up; they were Blackfeet of the north, and did not seem to be very well pleased that the Piegans had captured the prize; they soon rode away to their camp, and we went to ours, accompanied by Medicine Weasel.

. . .

One evening a vast herd of buffalo had been discovered two or three miles back from the river—a herd so large that it was said the valley of Cow Creek and the hills on each side of it were black with them as far as one could see. Soon after sunrise many hunters, with their women following on travois ° horses, had gone out to run this herd and get meat. An hour or so later they charged in among them on their trained runners, splitting the herd in such a way that about a thousand or more broke straight down the valley toward the camp, for the nearer to camp the killing was done, the easier it was to pack in the meat. Down the valley the frightened animals fled, followed by their pursuers. We in camp heard the thunder of hoofs and saw the cloud of dust before the animals came in sight. Our lodges were pitched on the lower side of the bottom, between the creek and a steep, bare, rocky ridge. Every man, woman, and child of us had hurried outside to witness the chase.

It was really far more exciting to see such a run near at hand than to take part in it. First of all, the huge, shaggy, oddly shaped beasts charged madly by with a thunderous pounding of hoof and rattle of horns, causing the ground to tremble as if from an earthquake; and then the hunters, their long hair streaming in the wind, guiding their trained mounts here and there in the thick of it all, singling out this fat cow or that choice young bull, firing their guns or leaning over and driving an arrow deep into the vital part of the great beast. The plain over which they passed became dotted with the dead, with great animals standing head down, swaying, staggering, as the life blood flowed from mouth and nostrils, finally crashing over on the ground, limp and lifeless heaps.

That is what we, standing by our lodges, saw that morning. No one cheered the hunters, nor spoke, nor laughed. It was too solemn a moment. We saw death abroad; huge, powerful beasts, full of tireless energy, suddenly stricken into so many heaps of meat and hide. Paradoxical as it may seem, the Blackfeet reverenced, regarded as "medicine," or sacred, these animals which they killed for food, whose hides furnished them with shelter and clothing.

A band of horses drinking at the river became frightened at the noise of the approaching [buffalo] herd. They bounded up the bank and raced out over the bottom, heads and tails up, running directly toward the [buffalo] herd, which swerved to the eastward, crossed the creek, and came tearing down our side of it. The rocky ridge hemming in the bottom was too steep for them to climb, so they kept on in the flat directly toward the lodges. . . . Women screamed, children bawled, men shouted words of advice and command.

. . .

Now, the leaders of the herd reached the outer edge of the village. They could not draw back, for those behind forced them forward, and they loped on, threading their way between the lodges, nimbly jumping from side to side to avoid them, kicking out wickedly at them as they passed. For all his great size and uncouth shape, the buffalo was quick and active on his feet.

. . . We held our breath anxiously, for we well knew that almost anything—the firing of a gun or sight of some suspicious object ahead—might throw the herd into confusion. If it turned or bunched up in a compact mass, people would surely be trampled to death, lodges overturned, the greater part of the camp reduced to ruin. Finally the last of the herd passed beyond the outer lodges into the river and across it to the opposite side.

No one had been hurt, not a lodge had been overturned. But long scaffolds of drying meat, many hides and pelts of various animals pegged out on the ground to dry, had either disappeared or been cut into small fragments. That, indeed, was an experience to be remembered; we were thankful to have escaped with our lives. . . .

The next day the trees and high bushes bordering the river were bright with the people's offerings to their Sun god. They gave always their best, their choicest and most prized ornaments and finery.

• • •

Nät-ah'-ki and I went once after buffalo, camping with Red Bird's Tail, a genial man of thirty-five or forty. There were few lodges, but many people, and we traveled as light as possible. We . . . camped on the head of Armells Creek. . . .

• • •

. . . The sun shone bright and warm, there was a big herd of buffalo nearby, everyone rode out from camp in the best of spirits. I had changed horses with Nät-ah'-ki; while mine liked to run as well as hers, it had a tender mouth, and she could easily control it. Once into the herd, I paid no attention to anyone else, but did my best to single out the fat cows, overtake and kill them. I did not need the meat nor robes, but there were those with us who had poor mounts, and what I killed I intended to give them. So I urged the little mare on, and managed to kill seven head.

When I stopped at last, no one was near me; looking back I saw the people gathered in two groups, and from the largest and nearest one arose the distressing wailing of the women for the dead. I soon learned the cause of it all; Young Arrow Maker had been killed, his horse disembowelled; Two Bows had been thrown and his leg was broken. A huge old bull, wounded and mad with pain, had lunged into Arrow Maker's horse, tearing out its flank and knocking the rider off on to the backs of

A Plains Indian with horse-drawn travois. *The Bettmann Archive*

its close-pursuing mates, and he had been trampled to death by the frantic-running herd.

Two Bows' horse had stepped into a badger hole and he had been hurled to the ground, his right leg broken above the knee. Some of the women's horses were dragging travois, and we laid the dead and the injured on them and they were taken to camp by their relatives. We hurried to skin the dead buffalo, some of the hunters taking no more of the meat than the tongue and boss ribs, and then we also went back to the lodges, silently and quietly. There was no feasting and singing that night.

They buried Arrow Maker in the morning, placing the body in the fork of a big cottonwood, and then we prepared to move camp, which took all the rest of the day, as meat was cut and dried to reduce weight, and the many hides had to be trimmed, the frozen ones thawed and folded for packing. There was not a man in camp who knew anything about mending a broken leg, but we splinted and bound Two Bows' fracture as best we could. On the succeeding morning we broke camp early and started homeward, every one frantic to get away from the unlucky place before more misfortune should happen. The injured man was made as comfortable as possible on a couch lashed to a travois.

In the afternoon a blizzard set in, a bitterly cold one, which drifted and whirled the fine snow in clouds around us. A few decided to make camp in the first patch of timber we should come to, but the rest declared that they would keep on through the night until they arrived home. They were afraid to stop; more afraid of some dread misfortune overtaking them than they were of Cold Maker's ° [personification of winter] blinding snow and intense cold. . . . Red Bird's Tail was one of those who elected to keep on.

The low flying snow-spitting clouds hid the moon as we hung on to our saddles and gave our horses the reins, trusting them to keep in the trail which Red Bird's Tail broke for us. We could not have guided them had we wished to, for our hands became so numb we were obliged to fold them in the robes and blankets which enveloped us. . . .

Red Bird's Tail and many of the other men frequently sprang from their horses and walked, even ran, in vain effort to keep warm, but the women remained in the saddle and shivered, and some froze hands and faces. While still some six or eight miles from home, Red Bird's Tail, walking ahead of his horse, dropped into a spring, over which the snow had drifted. The water was waist-deep and froze on his leggings the instant he climbed out of the hole; but he made no complaint, walking sturdily on through the deepening drifts until we finally arrived home. It was all I could do to dismount, I was so stiff and cramped and cold; and I had to lift Nät-ah'-ki from her saddle and carry her inside. We had been on the trail something like seventeen hours! I roused one of the men to care for our horses, and we crawled into bed, under half a dozen robes and blankets, shivering so hard that our teeth chattered.

When we awoke it was nearly noon; and we learned that a woman of our party had dropped from her horse and Cold Maker had claimed her for his own. Her body was never found.

Subsistence hunting is not all pleasure. A sportsman can postpone his trip if the weather is bad, or when he does not feel well. A hunter, needing to provide for family members as well as for himself, does not always have the same option. Hunters must go out with some regularity because their societies usually have little surplus food. If an epidemic (such as smallpox or influenza) hits a hunting band, a major cause of death may be starvation, not disease. Starvation also threatens if the weather is so bad that everyone is confined to camp for several days in a row.

On the other hand, daily hunting is rarely necessary. Hunters and gatherers have been pushed by stronger agricultural peoples into relatively poor environments, yet studies have found that even under these conditions, most hunters and gatherers have to work only a few hours a day a few days a week to provide an adequate diet (Holmberg 1969: 75–76, 248; Lee 1968: 37).

The Indians described in the excerpt were an affluent group of hunters and gatherers. They had techniques for storing and preserving food; they had horses, guns, bows and arrows, all of which made their hunting quite efficient. Yet even for them, the hunt— exciting, challenging, even inspiring—could also be difficult, frustrating, and sometimes deadly. Hunters on foot usually have a more difficult time. The anthropologist George P. Murdock thought horse transport made such a difference in life pattern that he refused to include mounted hunters in his compilation of hunters and gatherers. He also excluded groups that obtain their food from intensive fishing and those that engage in any agriculture at all, even though they obtain most of their food from hunting and gathering (Murdock 1968: 15).

Not all anthropologists agree with this classification. Some feel there is a significant difference between people who harvest what resources the environment naturally provides and those who modify the environment in such a way that it produces what they choose where they choose. Using this distinction, one can study the range of variation possible in societies based on harvesting natural resources as compared with those based on the domestication of plants and animals. Groups that use both methods may be either kept in a separate category or assigned to one or the other on the basis of an arbitrary distinction: all those who obtain more than half their subsistence from harvesting natural resources assigned to the hunters and gatherers; the rest to the food producers, for example.

Comparative study of different hunting and gathering societies can help isolate factors significant in the formation of social classes, complex political structures, and so on, and thus lead to a better understanding of how civilization began and what its dynamics are. This is important because man has been an urban, industrialized creature for only a short time. For two million years, perhaps more, man harvested his natural environment, as had his primate ancestors before him. What effect has this way of life had upon him? What demands did it make on him? What opportunities did it offer him? What kind of individual was most likely to be successful at this type of life? Why did man leave hunting and gathering for agriculture?

EARLIEST SURVIVAL TECHNIQUES: QUESTIONS AND CONTROVERSIES

Man's earliest phase of development is obscured by time. The role played by hunting is not clear, and reputable scientists sometimes find themselves embroiled in bitter controversy about it. Man's closest relatives are all foragers.° They hunt, if at all, only rarely (Hulse 1971:208). They never scavenge (eat meat not killed by their own efforts). When did man first begin to hunt? How important was the contribution of hunting to his diet and development? Was all the meat in his diet from hunting, or was he also (or entirely) a scavenger? Were the things he made used primarily as weapons, or were they simply tools for peaceful foraging? All these questions are currently being hotly debated, but one thing seems clear. If man was hunting in the early stages of his development, he was not using his teeth as weapons. Loss of the primate fighting canines was among the first of the physical changes that slowly differentiated man from his closest relatives. It is generally assumed that the loss was possible only because man's ancestors began to make extensive use of tools (but there is an alternative explanation—see page 16).

In spite of the controversy, most researchers agree that at some point in time, descendants of a generalized primate (one not specialized in the direction of either apes or man) began to deviate from the general pattern of primate behavior by walking erect and using tools. Why this happened is not entirely clear. Some scientists suggest climate variation forced the creature to change (Ardrey 1961:264–265); still others suggest the change was the result of random mutations that persisted and spread because they enabled the group to exploit an environmental niche untapped by other primates (Campbell 1966:29–30).

Apparently there were at least two varieties of manlike creatures in Africa between two and three million years ago. They were bipedal, with small canine teeth, and all apparently used tools of some sort (Chard 1969:62–63). One of the varieties (*Paranthropus* ° or *Australopithecus robustus* °) was large and powerful; the others were smaller and more delicate (*Australopithecus africanus*,° *Telanthropus*,° *Homo habilis* °) (Howell 1965:62–63; Le Gros Clark 1967: 31). There is still some controversy over which (if any) was man's ancestor, but the largest one definitely seems to be out of contention, since in certain characteristics it was already too specialized in a direction away from that leading to man. Since the manlike creatures were all effectively erect and used tools, but yet were not all ancestral to man, apparently these two characteristics alone were not sufficient to cause human development. Many animals eat meat, so it is also apparent that meat eating alone was not sufficient to produce man. It has been suggested that all three characteristics— erect posture, tool using, and meat eating—were necessary for the development of man. The evolutionary selection process, favoring those individuals best able to do all three things (and probably others we are not yet aware of), enabled them to have more offspring and pass on their genetic differences to an ever-increasing number of individuals. Thus man evolved and spread (Chard 1969: 70–71).

There is controversy over how much meat there was in the diet of man's ancestors and whether it was obtained by hunting or by scavenging. Because the subject is *man*, even scientists have difficulty remaining objective. Some who think the development of man began as a result of deliberate hunting for food also seem to believe that any carnivore must accept killing, violence, and bloodshed as natural. They therefore suggest that more than two million years of selection for the best hunter and the most successful carnivore in the group has made a taste for violence part of man's biological endowment. Other scientists, deploring the violence man displays, reject this explanation as an attempt to excuse and condone his aggressions. These scientists insist that man's immediate ancestors were peaceful foragers and got their meat by scavenging, not hunting. Therefore, they say, man is innately peaceful; it is society that turns him into a killer. Thus political, religious, and humanitarian views enter the arena of the study of the development of man, causing individuals to promote certain hypotheses not so much because the evidence supports them, but because they as individuals *prefer* one interpretation over another.

The entire question is complex, with little concrete evidence to support either side. There is no doubt that man has been a hunter for at least the last half-million years of his existence. But half a million years is a short time in terms of evolutionary change and could not be expected to have the same effect as two million or more years of selection. In addition, many of the assumptions on which the arguments are based have not been tested. For example, is a carnivore unique in accepting violence and bloodshed? Some generally tranquil grazers show a considerable capacity for violence at certain times of the year (usually the mating season) or in defense of their young. If the acceptance of violence cannot be limited to carnivores, then either carnivorous or vegetarian ancestors could account for man's pugnacious behavior.

Can one assume that the violence involved in hunting—normally directed toward other species of animals—encourages in-group violence of the sort that plagues man? Not all hunting animals engage in violence against their own kind; even the killer whale is good to its mother. Perhaps some of the difficulty with man lies in his narrow definition of kinship, which is often limited to his biologically close relatives. Quite a few human groups call themselves "People" or "Real Men" and designate different groups by "Enemies," "Almost-people," "Not People," "Savages," or other names that safely remove them from consideration as fellow humans (Dobyns and Euler 1970:2–4).

Can one assume that violence is the *only* characteristic selected for in hunters? Many of the hunting techniques used by man (and even by some other carnivores) require close coordination and cooperation among a number of individuals. Under these circumstances, evolution would select for cooperative individuals as well as for violent ones. (The suggestion has been made that the loss of the fanglike canine teeth resulted from hormonal changes necessary to curb in-group aggression and to increase cooperation [Holloway

1967:63–67].) There is no real evidence that violence and coopera-tion are mutually exclusive, however. Many human groups that have been ferocious to outsiders have been models of cooperation among themselves.

Even if all the assumptions about the relationship between vio-lence and hunting should prove to be correct, can it be assumed that these characteristics have become part of man's *biological* heritage? Man is noted for lack of instincts and for the importance of learning in determining his behavior. Is there any evidence that violence is an exception? Some people feel that there is. If violence does not have some instinctive basis, why does it seem to be so easy to teach to each generation? And why is it so difficult to develop a peaceful society? If man is basically a peaceful gatherer, his history shows precious little evidence of it. Regardless of the type of economic or political system he has had at any particular time, man seems to have behaved violently toward other men.

If the basis for man's violence should prove to be instinctive, does this mean that nothing can be done about it? Sex is instinctive, but to admit that does not automatically condone promiscuity. Hu-mans have apparently always regulated sexual behavior; societies have fallen into difficulties only when they have tried to ignore the drive or to eliminate it entirely. Scientists who accept the position that man is instinctively aggressive do not necessarily condone in-discriminate violence. Instead, they suggest that aggression can neither be ignored nor eliminated; like sex, it must be channeled into socially beneficial rather than disruptive patterns (Lorenz 1963:49–56).

Like many controversies, this one thrives on the lack of data. We do not yet know *how* early man got most of his meat—by hunting or by scavenging. We do not know precisely how he used the tools he made; nor can we tell what other tools—of more perishable ma-terial and so unpreserved—he had. It is difficult to imagine how the lighter varieties of manlike primates could have either hunted or scavenged without some sort of weapon. They were too small to kill any large animals unaided, and would have had difficulty com-peting with other scavengers for dead animals even after the preda-tor abandoned his kill. Possibly man's ancestors threw rocks to chase predators or scavengers away, to kill small animals and stun larger game. (Man can naturally throw more accurately than any other primate, although the chimpanzee can be trained to do quite well [Hulse 1971:176].) The tools that have been discovered in asso-ciation with these manlike primates may have been used for butcher-ing, skinning, or opening hard-shelled nuts or fruits, rather than as weapons. Future archeological research may provide more answers.

TECHNICAL ADVANCES

Whatever the behavior of man's immediate ancestors, early man himself was definitely a hunter. The record becomes more complete as we approach the present, of course, so there are more data to use for speculation. Half a million years ago, man was hunting very large animals, like mammoths, cooperatively. He had some use of fire, and probably knew how to make it. His weapons were improved over those of earlier periods, and he may have had some form of language (Howell 1965:83).

The discovery and control of fire was one of the more significant early technological advances made by man, for shelter is one of man's basic survival needs. Control of fire made it possible for man to live in areas where he could not survive without some protection.

The burial ground of the Wind River Indian Reservation in western Wyoming, in which iron bedsteads have been used as grave markers. *United Press International*

He could occupy roomy caves that would have been too damp and cold otherwise. He could drive (and keep) out formidable predators. Food is also a basic need. With fire for cooking, man could eat otherwise inedible foods, and could make other foods more digestible. The presence of charred animal bones at Chou-kou-tien suggests cooking food was one of the early uses for fire, but of course we cannot be certain (Weidenreich 1939:53, 56; Roper 1969:436). In historic times, fire has been used as a hunting weapon. We do not know that it was so used early in man's history, but it might have been. Fire in a shelter at night serves to lengthen the day—perhaps to encourage the development of language, but at least to give man an advantage over other animals by providing him with more functional time. Fire by night and smoke by day could also signal the location of the main group and thus enable wide-ranging hunters to find their way back to camp more easily. Fire could be used to protect women, children, the elderly, and the disabled, thus making it possible for the hunters to leave them for longer periods without endangering their survival.

The development of language was another highly significant step in the evolution of man. Its origin (like the origin of man himself) is still subject to controversy. Since language left no direct traces until writing was invented, its existence must be inferred from indirect evidence. Some individuals have suggested that proof of hunting cooperation demonstrates the presence of language, but this is a weak argument, since other predators hunt cooperatively without language. Language makes man time and space free. He does not have to be in the presence of a particular stimulus to communicate about it. He can talk about events and objects from the past or future, and he can even speculate about imaginary or intangible things such as pride, X-rays, and unicorns. About 100,000 years ago, some kinds of men buried their dead in an elaborate manner, occasionally surrounding the bodies with animal skulls or grave goods ° (Chard 1969:123). It is difficult to imagine a reason for this unless there was some sort of belief system surrounding the dead. The existence of such a system virtually demands language, for how could shared complex beliefs develop without some means of communicating abstract concepts?

The use of language gave man a tremendous survival edge. For the first time, an individual could pass his knowledge along to others by some means besides action and imitation. Members of a group could pool their knowledge more effectively, could discuss and ponder the significance of some unique event, and could speculate about the future. Man with language is no longer bound to the present as are other animals; he is free to deal conceptually with the past and the future. When man finally developed language, he could accumulate traditions and his offspring could build on what he had learned, unlike other animals, who were forced to repeat the same learning generation after generation. The advantages for survival are obvious. A deer that has never experienced a forest fire must escape through its own native intelligence and good fortune, unless some other deer that has escaped one is around to provide a model. Without an actual fire, the experienced deer has no way of passing the knowledge along to the others of his kind, so his valuable information dies with him. Man, on the other hand, can prepare his offspring to cope with events that might not be repeated for years. Theoretically, a man might indirectly save the life of his great-grand-children through information transmitted down two generations.

In addition to the development of fire and language, man also steadily increased the complexity of his tools. The hand-held stone point was improved by the addition of a handle, making a knife, spear, or javelin. The *atlatl* ° (spear thrower) was invented. This artificially extended the length of a man's arm and thus gave more force to the thrown missile. Ultimately, the bow and arrow were developed (apparently in northern Africa about 30,000 years ago [Chard 1969:135]) and spread throughout the world. The bow added greatly to the range and force of man's weapons.

By the time the bow and arrow were invented, man was physically *Homo sapiens*, the modern species. The establishment of *Homo sapiens* all over the world occurred with surprising rapidity and has led to controversy over what happened to preceding forms. It has been suggested that they evolved into modern man, were absorbed by modern man, died out naturally, or were killed off by modern man. The weight of expert opinion seems to be gradually shifting to support the position that earlier forms, called Neanderthals ° or Neanderthaloids, evolved into modern man (Brace 1964:19), but there is still resistance to this hypothesis. Many scientists seem reluctant to admit a Neanderthaloid into their family tree.

ANALYZING EVIDENCE: THE PIEGAN PATTERN

The history of the development of man includes the development of culture. Man cannot be studied as a biological organism alone; culture has coexisted with him from his beginnings. Culture and man have changed together, and one author has even made culture part of the definition of man by suggesting that man crossed the threshold of humanity when he could no longer survive without culture (Chard 1969:75). It has also been suggested that the biological development of man was caused at least in part by culture, and that without it, man would not have become the physical being he is (Chard 1969:74, 75).

Archeological evidence is therefore not the only data that have been used in the attempt to reconstruct man's early life patterns. Researchers have looked to the cultures of historic or modern hunters and gatherers for analogies to help them understand the way man lived for most of his history. This approach must be used with caution, because modern hunters and gatherers have as long a history as anyone else, and there is no way of being certain what changes may have taken place during that time. Nonetheless, it would be foolish to overlook any opportunity to learn more about the dynamics of hunting and gathering patterns. What do hunters and gatherers have in common? In what ways do they differ? What is the range of variation that seems possible within the pattern? What are the attitudes of hunters and gatherers toward violence, death, cooperation? Since cooperative hunting techniques require organization in a way that individual hunting does not, what forms of organization appear most often in hunting and gathering societies?

The excerpt at the beginning of this chapter answers some of the questions for one group of hunters and gatherers—the Piegan Indians—at one period of time (the end of the nineteenth century) and in one general location (the northern plains of the United States). No claim is being made that these Indians were typical of all hunters and gatherers, and in any case, one brief excerpt on one society cannot possibly provide definitive answers to any of the questions. In analyzing the excerpt, however, one can practice gathering bits of information on significant questions from the observations or descriptions of societies. Answers suggested by the analysis can be checked against other observations or descriptions of the Piegan, then compared with similar data from other societies. Science proceeds through the patient compiling of data until the pattern finally becomes clear.

Division of Labor

To analyze the excerpt, one can first ask: Who does what in the society? What is the normal division of labor? The excerpt indicates that both men and women were involved in providing the basic necessities of food and shelter among the Piegan, but they did not duplicate each other's efforts. The labor of one sex complemented that of the other.

Men provided meat and skins. Other parts of the book from which the excerpt is taken indicate that men also provided horses (mainly by stealing them from other tribes), engaged in both offensive and defensive conflicts with other tribes, and traded, both with other tribes and with non-Indians. Women sometimes joined them in the trading, but did not normally take part in the rest of the men's activities. Women sometimes accompanied the men on long hunting expeditions, but, according to the excerpt, only to do the cooking.

Women gathered fuel for cooking and heating. They cooked daily meals, and they preserved food for future use by drying and storing it in rawhide containers they made themselves. Women also tanned the hides men provided and then made clothing and other articles from the tanned skins. Using trade beads and dyed porcupine quills, women decorated the articles they made. They also made the shelters, which were of tanned skins stretched over poles. (The male usually had the job of finding the poles, although the excerpt does not mention that.) Women put up and took down the lodges, and normally loaded and unloaded the horses. Men occasionally helped with some of these activities, but generally, according to the excerpt, women took pride in doing their own work, and the book indicates they were embarrassed to accept male assistance unless absolutely necessary. Neither the excerpt nor the book mentions the women's contribution to the food supply by gathering berries and other vegetable products, yet these formed an important part of the diet and a significant supplement to the meat provided by the men. Some chores, such as gathering wood, carrying water, and providing occasional meat by snaring small game, were often performed by the children, but neither the excerpt nor the book mentions these.

This division of labor is typical among hunting and gathering peoples. There is no hunting and gathering society that makes hunting large game a regular part of the woman's role, for example, nor one that confines men to activities around the home base. This is probably related to another normal part of the female role, bearing and rearing children. It is difficult to imagine a woman eight months pregnant stalking a deer with any ease, and a woman burdened with a toddler and an infant would have trouble dodging the charge of an enraged buffalo. Such activities would not promote the survival of the children, either.

These differences in activity patterns have often fooled observers

An Eskimo family in the Thule region of northern Greenland. One of the major activities of Eskimo women is repairing and maintaining clothing. *De Wys, Inc.*

who did not participate fully in the lives of the people they described. Such outsiders rarely accompanied the men hunting, where they were more likely to be a hindrance than a help if they did not know the customary procedures. Because the outsider usually observed hard-working women (whose normal activities were performed around the camp) and resting, relaxed men, much of the literature paints the women of "savage" societies as overworked slaves to their lazy mates. The excerpt calls this view erroneous; the writer points out that the women worked at their own pace, and did it from choice. It also makes clear that the "lazy" male was often away, engaged in exhausting and dangerous pursuits from which he might not return at all. In camp, he felt entitled to relax, and his wife, who often remained snug at home while he was risking his life, seldom begrudged him his leisure.

In hunting and gathering societies, female activities are almost always important to group survival. Usually females contribute to the food supply by gathering vegetable products. When the environment permits, they may also engage in shallow-water fishing or snare small game. In many societies, the female contribution means the difference between survival and starvation, or between scarcity and plenty. Even when her contribution to the food supply is minimal (among Eskimos, for example), her work is still essential. Life in the Arctic is so precarious, hunting so demanding and time-consuming, that the male food provider could not survive for long without the activities of the women, who spend all their time making, repairing, and maintaining clothing; processing food; and keeping a warm home base, in addition to caring for the children (Freuchen 1961:55).

Although Eskimos may be extreme in the amount of interdependence of the sexes, hardly any hunting and gathering society could afford to have half its adult members unproductive. A few societies can barely afford any unproductive members at all, and are occasionally forced to abandon the ill and aged. (Some anthropologists who have worked with such peoples have suggested that they do not really *have* to abandon the sick and aged; they simply do not want to be bothered caring for them. It is difficult for people steeped in Western traditions to accept this explanation, but it seems to be correct [Holmberg 1969:225–226; Lee and DeVore 1968:91].)

Members of a society in which the male obtains all or most of the food will necessarily be concerned with preserving his life first, because without the food producer, everyone in the group will die. In a crisis situation, therefore, only the adult male is indispensable. In societies in which both men and women contribute significantly to the food supply, able-bodied adults of both sexes may receive approximately equal priority, but the aged, the sick, and children are still expendable. Under these conditions, attitudes toward life and death are far different from those in modern industrialized societies. Only the affluent can be permitted the luxury of "women and children first."

The Piegan excerpt suggests another characteristic that may be common to most hunting and gathering societies—a difference in the steadiness of the activity of men and women. Women work day after day with little variation in the *total* amount of activity, although the *type* of work frequently varies. Men, on the other hand, tend to work very hard for one period of time and then relax for another period. In one study where time spent in various activities was measured, it was found that hunters averaged about as much time resting as they did in hunting, but that the daily routine varied sharply. Hunters sometimes went out several days in a row—particularly when they were unsuccessful—but after a fortunate kill, a man might remain in camp eating and sleeping for several days (Holmberg 1969:75–76).

It would be interesting to know if this difference in male-female activity patterns is typical of all hunting and gathering societies and if so, what effect (if any) it had on man's development. What adjustments (if any) were required by the change to an agriculturally based system with quite a different activity pattern?

Environmental Constraints

Certain environments limit the number of possible solutions to the problems of survival. Without sophisticated technological control over heat, Eskimos can never be an agricultural people in the Arctic. Most of the year they do not even have a chance to *gather* plants. Hunting, and trade, remain the only sources for food. Desert environments similarly limit survival possibilities without sophisticated control over water. The environment also limits the possible solutions to the problem of shelter. Grass huts are neither practical nor possible in the Arctic, where the climate demands protection against cold. On the other hand, snow houses and fur clothing would be equally impossible or impractical in tropical rain forests.

The environment, although it limits, does not *determine* the solutions to the problems of survival. Given a moderately rich environment instead of the Arctic or the desert, a number of different solutions are possible. For example, in the southwestern United States, the environment has been successfully exploited by hunters and gatherers, subsistence farmers, commercial farmers, stock raisers, merchants, and manufacturers. The northeastern coastal region has included the same range of possibilities, plus that for fishermen. The limitations of man's environment are modified by his culture,° especially his technology. One can say either that the environment limits the size of the population a given technology can support or that the technology limits the size of a population a given environment can support. The two are in a dynamic interrelationship that is difficult to disentangle even for the purposes of analysis.

In areas where numbers have had to be strictly limited in order for the group to survive, infanticide has often been used as a means of population control when other techniques were not available. People do not normally prefer infanticide and will stop the practice if their technology changes. On the other hand, infanticide has been adopted in areas under new population pressure when the alternatives of contraception or abortion were not available (Lee and De Vore 1968:11).

Where infanticide is an accepted practice, general attitudes toward the preservation of life often differ from those in Western civilization. Another factor is also operative, however. In some societies, a baby is not regarded as a member of the group, or even human, until some time (occasionally up to several weeks) has passed. If the infant dies before that time, it is not publicly mourned and no funeral rites are held; the body is simply discarded (Hart and Pilling 1964:91). Such an attitude is difficult for people in advanced, high-technology Western societies to understand. Even in the United States, however, there is a sharp difference of opinion between those who believe human life begins at the moment of conception (and therefore regard abortion as murder) and those who believe human life begins only after birth, or when the fetus can survive outside the womb, or when brain-wave activity can be detected. Members of different societies can be placed along a continuum according to the point at which they believe human life begins. Roman Catholics might be placed at the earliest extreme, since they believe life begins at conception. There are some groups, however, that believe pregnancy begins when a spirit enters the womb (Hart and Pilling 1964:14).

What is the "right" answer to this question of when human life begins? Each group can and will defend its position, but members of the other groups usually will not accept the justifications, the "evidence" offered, or the assumptions on which justification and evidence are based when these contradict their own. It appears, then, that the "right" answer depends on which premises, evidence, and definition of "human" one accepts. (The same cannot be said of *all* differences between cultures, however; some are susceptible to objective evaluation. This will be discussed at greater length in Chapter 8.)

Sources of Survival

What do hunters hunt? How does this affect the way they hunt? The Piegan excerpt describes a society heavily dependent on a single animal—the buffalo, more accurately called the American bison. The buffalo was not only the main source of meat, but also provided clothing, shelter, storage containers, and various tools through the use of skin, bone, muscles, and internal organs that were not eaten. In addition to buffalo, Piegan hunters killed deer, elk, antelope, and mountain sheep, although these did not play a major role in the economy. Since porcupine quills were used in decoration, that animal must have been hunted, too. The book indicates that various predators, such as mountain lion, wolf, wolverine, and bear, were also killed, but only for their skins. Since the bear was thought to be supernaturally powerful, he was rarely hunted and was more often killed in self-defense.

Several societies have been heavily dependent on a single source of food—the Chipewyan Indians on caribou (Oswalt 1966:19), prehistoric Magdalenian peoples on reindeer (Chard 1969:25), the California Indians on acorns, the Northwest Coast Indians on salmon, and the Eskimo on seal (Spencer and Jennings 1965:124, 169, 233)—but such dependence is neither inevitable nor universal. Many societies exploited their environment so fully that few animals or plants remained unused, and the most important food source at any particular time depended on its relative abundance then. A band that exploits its environment extensively is usually more secure in regard to food than one that relies heavily on one source. A recent symposium on hunters and gatherers revealed that the only societies that ran a real risk of starvation were those depending almost exclusively on meat obtained from relatively few kinds of animals. Those that relied on both meat and plant food, although they might suffer meatless days and times of scarcity, were never in any real danger of starvation (Holmberg 1969:83; Lee 1968:40–42).

With the buffalo gone, Piegan culture collapsed. Their life pattern was so dependent on the buffalo that they could not maintain it without them. Although the situation would not have been such a disaster had it not been complicated by hostile pressure from non-Indians, the disappearance of the buffalo alone would certainly have forced a major adjustment. The disappearance of the mammoth in the distant past, the permanent migration of the reindeer from southern France in the even more distant past, changes in caribou migration routes in historic times—all these have had repercussions on the culture and survival patterns of the people dependent on those animals. Just what changes were made, or how disruptive the consequences were, we do not know, except in the case of certain American Indian groups where the process was observed and documented. The changes must have been profound, however, since the artifacts characteristic of the mammoth hunters or the reindeer hunters cease to appear archeologically, and are replaced by others.

Food Customs

The excerpt mentions briefly another characteristic typical of many hunting and gathering peoples—generosity. The author killed seven buffalo one day not because he needed meat or hides, but because he wanted to give them to other people. Almost all hunting societies try to make the sharing of game animals desirable to their members, and some make it obligatory. It is not always popular, and descriptions of life in other societies frequently contain anecdotes of attempts to avoid mandatory sharing of food by various devious means, such as eating late at night, eating away from the main camp, sneaking into camp, or hiding food (Holmberg 1969: 87–88). Yet sharing game is a form of insurance. No hunter is so skilled that he can always be sure of success; any hunter may have periods of sickness or be incapacitated as the result of an accident so that he cannot hunt effectively. One who has shared game can demand a return when he is empty-handed. The gift of game almost always creates an obligation on the part of the recipient either to return the gift in kind when possible or else to return it in some other form—performing a service for the giver or doing a favor for a member of his family. A society in which each individual hunted only for himself and his family, and in which each family had to depend only on its own members, would not have the survival potential of one in which game was regularly shared. In addition, unshared food would often be wasted when a hunter from a small family killed a large animal. Unless the society had efficient food preservation techniques (and few do), his small household would not be able to eat all the meat before it spoiled. Sharing meat with the whole group is thus a more efficient utilization of the resources and consequently promotes group survival. This may be the reason why there are so few "selfish" hunting and gathering societies; they simply did not survive.

Food is, of course, basic to individual survival. In all but modern affluent societies, most individuals are directly involved in the food quest. In such societies, hospitality is usually obligatory. Even in urban United States, some sort of food or drink is normally offered to visitors, but the significance of the offer has declined to such an extent that in most cases it can be rejected by a simple "No, thank you." If the visit is prolonged, however, the refusal often causes some anxiety and the host or hostess usually asks again, "Are you sure you won't have something?"

In many other societies, an offer of food is equivalent to an offer of friendship, and refusal is a rejection of friendship. It is therefore potentially dangerous to refuse food or drink. One of the hazards (and sometimes pleasures) of cross-cultural research is the variety of food items presented to the honored guest (the researcher). Almost all anthropologists have anecdotes about items they have been expected to consume (sheep's eyes, honey ants, and grubs are among the more disconcerting to American anthropologists). But although people in many societies eat things regarded as inedible in the United States, almost all societies reject some edible items in the environment. No one has yet determined why this characteristic should be so universal. The reasons for specific prohibitions are varied, and not always clear; frequently, a member of the society can only say that the item is "no good" or that it is just "not eaten." Occasionally, something edible is believed to be poisonous. Tomatoes were not eaten in the United States for many years in this mistaken belief. Their red color was thought to confirm their poisonous nature, since "everyone knows" that red is one of nature's danger signals. The Siriono in eastern Bolivia refused to eat snake meat on the same erroneous grounds (Holmberg 1969:78).

Sometimes esthetic reasons are given for not eating an item. Asians are generally squeamish about drinking the mammary secretions of a cow, although people in the United States enjoy the taste of milk. Americans are squeamish about eating buzzards or other scavengers because of their food habits, yet will usually consume pork products from an animal whose food habits are equally questionable and whose meat in addition often carries a dangerous parasite (trichina) that can infect humans. The esthetics of eating parasite-infested meat apparently does not bother most Americans, although stories of Eskimos eating maggoty meat are apt to nauseate the same people.

An item may be rejected because it is not regarded as fit food for humans. Dog and cat meat is generally rejected in the United States, and meat from some other animals such as snakes, horses, squirrels and even rabbits is rejected in certain regions, or by certain segments of the population. All these animals are quite edible, and most are eaten in some parts of the world. (If a forbidden item is unwittingly eaten and the individual subsequently learns what he has done, he may become ill even if he enjoyed the food before he knew what it was.)

Religious prohibitions against certain items frequently occur. The Judao-Arabic proscription of pork is well known, and the Christian Bible lists additional items still prohibited to orthodox Jews.

The majority of the items on the list are not regarded as fit for human consumption in most Christian countries today, even though the prohibition is no longer consciously religious. (Examples of these items are camel, mouse, lizard, mole, bat, eagle, vulture, owl, pelican, and stork.) Most of these items were or are eaten in some parts of the world. A few of the items on the proscribed list are eaten today in Christian countries, although they are not usually part of the general diet; they tend to be regarded either as gourmet food or as food for the poor (examples are rabbit, tortoise, and snail). At least one group of items permitted in the Christian Bible is entirely rejected in the United States—the group of insects including beetles, locusts, and grasshoppers (Deuteronomy 14:4–20; Leviticus 11:3–30). Some items regarded as "sophisticated" delicacies in the United States today (chocolate-covered ants, for example) are simply affectations. *Nobody* in hunting and gathering societies (or even simple agricultural societies) eats such things. Australian aborigines still eat honey ants, but *not* chocolate-covered.

No general food prohibitions are mentioned in the Piegan excerpt, but an incident in the book from which the excerpt was taken reveals at least one. At a treaty ceremony with Crow Indians, the Piegans were both revolted and fascinated by the Crow dog feast. According to the author, the Piegans regarded the dog as partly sacred, never to be killed and certainly not to be eaten. The Piegans left hurriedly before the actual feast, and the author reported that some were nauseated at the very idea of the dinner. Other tribes in addition to the Crow regarded the dog as edible and even as a luxury food (Jameson 1909:175).

Many food tabus among the North American Indians were specific to certain individuals as part of their relationship with the supernatural. Individuals often sought personal help from supernatural beings. To establish and maintain the relationship, the individual usually had to follow certain procedures, among which food tabus were frequent. The excerpt, for example, mentions a special tabu on buffalo meat. When the *white* buffalo was killed, the tongue (one of the best parts and regarded as a delicacy) was offered to the Sun, but the rest was left on the prairie. No one was permitted to eat it.

Hunting Tools and Techniques

What tools and techniques do hunters use to hunt? Horses were an essential part of Piegan technology. The horse enabled them to get close to game, to keep close after the buffalo began to

Indians hunting the bison. *Courtesy of the American Museum of Natural History*

run, and to carry large amounts of meat back to camp. Not surprisingly, horses were highly valued, and individuals constantly tried to increase their herds. The excerpt indicates that they tried to spare the horses when they could, showing that they knew something about caring for animals. On the hunt for the white buffalo, the men walked the horses as much as possible to save them for the run they knew was coming. When they stopped to wait for the buffalo to come closer, the Indians "as usual" removed their saddles (these were obviously not the bareback-riding television Indians). On the other hand, the excerpt also indicates that they used quirts freely to force their horses on after they began to tire. Many peoples of the world—not just hunters and gatherers—are known for their casual (by American standards cruel) treatment of animals. The Piegans were no exception.

The culture of the Piegans was almost as dependent on the horse

31

as it was on the buffalo. The introduction of the horse radically changed the life of many North American Indian groups, some of whom had previously been small-scale farmers. Only a few hunters and gatherers have had animal transport, and all the examples date from relatively late in man's history. Animals large enough and fast enough to serve a hunter's purpose were not domesticated early anywhere, and did not exist in the New World until the Spanish brought in horses. Other forms of transportation—boats, canoes, kayaks, dog sleds, travois—also developed relatively late. So far as we know, all early hunters traveled only by foot. The new means of transportation affected man's range, his affluence, and some of his behavior, yet hunters with these more advanced transportation techniques still share many characteristics with hunters on foot. The Piegans provide a good example.

According to the excerpt, the Piegans had guns as well as bows and arrows. Interestingly enough, many preferred to use bows and arrows for hunting buffalo because they could shoot more arrows than bullets in a given period of time. Guns had the advantage of being effective over longer distances, but they were both noisier and slower. In general, even after the repeating rifle eliminated the difference in speed of firing, Indians continued to use bows and arrows in situations where noise was a factor and distance was not. They shifted to guns when firepower and long range were more important. A steady supply of ammunition was also an important variable in the adoption of the gun. A man could always make his own arrows, but after the development of the cartridge containing both powder and bullet, the average individual (Indian or not) could no longer make his own and had to obtain supplies by purchase or theft.

The rifle is a late technological development. Bows and arrows are much older, but man was a hunter long before even they were available. The spear thrower was the first advance over hand-thrown missiles, just as the composite spear (stone or bone points on a wooden shaft) had been a technological advance over wooden spears or unshafted stone points. The spear supplemented or replaced the bolas,° stone balls tied together on long strings and thrown to entangle the legs of game animals. The bolas is still used in South America (Martin, Quimby, and Collier 1947:247). Early man may also have used the sling, but there is no archeological evidence of this. He probably had many tools and weapons made of perishable materials such as plants, leather, and wood that have not survived. Some form of throwing stick is certainly possible. In historic times, such a weapon has been reported from places as far apart as Australia and southwestern United States (Simmons

1966:11). So much time has passed since the period of early man that it would be more surprising to find evidence of these perishable materials than it is not to. Traps, nets, snares, and poisons are all hunting techniques that leave little or no archeological traces. Some remnants of fish weirs ° have been found, but they are only a few thousand years old (Martin, Quimby, and Collier 1947:93). Other than these, there is little direct evidence as to the full variety of techniques early man may have employed.

Land animals, fish, water mammals, and birds are snared, netted, trapped, speared, poisoned, or shot by modern hunters. The blowgun and sling are usually limited to use on land animals or birds, whereas the hook and line or harpoon tend to be limited to use on fish or water mammals. With these exceptions, virtually all techniques used on land have been adapted to water use, and vice-versa.

Some animals are more efficiently hunted cooperatively; others, individually. Animals that move in herds and animals that are either very large or very small are usually more effectively hunted in groups. The group can surround the game, drive it into a trap or bog, or frighten it over a cliff. Buffalo were hunted this way before Indians had horses, and apparently mammoths were driven into bogs in the same way as early as 300,000 years ago (Howell 1965: 94–95). Rabbits and other small game are still hunted by surrounding an area with a circle of people who gradually close in. For this type of group hunting, as well as for some others, virtually every member of the society, including women and children, is involved. Dangerous animals (bear or tiger), besides being surrounded and frightened by noise makers, may also be hunted by small groups of men who protect one another and jointly bring down the game (Steward 1968:326–327). Medium-sized animals (deer, elk, antelope) are probably more often hunted by individuals.

Most societies employ a variety of techniques and consequently organize their hunters in various ways for different situations. The excerpt provides an example of this. The author usually went hunting with a group rather than alone. When he was part of the group, he cooperated with the others and accepted certain rules. In hunting the white buffalo, for example, everyone agreed not to start the buffalo running until either the white one was found or they were ready to give up the search. In general among Plains Indians, no one was allowed to hunt individually before a tribal hunt, because if the buffalo were frightened, the whole tribe might go hungry for a time. The Cheyenne Indians even gave one of their military associations the responsibility of policing the camp during the time just before the hunt to see that no one sneaked out early (Hoebel 1960:53). Cooperative hunting is practiced by many peoples (see the excerpt on Pygmies in Chapter 4), and always places some restrictions on the behavior of the individuals involved.

On the other hand, the excerpt indicates that along with the cooperative hunting went a great deal of individuality. Once the buffalo run started, each hunter was on his own, and the game he killed (through his endurance, skill, and the ability of his horse) belonged entirely to him. This made his generosity all the more admirable. He did not *have* to share his kill, so if he did, he was highly respected for it. In this attitude, the Piegan resembled many other hunters and gatherers. The excerpt indicates that among the Piegan a man was free to hunt by himself whenever he cared to. He was also free to hunt with only one or two friends instead of a larger group. Hunters and gatherers tend to be pragmatic; if the usual procedure fails for any reason, almost all such societies have an alternate technique.

Attitudes and Beliefs

What were the attitudes of the Piegan toward violence? What data does the Piegan excerpt provide on this question? Of course, any attitude revealed by this excerpt could be unusual and atypical. It *is* one example, however, and the controversy can only be settled by the examination of actual cases, not by armchair discussions of what human behavior "logically" should be. The excerpt makes only a few specific statements about attitudes toward killing game. Once, when the buffalo were headed toward camp and people could see the killing, "No one cheered the hunters, nor spoke, nor laughed. It was too solemn a moment. We saw death abroad; huge, powerful beasts, full of tireless energy, suddenly stricken into so many heaps of meat and hide." That hardly sounds as if the Piegan took killing lightly. Again, when Medicine Weasel killed the white buffalo, "He was so excited, he trembled so, that he could not use his knife, and some of our party took off the hide for him . . ."

Of course, killing a white buffalo was something quite special, but even so, the killing obviously was not taken lightly. (The same passage, incidentally, disposes of the myth of the stoical Indian.) The book makes it clear that animal killing was frequently a highly emotional experience. Nonetheless, the Piegan engaged in considerable violence against other people. They gloried in raids against other tribes; they responded to conflicts within their own group by assault, corporal punishment, suicide, and murder. Killing a Piegan exposed one to retaliation from the victim's relatives, but aside from concern over this danger, killing a human does not seem to have been taken as seriously as killing a white buffalo.

The Piegan example does not contradict the hypothesis that hunters are apt to be violent against humans as well as against animals, but neither does it fully support the suggestion that intra-human violence results because hunting leads people to take violence and killing casually. The excerpt indicates that the whole relationship is more complex than it first appears. The Piegan attitude toward violence is not a simple one of "accept" or "reject." Instead, members of the society seem to classify cases of violence according to the perceived necessity for it. In the book, attitudes toward any specific act of violence between humans vary from complete acceptance through reluctant acceptance to complete rejection, according to the circumstances. Most societies seem to make a similar distinction between acts of violence that are regarded as fully justified and those that are in every way repulsive. Is it possible to channel an instinct in so many diverse ways? Human sexuality, certainly based on a biological drive, shows much the same kind of variation. So the argument continues. The Piegan excerpt does not solve the problem; it only adds some depth.

The anecdote about the stampede mentioned in the excerpt suggests that the Piegan shared what seems to be an almost universal human tendency. The buffalo had been driven near the camp by the hunters so they would not have to pack the meat far once they had finished their killing. The desire to save time and energy is a characteristic that has affected the direction of culture since man became man (Titiev 1963:378–379). Given a choice of alternatives, man has almost invariably chosen that which would take less time and less human muscle—except in the areas of art, recreation, and religion, in which the choices are usually made on some other basis (see Chapter 8 for further discussion).

The excerpt also suggests that the Piegan were not expert conservationists, at least not by conviction. The white buffalo was madly pursued, although if left alone, white buffalos might have appeared more frequently in the future. Fat cows were singled out for killing as often as possible, since the meat was tenderer and had more flavor. Studies show that most subsistence hunters have this approach to game. It is only the herdsman and sportsman who are concerned about keeping productive cows and their offspring alive to ensure future plenty. Hunters and gatherers tend to resort to fertility magic instead. Reported instances of subsistence hunters concerned with conservation are rare, and usually refer to protests against outsiders killing off game the hunters regard as rightfully theirs. On the other hand, subsistence hunters rarely kill for sport and seldom waste any of their kill.

The description of the hunt for the white buffalo and that of the ride through the blizzard reveal why so many hunters and gatherers place a premium on strength and endurance, especially for males. Hunting and gathering societies often incorporate endurance training into their child-raising techniques—making young boys roll naked in the snow every morning, or go all day on a minimum of food or water. Sometimes the ceremony marking the change from child to adult also incorporates a test of courage, strength, or endurance (see Chapter 5). When adults frequently have to call on resources of courage and physical endurance to survive, this is likely to be reflected at some point in child training.

Beliefs about the supernatural are closely interwoven with pragmatic hunting knowledge among the Piegan. The white buffalo hunt provides one example; the incident in which Young Arrow Maker was killed and Two Bows wounded another. Trouble indicated to the hunting party that the supernatural environment was hostile. They did not know why and did not try to find out; they simply wanted to get away quickly. Most were willing to risk the dangers of the blizzard to put as much distance as possible between themselves and the dangerous location. When the buffalo stampede passed through camp without doing any major damage, people attributed their safety to supernatural intervention and responded with sacrifices to indicate their gratitude. Interestingly enough, no one seems to have blamed either the supernatural or the hunters for directing the buffalo into the camp in the first place. If people had been harmed, the supernatural rather than the hunters would probably have been blamed.

In most hunting and gathering societies, both hunting skill and favorable relations with the supernatural are thought to be essential to success. A successful hunter is confident of supernatural favor; an unsuccessful one usually consults specialists to find out what his problem is. Specialists are expected to perform ceremonies to ensure success, to increase or attract game, and so on. The excerpt mentions that a "medicine man" accompanied the group on all the long hunts, and members of the party passed the evening in prayer or in singing special songs associated with hunting success.

Most writers now assume that the Paleolithic ° cave art in southwestern Europe was part of hunting magic, performed either to celebrate success or to ensure it. Some art may also have been associated with fertility magic, to ensure plenty of game. All hunting peoples have had enough experience to realize that the most skillful hunter may return empty-handed at times. Resort to the supernatural can restore a man's confidence, maintain it, or explain his misfortune and thereby reduce anxiety.

Unusual animals such as the white buffalo are often thought to have supernatural qualities themselves, or at least to enjoy a special relationship with the supernatural. An animal that is peculiarly hard to kill or one that behaves in an uncharacteristic way is also often thought to have special powers, and the individual who kills such a beast may strengthen or prove his own power by doing so. Of course, he may also run the risk of antagonizing the supernatural by killing a favored animal. Greek mythology contains several stories illustrating this danger (Leach 1949:76), and most schoolchildren are familiar with the tale of the Ancient Mariner. In societies where the dangers are emphasized, killing a special animal may be an omen of disaster.

Some hunting societies believe in a generalized spirit for each animal: a giant beaver, symbolizing all beavers; a special elk, representing all elk. The body of a slain animal must be treated with proper respect, or all animals of that type will avoid the hunter in the future. Quite a few hunting societies believe that animals allow themselves to be caught or that their representative spirit sends his "people" to the hunter for man's benefit. Consequently, Eskimos give seals a "drink" of fresh water to encourage other seals to let themselves be caught, and in the 1600s Huron Indians would not allow the bones of deer, moose, or fish to be thrown to the dogs for fear others of their kind would learn of it and refuse to allow themselves to be taken (*Jesuit Relations* 1897, 10:167). Some societies also extend feelings to plants and perform rituals before gathering them.

The excerpt reveals that the Piegan thought the supernatural controlled the weather (a widespread belief in the modern United States, too—witness prayers for rain during drought). When the chinook began to blow and cleared the air of the frost haze that had been hampering the search for the white buffalo, one of the men exclaimed that since he had prayed for the "black wind," its appearance proved his power. (Of course, if it had not come, it would simply have shown that his power was weak. Either way, the belief in the supernatural was supported.)

THE CHANGE TO AGRICULTURE: WHY?

One interesting discovery in recent studies is that most hunters and gatherers live well on a minimum of effort. Only those in rigorous environments where plant food is unavailable most of the year live a precarious existence (Lee 1968:42). The old idea that hunters and gatherers lack the necessary leisure to be able to build a complex society is apparently incorrect. Something else must be missing.

Along with leisure, a large population and a surplus food supply are regarded as necessary for the development of civilization. If hunters and gatherers worked as long and hard as farmers do, they too could produce a considerable food surplus. Since the population of hunters and gatherers is usually only about 20–30 percent of the carrying capacity of the land, they should also be able to increase their population without putting too much strain on the ecology. Yet they do not (Lee and DeVore 1968:11). Why not? It has been suggested that population is determined not by the average carrying capacity of the land, but by the minimum. That is, the worst years, not the best, determine what the population size will average. If this hypothesis should be correct, then hunters and gatherers could not increase either their food stores or their population safely because a bad year might come along and destroy all they had gained. This hypothesis has not yet been thoroughly investigated, however (Lee and DeVore 1968:84–85).

The other side of the question is almost equally puzzling. Why, after more than a million and a half years as a successful hunter, did man suddenly turn to agriculture, begin to work longer and harder, and build surplus food stocks? Since the question in this form is so new (because the extent of leisure time and potentials for surplus food production and increased population among hunters was not realized before), we have no answers yet, and little speculation. Changes in values and motivation could have been responsible, but the factors that might have produced these changes have not yet been identified.

Most kinds of hunting require considerable mobility, which is not compatible with large accumulation of goods of any type, particularly when no animal transport is available. Hunters and gatherers in a stable relationship with an environment that ensures them an adequate and steady food supply also do not need to plan for the future, or stock food (Steward 1968:328). Sedentary hunters who exploit a seasonal abundance, preserving and storing enough food to last them through the season of scarcity, are an exception. They almost alone among hunters are apt to have highly complex societies, with a considerable difference in power and wealth between various segments of a large population. Tribes such as the Haida and the Tlingit (Southwest Canada and Alaska) lived in just such a favored environment and developed a complex, elaborate social system based on the seasonal abundance of salmon (Drucker 1963). Without techniques for preserving and storing fish, these peoples would have fed heartily for part of the year, but then would have had to travel in search of food. On the other hand, location on a bay near the mouth of a river with easy access to a forested hinterland may have permitted sedentary living even without any efficient food-preservation technology. Fish, sea mammals, shellfish, and game would then have been available with a mimimum amount of travel. Sedentary hunters and gatherers can also accumulate a considerable store of material goods, and engage in long-range planning. It is possible that it was a society of this sort that first turned to agriculture but a system doing so well is less likely to change.

Another type of hunting and gathering society that may have been the first to turn to agriculture is one that depended heavily on plant products instead of game. These people, more gatherers than hunters, may have begun to interfere slightly with nature by pulling weeds or cultivating the ground around the wild plants they intended to harvest later. With their knowledge of plants and especially of growth cycles, they could easily have taken the additional step of occasionally planting seeds. Some modern groups of hunters and gatherers actually do plant seeds and then leave to forage elsewhere, returning when the crop (if any) is ready to harvest. This is called incipient agriculture, and it has been suggested that this pattern in the past first led man to domesticate plants (Armillas 1964: 292–300).

SUMMARY

The survival of the individual is basic to the survival of groups. Food, water, air, and usually shelter are basic to the survival of the individual. In this chapter, we have dealt mainly with the topic of food, since it has posed the most immediate and persistent problem for man. Until recently, man was able to take air and water for granted (except in the desert). Actually, pure water has been a problem ever since man began to congregate in cities, but only a few of the ancient cities of the world (and not all the modern ones) show any awareness of the difficulty. Cities in technologically complex societies at one time had virtually solved the problem of water pollution, but recently increasing population and additional sources of pollution have created new dimensions of the problem so that urban man is once again faced with the difficult task of obtaining pure water.

Shelter from the elements and protection from predators has

posed more of a problem to man in the past than it does at present. Once the problem was solved, however, it tended to stay solved for some time. That is, once man found a particularly good cave, or built a durable house, the problem was solved for generations. Some caves show occupational sequences covering thousands of years. Even man-made shelters have sometimes been occupied for hundreds of years. Temporary shelters, although they do not last long, have the advantage of being easily built by almost anyone out of the materials at hand. The shelter problem has therefore only occasionally been serious and recurrent for man.

Food, however, is a daily requirement if man is to continue to function at full efficiency. Although the problem of food supply may be solved for months or even years through the use of preservation techniques such as drying, freezing, pickling, dehydrating, smoking, salting, and canning, no technique has yet solved the problem for centuries, let alone millennia. Consequently, this chapter and the next concentrate most heavily on man's solution to the problem of obtaining food.

Man has had a long history as a hunter and gatherer. He started (and continues) as an animal living off his environment, but with a gradually increasing development of and dependence upon his culture. This adds a variable that through the centuries has become increasingly important. With the aid of culture, the power of the environment to determine man's physical form began to diminish. More and more, the environment simply provided a framework within which a number of different solutions to survival were worked out. Culture became a screen interposed between man and the direct effects of his physical environment. He began, in fact, to change the physical environment itself. Man did not grow fur to survive in a cold climate; he built a fire to heat his environment, a shelter to protect him from cold and storms, and he used the furry skins of other animals to keep his body warm. He did not grow water storage areas inside his body so that he could live in deserts; he made watertight containers and aqueducts to carry water into arid environments. He made weapons with which he could kill animals otherwise too strong, too large, too fast, or too fierce for him.

The problems of survival remain the same for him as for all other animals, but with culture, man no longer has to depend on his own physical equipment to solve them. He has been increasingly dependent on his culture for more than two million years of development. In the most technologically complex societies of the present day, this screen of culture has cut man off so effectively from the direct influence of his environment that some people have forgotten how intimately and ultimately he is involved in it. Fortunately, some individuals have never lost that awareness and have succeeded in alerting people to the damage man has been doing to his environment. In the United States today, probably more individuals are conscious of their relationship to the environment than at any time since man was exclusively a hunter and gatherer. Certainly there is more widespread concern now about the quality of the environment than there has ever been in the past. Man has been a polluter for hundreds of thousands of years, but because his numbers were relatively few, he did little damage and was able to remain unconcerned about what damage he did do. He has only recently begun to accept some responsibility for his actions in this area, and one hopes he has accepted it in time.

2 Survival:
Food Producers

Hunting and gathering is not the only way man obtains food. Producing food in quantity is another way of providing for basic nutritional needs. It therefore contributes to individual and ultimately to society's survival. The domestication of plants and animals, which was a relatively late discovery in the history of man, has had profound consequences for his way of life. Its demands are different from those of hunting, but it also provides him with new opportunities for settlement, clothing, and housing.

In the following excerpt, take particular note of what foods are consumed, what material goods are available, how they are obtained, and what is done to prepare raw materials for consumption. Also pay attention to who does what in this type of subsistence system. Be alert to the various ways in which food production differs from hunting and gathering, but also look for ways in which the systems are similar, particularly in the demands they place on the people who follow them.

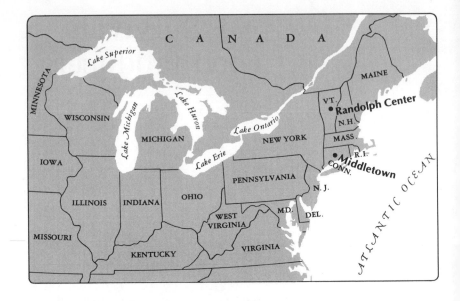

A Rural Childhood in Vermont

All five of us went to normal school—my three sisters, Rebecca, Adelaide and Martha, as well as Closson and I.* But we boys always had to hustle home, get into overalls, and do chores, no matter what the weather was like. . . .

. . . I loved the farm animals, and Martha and I spent much of our spare time during the winter training calves to drag us around on our sleds. We had one black and white heifer we could drive anywhere. Years later Father took that grown-up heifer out with some of the herd, to lead them down a road to a distant pasture. He had a terrible time with the one we had trained. At last he gave up and rushed into the house dripping with perspiration and wildly excited. While he was being calmed down, I sneaked to the barn. Imagine Father's chagrin when he saw me driving the recalcitrant cow down the road with a horse's bridle on her head and the reins through a saddle on her back!

• • •

Father was a small man with a majestic beard and an excitable manner. He met large issues calmly but was in a continual ferment over trifles. His native Vermont reserve was shot all through with a strong dash of peppery temperament . . .

---

* Abridged from *Forty Years a Country Preacher* by George B. Gilbert (New York: Harper & Bros., 1939), pp. 10–11, 15–23, 35–38, 41, 134–137, 141, 145–147, 192, 242–244. Reprinted by permission of Mary Virginia Gilbert.

To understand Father one would need to know something of his own bitter childhood. At the age of three he walked to school, a considerable distance, experiencing the rigors of a New England winter almost before he was free from his cradle. One day his father picked him up when he got home from school, kissed him and told him that his mother was dead. After that he had a stepmother who was so cruel to him that it shaped his attitude to women for the rest of his life. In his teens he ran away from home and by the time we got to know him, there was little softness left in Father. But life under his roof was never dull, for he had the knack of dramatizing every simple event around the farm. . . .

He had all the ingrained pessimism of the farmer and the beauties of nature left him cold. If he looked at the sky at all, it was merely to see whether it was going to rain, and usually he was sure that it was. The flowers and birds might have been so much cardboard, except that the birds would undoubtedly damage the corn and the flowers were traps for weeds. If a stretch of fine days came along, it was a "weather breeder" sure. We would have to get the corn in before it rained, or rescue the buckwheat from the deluge. A sunny stretch was bound to presage drought. Early in the fall he began to worry about frost. . . .

. . . One night he got us up at three o'clock to go down back of the barn and cut corn as, sure enough this time, the frost had come. We had no mittens, since it was too early for our woolens, so I remember Father holding the lantern while we boys, half asleep and shaking with cold, gripped the icy stalks with one hand and tried to wield the cutter with the numb fingers of the other.

. . .

The old north bedroom where Closson and I slept was terribly cold. Our covers were usually like ice. We slept on corn husk mattresses with socks on our feet and long woolen toques ° with tassels on our heads. . . .

The winter cold of these days lives more strongly in my memory than the blossoming springs and fine autumns we had in Vermont. Father was more solicitous of his horses than his sons, so when Closson and I wanted to go somewhere, we generally had to walk, no matter what the weather was like. It was bad enough doing the mile and a quarter trek to school in the snow, trying to keep in the narrow ruts made by sled tracks, but getting back late at night in the dark from a church function was worse. Often there would be an icy crust on which I kept slipping, and the wind would cut right through me. I remember once getting so discouraged that I sat right down in the snow, despairing, and after a while crawled along on my hands and knees. It really seemed as though I never could get home that night. But I didn't get any sympathy from Father. "Nonsense," he would say, dismissing the subject, when I dared to complain of the cold.

. . .

Our sufferings were greatly aggravated by chilblains ° [painful swellings or sores caused by exposure to cold]. Can I ever forget them? We
wore hard, cold, cowhide boots made by our Grandfather Blodgett, and
sometimes rolled on the floor with pain, in spite of the woodchuck grease
rubbed into the leather to soften it. There was one pair in particular
from which we all suffered in turn, boys and girls. No one could tell on
whose feet those awful shoes would land. They must have been a child's
size twelve, and were made of heavy, unsplit cowhide just as stiff as a
board. There were cut holes for the strings and no shaping in the back
to fit the heel. Just low and painfully straight. How we hated them!
They were summered in an old chest over the shed. Four of my generation had worn them and finally they fell to poor Martha. One thing I
know, they never wore out. The one redeeming feature was that after
going barefooted all summer, our feet would spread and the abominable
shoes would not go on, no matter how much woodchuck grease, well-
colored with lamp black, Father might apply from his three-legged iron
kettle with its rattail handle, all of which gave off a worse smell than the
fried salt pork we had every morning. But when I was about twelve
years old along came a new kind of shoe—a felt moccasin covered with
rubber. I shall never forget the difference this made to me. My feet
were warm at last. I was no longer driven half crazy with chilblains
and blisters.

. . .

. . . We had two fine maples and some big elms on the farm. There
was a maple right in front of the house and a swing hung from one of its
limbs. If a rope broke when the beds were being corded, we got the
worn pieces to make swings for ourselves. . . . in my boyhood no one
would think of buying a new rope for a swing. That would be mad ex-
travagance. We made up all of our own games, of course. We hunted
through the barn for odds and ends to help in making sleds and for pieces
of straps to hold on old skates. . . .

I can never forget the rattrap Father made. He got a big box, at least
a yard square, made a sliding door for it, and put a hook over the door.
This he put up in the cellar. A string ran up from the sliding door,
through a knothole in the floor, and was tied to the bedstead right by
Father's pillow. Some corn meal was put in the box as bait for the rats,
and any old time that Father happened to wake up in the night, he pulled
the string, just on general principles.

The morning after the box was first set up, there was a grand rush
for the cellar. We hit the box and listened. Yes, it was occupied all right.
We heaved it step by step up the cellar stairs and into the living room.
Closson had been dispatched to the hay mow to hunt for the cats. . . .

They were to help conduct the massacre when the box was opened.

The women came downstairs from their bedrooms, and the men of the house armed themselves with clubs. The cats were all present or accounted for, and we opened the door of the box. Man alive, what a time we had for a few minutes! Men, boys, cats, rats, chairs, weeping and wailing and gnashing of teeth! We went through that performance a dozen times, whether there was one rat in the box or eleven, which was our score on one occasion. The women soon learned to absent themselves from those rat-killings, and to show up only after the carnage was over. . . .

Another time, Father and I went down to the cellar to open a barrel of cider. Cider, of course, begins to "work" [ferment] about three or four days after it is made. Father had rolled a barrel of it to the foot of the cellar stairs and I noticed that there were decided signs of pressure and agitation within. But he said nothing until after supper that night. Then he exclaimed, "By thunder, George, I forgot about that barrel of cider. We've got to knock the bung ° out of it. Get a hammer and a lantern."

He took the light and I followed him down the cellar stairs with the hammer. We rolled the barrel over on its side and worked it around until the bung was on top. Father reached for the hammer. Now, you don't hit the bung itself in a cider-barrel. You strike the stave near it, with a downward blow. Father was never a man to do things by halves. When he hit a barrel, it stayed hit. And he hit this one. Bang! The thing blew out like the rear tire of a Model T. A two-inch stream of overworked cider hit the ceiling. Father, acting on impulse, pushed his hand down over the hole, to stop it. He might just as well have tried to stop the Mississippi, for he merely spread the shooting stream sideways. I ducked to the floor and Father got the full benefit of the flood. He was literally soaked with cider. His whiskers dripped streams of it. . . . He was a sight to behold. The deluge put out the lanterns and we groped our way upstairs, in the dark.

Well, I never found that bung. Out of sheer curiosity I used to look for it, but it never did turn up. The force with which it hit the ceiling may have broken it to bits—who knows? Neither did I ever refer to this incident in Father's hearing. Whenever I thought of it, I had to get out of his sight, back of the kitchen stove, until I could quiet down. No one ever laughed at Father and survived.

. . .

Mother and Kate Robinson, who worked for us, were great cheese makers. This was always an elaborate ceremony. First, when a calf was killed, its stomach was stretched on a board, as one might stretch a woodchuck skin. There it dried and the pieces were then used to make cheese. One piece of rennet,° an inch square, was put in four-and-a-half quarts of milk to curdle it for the making of a pound of cheese. When the milk was properly curdled, it was poured through a basket to remove the whey. Then the curd was seasoned with salt and sage, both well mixed together with the fingers. (The sage was raised in the garden, dried in the attic, and crumpled up, ready to sift into the curd when needed.) The cheese was then put in a round wooden cylinder and thoroughly pressed down until hard, remaining in this state at least overnight. Finally, the cheese was removed and covered with a cloth, ready for use. It was cut with an army sword, a flourish favored by Father.

The churning was a great headache to Closson and me. We had the usual barrel churn that flopped over and over. If you didn't get the cover on just so, with all the "fingers" under the "hooks," then off it would come, as you turned the churn over, and the whole mess would go all over the floor. Besides the loss of the cream, there was the task of cleaning up, with the prospect of Father's fury hovering over us like a thunderbolt. "Has it come to butter yet?" was the cry that pursued us all over the farm for years, it seemed to me. Sometimes the wretched mixture would take a whole day and would even run over to the next—stubbornly

A barrel churn, used to make butter. *The Bettmann Archive*

frothing and foaming, everything but coming to butter, and in the end going to the pigs. Closson would get so bored that he would try to read and churn at the same time.

· · ·

. . . I prefer to remember the good times we had sugaring. During my normal school days, I used to work at it all night, leaving home in the morning just in time to get to class. I love sugaring, as I suppose all boys do who have tried it. There would be a fine crust of snow at that time of year, and we would slide over it through the bare maples. Afterwards would come the big roaring fire, the steam, and plenty of syrup around for us to spread on our slices of bread.

On Saturdays Mother sent us our dinners from the house. There would be a six-quart pan with mashed potatoes and now and then a fried egg, depending on how Father's hens were doing. . . .

· · ·

In those days there was no such thing as an evaporator with a regulated flow of sap. If the sap got scorched, that meant a lot of trouble. . . . But the great thrill came at "sugaring off," when the sheet-iron pan was pulled off the fireplace and the syrup dipped out. Father would stand by the pan with a long-handled dipper, stirring the boiling mess to and fro, holding it up every minute or two to watch the syrup drip off the edge. If two or three drops ran together and made a big flat drop, it was called an "apron." This meant that the sap was boiled down enough for syrup, but if the drip came off the dipper and made a long "hair," it was done well enough for granulated sugar. Father would get excited when it aproned. "She's down," he would yell, and we would run around to the other side of the fireplace to lift up each end of the pan, so that he could push a board through. Down would come bricks, ashes and all sorts of debris, right into the tops of our boots. A delay of half a minute meant that the mixture would be scorched and spoiled so we had to work fast, no matter what the consequences to ourselves. The last run of sap, when the leaves had started, made a ropey syrup that turned into vinegar. We were sorry when sugaring time was ended. It was hard work but great fun.

· · ·

Father preached education to us all the time. Both he and Mother had high respect for academic attainment, so it was not strange that Closson and I should turn our attention to teaching . . . My first school was at Brookfield. . . . I was sixteen. . . .

. . . It was a winter term. I had twenty-four scholars representing eight or nine grades. . . .

· · ·

. . . In summer I worked on farms for a dollar a day. One season I loaded and pitched off 119 big loads [of hay], earning enough to pay for a two-horse spring-tooth harrow ° for Father's farm. It was a grand affair that ran on four wheels and had a seat. After studying it carefully, Father put the seat down cellar and stowed it well out of sight over a beam. Nothing as lazy as this could get a footing on his farm. . . . Father was ever a critic of the soft and effete.

· · ·

[After the author married, he bought himself a farm.] . . . As I approached the place on foot, I kept my eyes open. Father had told us many a time: "If ever you buy a house, boys, look well to the cellar and the underpinning. And if ever you buy a farm, look well to the water supply—a farm with stock takes an awful lot of water."

· · ·

Before I bought the farm I asked the owner's son how wide the farm was, for I knew its depth. "Why," said he, "if you start hoeing a row of potatoes on a blazing hot day, you'll think it long enough." And he was right. It was forty rods across [660 ft]. . . .

· · ·

. . . how we slaved on that farm during the next few years! It didn't have a single fence, and the land was run down. At the start we sold butter and buttermilk, cream, eggs and lambs. . . . The blankets we have on our beds were made from the wool of our own sheep. One year we had cloth made from our sheep's wool and we all had suits of it.

· · ·

As we had a brook and a good deal of water, we went in for geese. . . .

· · ·

At one time or another we have had all sorts of animals on the farm, even a Shetland pony and an Angora goat, but now we confine ourselves to sustenance farming. We have a horse and enough hens to supply the table with eggs and chickens. We generally raise two pigs every summer, and smoke our own ham and bacon. We have our own beef and we sometimes can thirty or forty jars of it. When we kept sheep we had sheep bakes every year, but we gave them up because with sheep the ground soon becomes infected and they need to be moved around. Our land is not extensive enough for that.

· · ·

. . . I've always liked to fish and as far back as I can remember I've been crazy about a pond, so when I got to wondering one day what I could do with that old hen yard, suddenly I thought of pond lilies and how I had always longed for them. Father never would bother with flowers in Vermont. A garden to him was a place to grow good filling

Maple syrup gathering in New England in the early part of the century. *The Bettmann Archive*

vegetables, and not rows of flowers. Anyway, the pond lily is a fine bloom to raise if you have water. You don't have to hoe or water it.

. . . You need soft mud for the lily roots and rather stagnant water, so it doesn't do to clean out the pond too thoroughly—they thrive on decaying matter. . . .

The big pond [the second pond] is about 200 feet long and 60 feet wide. We had to dam up our brook, just as we used to do in Vermont, and with pretty much the same results at first—the rains would come, the floods would flow, the dam would be washed away. Remembering how many times this happened in my boyhood, after one washout on my own farm, I decided that we must dig the hole aside from the main channel of the brook; otherwise it would soon fill up with mud. We started digging on the flat near the brook and we worked on it off and on for ten years. The pond from the first took its place as one of the most important activities of the farm. Its enlargement, care and use were discussed as much as the crops. Just as the boys helped me with corn, potatoes and hay, so I helped them with the pond. Sometimes we used wheelbarrows, but most of it was done with horse and scraper. Help came from an unexpected source when the neighbors found that it was a fine place to cut their ice. Instead of going farther afield, they came to our place, often with two horses and a big scraper, and between one thing and another the hole steadily grew bigger and deeper until it reached its present proportions.

It has provided good swimming and skating for the whole neighborhood. . . .

. . . We always have a row boat on the pond, and visitors think there ought to be fish in it, but fishing and a good swimming pond do not go together. Even with the brook running in, it will fill up with mud at the bottom, and for good swimming, of course, it has to be cleared out. Fish require weed growth. . . .

. . .

On the old farm in Vermont we had a pump that brought up soft rain water from the cistern in the cellar to the kitchen [for washing] but we had to go down cellar for all our drinking and cooking water, and lug it up the stairs in kettles and pails. It was a great nuisance. When I began earning money, one of the first things I did for Mother was to put in another pump at the other end of the kitchen sink with a pipe running down cellar to the drinking water. This was a great help to her. It is terrible to reflect on the tons and tons of water that have been lugged up just such stairways by generations of women and children, lifting the pail up one stair at a time. An investigation made in Litchfield County showed that in one year a woman carried thirty-six tons of water from the outside well into the house—something like ten pails a day.

. . .

[The author's father, who was a Democrat in Republican Vermont, was appointed postmaster by President Cleveland.] Father lost the post office when Cleveland went out, and the building [that he had constructed on rented land] had to be moved off the rented ground and down the road a mile and a quarter to our farm. It was a job we never would have tackled had we known what was coming, but we had a lot of fun out of it too—thanks to Charlie Blodgett, comical, dirty, fat and disreputable, but a soul I hope to meet in heaven. I learned one of the most valuable lessons of my life from Charlie, and that was to maintain perfect cheerfulness under the most trying circumstances. . . .

. . . even Charlie was stumped by that plagued post office. Day after day we struggled with it, Charlie cursing like mad—hot, red and filthy, but always cheerful . . .

We worked with planks and rollers, moving the post office on a capstan,° with a horse going round and round. When we got it down to the edge of the hill we decided to have a bee and get people to bring their oxen and horses to help in our mighty task. I was dispatched to ask the people to come, and the bait was the dinner we would give them. The people grumbled. They didn't see why they should use Republican horses to pull a Democratic post office. Well, we finally hitched on seven pairs of horses and seven of cattle and did we have a time! We had to feed this army of men and animals. . . . Charlie . . . did turn a heartbreaking job into a holiday. Father in the same circumstances would have had a thousand fits, but Father was steering clear of this undertaking. . . . Well, in the end Charlie's horses triumphed and the building found a resting place after a week's labor.

The moving bee took place less than eighty-five years ago, and Gilbert was running his own farm less than sixty years ago, during the childhood of individuals still alive today, yet for most of us, it sounds like a different world. The percentage of people working on farms in the United States has steadily decreased during the last half-century to less than 6 percent today (Toffler 1970: 13–14). Some figure near this percentage is common among the highly industrialized nations, but it is unique to them and has only been true during the last few decades. Most people in the world today are still directly involved in the food quest, but—unlike their early ancestors— as farmers instead of as hunters and gatherers.

Man domesticated plants and animals after about two million years of hunting and gathering, and the world has not been the same since. The pace of change has steadily increased; children now live in a world dramatically different from the one their parents knew, and their children will inherit one still different. The excerpt illustrates the extent of change during just the last two generations. To people over forty, some elements in the excerpt may be familiar, but the younger the reader, the stranger the life described seems. For example, in this day of the school bus and the automobile, how many children have had to walk miles through ice and snow to get to school, or have had to make their way home on foot on a bitter winter night? How many people under fifty have churned butter by hand? Or made cheese at home? Or worn home-made shoes? Or used woodchuck grease as a lubricant? No doubt some have, but there are not many. There are fewer under forty, fewer still under thirty, and hardly any under twenty, at least in the United States.

THE SHIFT TO FARMING: CONTINUITIES AND CHANGES

The shift from hunting and gathering to full-time farming took generations in some areas, and although it carried the potential for drastic change, this was not apparent at first. A comparison of the excerpts in Chapters 1 and 2 reveals that some aspects of life were surprisingly similar for both the hunter and the subsistence farmer. Note, for example, the parallel need for endurance, courage, and perseverance. The farm boy as well as the hunter had to cope with extremes of weather, and had to complete certain tasks, regardless of climate or inclination. In some ways, the farmer's life in the excerpt is more demanding than that of the hunter. Hunters rarely have to get up in the middle of a cold night to save their food supply, as the farm boys did. When crops are ripe, they must be harvested or they will be lost—unlike game. In many parts of the world, planting cannot be postponed for long either. On the other hand, a farm community usually has a stored supply of food that will last for a while, and the people may not suffer so extensively from a protracted period in which no one can work (during an epidemic, for example), if it comes after the harvest. In addition, everyone—old men, women, and children—can help with many of the farm chores, whereas hunting often demands physically strong, individual effort.

The farm boy, like the hunter, must be able to face pain with courage. For example, the children in the excerpt suffered terribly from the cold during the winter, but endured it. The shoe incident, in addition to demonstrating courage and endurance, also illustrates another attitude frequently held by farmers. In spite of the pain caused by the hard, ill-fitting shoes, none of the children refused to wear them. Why not? Obedience and submission to parental authority are expected in many farming communities, and children rebel at their peril (as the author put it, "No one ever laughed at Father and survived"). Hunters and gatherers do not usually regard submission as so desirable. Societies that encourage originality or independence of thought and behavior are seldom agricultural (more than 50 percent of the productive adult population directly involved in farming). Conversely, societies that demand long-term submission of sons and daughters to parental authority are rarely based on hunting and gathering. Is there a causal relationship? Possibly. Unquestioning obedience may not be a useful attribute among hunters, who often have to exercise rapid and decisive independent judgment when pursuing game.

On the other hand, there may simply be a correlation ° resulting from the amount of mobility required by the different life styles. Normally, a hunter either follows game wherever it goes or, if he has moved on his own initiative, hunts whatever game is available. The farmer, however, is tied to a particular locality once his crops are planted. If he leaves his fields, he loses his harvest. When most of a man's food supply is obtained from farming, he *must* stay with his crop. He therefore cannot escape frequent confrontations with people whose interests may conflict with his own. Confrontations of this sort can easily be disruptive to the society. A clear-cut determination of who can give orders to whom and who must submit to whom eliminates a great deal of open conflict (Homans 1950:418–419), but for such a system to be effective, children have to be well indoctrinated in the appropriate rules and roles. If mobility, rather than the subsistence method, should prove to be the significant factor in developing attitudes of submission or independence, more independence and less submission should be found in societies with high mobility, and vice versa, regardless of the subsistence base.

The domestication of plants had other consequences. For example, attitudes toward land changed. A hunter is not particularly interested in the land itself, but in the animals on it. If they move to another area, he has no desire to control a geographic place empty of game. The attitude of the farmer is different, however. Often, he has invested a considerable amount of time and effort into making a particular piece of land productive and in caring for the crop itself (weeding and cultivating, protecting it from animal and human thieves). It is probably a general human characteristic to value something according to the amount of time and effort invested in it. Certainly, individual farmers who have spent time and effort producing a crop do not willingly give it up even when each one knows he could survive by hunting if necessary. Similarly, the more effort the individual farmer has put into making a particular spot of ground productive, the more likely he is to be reluctant to abandon it.

Thus, with the development of farming, men not only *had* to stay with their crops, they *wanted* to stay. Just as many hunting peoples develop a positive attitude toward the ability and opportunity to move freely, farming peoples often develop a positive attitude toward stability. They "grow attached" to their land. The peasant's craving for land is notorious. Land characteristically serves as a major basis for prestige and power in farming societies, or in those societies recently emerged from an agricultural orientation. (Land loses much of its importance as an indicator of status in highly industrialized societies, however. Factories, businesses, and money, among other specific status symbols, become more significant.) Thus agriculture fostered a fundamental difference in attitudes toward land and stability. The excerpt reflects some of the basis for this attitudinal change in descriptions of how hard the author worked on the farm he purchased, and how proud he was of the improvements he made.

Residential stability led to other unanticipated consequences. In Chapter 1, it was pointed out how generosity is highly valued among hunting peoples. The generous person attains prestige and receives esteem from his fellow-man. Among some farming peoples, however, the accumulation of goods began to take the place of generosity as a source of prestige. Perhaps the change was a logical one. Mobile hunters cannot accumulate much in the way of tangible goods because they are constantly faced with the problem of transporting them. Since farmers may remain in the same place for years, however, they can accumulate material things. (Students are often amazed at how much they manage to accumulate in their dorm rooms during one school year.) Furthermore, a farmer who continually gave away his produce not only would have nothing to show after a year of effort, but in addition might even lack the seed to plant the next crop. A successful farmer not only *needs* a surplus (to provide seed and to ensure against a bad year or two in which there might be no harvest), he also *wants* one, since it relieves his anxiety. Thus the emphasis easily shifts from generosity to accumulation.

In stressing the change from generosity to accumulation as a means for attaining prestige and power within the group, one must not overlook the continuing trends stressing cooperation. It is too simple to describe certain societies as altruistic and others as selfish or acquisitive. Human societies are invariably more complex. The society in the excerpt is one in which the accumulation of goods is important, private property is highly respected, and prestige is largely obtained from possessions. Yet cooperation is evident not only as an ideal, but in practice. Cooperation within the family was, of course, taken for granted. The family was an economic production unit, and all its members had tasks that contributed to the well-being of the family as a whole. Although the family was self-reliant, and valued being so, it still maintained cooperative relationships with other families. The excerpt mentions that neighbors found it convenient to cut their ice in winter from the Gilberts' pond, and the Gilberts were pleased to let them. The neighbors did not pay in coin for the privilege of using the pond ice, but they frequently went to the trouble of enlarging the hole as they were getting ice—thus saving the Gilberts a considerable amount of labor. In another example, community members, although political opponents of the Gilberts, helped them move their post office building in exchange for a dinner.

The pattern of labor exchange—a favor for a favor—is widespread among agricultural peoples. In return for the help of his neighbors during harvest and planting, a man works in their fields when called. Anyone who fails to contribute his fair share of labor is left out of this exchange system and may lose much of his crop in consequence. Like the system of shared game among hunting peoples, labor exchange provides social insurance. A man who is incapacitated can expect the same help from his neighbors as he would get if he were healthy, with the understanding that he—or his family—will reciprocate at the first opportunity. Exchange also makes possible a more efficient use of labor during peak agricultural periods, and therefore gives those societies practicing it a survival edge that may account for its wide distribution. Societies that did not practice it may not have survived.

Residential stability also fostered changes in relationships between people. With the increasing differential possible in possession of material goods, an ever-widening gap developed in farming societies between rich and poor. Hunters also have their poor, but the difference between rich and poor is not great in regard to material possessions or in the amount of food each consumes. The richest family has the same transportation problem as the poorest (particularly in societies without animal transport), and even the best of hunters would go hungry occasionally if he did not receive food from others. The same factors do not apply in farming societies.

Another change in the relationships between men that probably depended on residential stability was the development of slavery. Male slaves are not much use to mobile hunting bands. They have to be fed; one dares not send them out hunting because they probably would not come back; one dares not leave them behind in camp since they might not only escape, but take the women and children with them as captives. Female slaves usually rapidly improve their position by becoming mothers of hunters.

With the development of farming, however, the utility of male slaves increased enormously. There was plenty of hard labor for them to do; free men were not away hunting and so could supervise and guard them; and even better, slaves produced not only the food they ate, but a surplus as well. Female slaves usually produced more slaves, and did not improve their position so easily as they could in the hunting band. Consequently, slavery became an important human institution whose legitimacy was never really questioned until the morality of the concept itself was challenged by English and American Protestant humanitarians (Quakers and others) in the late 1600s and early 1700s (*Encyclopaedia Britannica* 1966, 20:780–781). The opposition to slavery gained strength with increasing industrialization. Slavery is almost as inefficient to industrialists as it is to hunters and gatherers.

Residential stability also apparently encouraged, or perhaps demanded, another change. Among mobile hunters, if people within the group quarrel and cannot be reconciled, it is fairly easy for the group to split. The enforced stability of the farmer may prevent this—except as a last resort. With the development of agriculture and residential stability, new techniques for resolving quarrels and conflicts had to be invented. The new institutions that were born led ultimately to the development of the formal legal and governmental structures we know today.

POPULATION GROWTH AND CONCENTRATION

Stability was not the only impetus to the development of formal legal and government structures; the size of the society was another factor. So long as a group remains small, informal means of social control are usually effective; but once the group exceeds a certain size, other methods must be developed or the society will split into smaller, more manageable units again. (This subject is discussed in more detail in Chapter 4.) With the development of agriculture, the overall human population increased enormously. The relation of population size to environment and technology is complex, and still not fully understood. In a given environment, the population size will vary according to the technology. Normally, a technology based on domesticated plants and animals supports a much larger population than a hunting and gathering one can in the same environment, but a growing population poses a series of problems even to farmers.

One effect of the concentration of population in sedentary villages and large cities was the increasing importance of epidemic disease. That this probably had genetic consequences is indicated by the history of depopulation in the New World after the introduction of Old World diseases. Illnesses that were relatively mild among the Europeans were deadly to New World natives who had never developed any kind of immunity—genetic or otherwise—to them.

So long as humanity lived in small groups, in scattered hunting bands that had little contact with one another, epidemic diseases were relatively limited in the amount of damage they could do. Once man began to concentrate in settled communities, however, sanitation problems increased the speed with which epidemics could spread, and people crowded together increased the number of potential victims. Villages and cities provided a more suitable environment for rats, mice, and the vermin they carry than did the mobile hunting camps. This increased the potential for certain diseases, such as plague and typhus, that may not have been serious problems before. The greater amount of long-distance trade, along with the habit of fleeing a city or village when an epidemic struck, also increased the distance over which an epidemic could spread. Disease has played a major role in human history, but only a few individuals have ever commented on its significance (Zinsser 1935:150–165; Dobyns 1966:441–442).

Invention of techniques for controlling larger numbers of people was probably a major factor in the appearance of urbanization, one of the characteristics of the life pattern we call "civilization." ° The word *civilization* as used here refers to a society with certain typical attributes. Those accepted by most scholars are monumental architecture and public works; formal governmental structure; formal legal structure; a significant increase in technical specializations other than farming; scientific advances, particularly in the fields of metallurgy, astronomy, mathematics; invention of writing; large complex social units, including cities, national states, and empires; and social stratification (Chard 1969:222). Not all civilizations exhibit every attribute, and no single element is diagnostic, but all civilizations have most of the characteristics mentioned or they are not defined as civilizations. Obviously, it is quite possible to have a civilization in this technical sense without members of it being "civilized" in a humanistic sense. The two meanings should not be confused.

Urbanization and civilization are not an inevitable consequence of the domestication of plants, since many societies based on agriculture have remained on a small-village level of organization for centuries and have never become urbanized. The small village is apparently a stable adaptation, evolving to urbanization only under the stimulus of other factors, which are not at present identified with any certainty. Agriculture of some sort does appear to be necessary for the development of a civilization, however, because apparently none based on hunting and gathering has ever appeared. Therefore, we say that agriculture is a *necessary* but not a *sufficient* condition for the development of civilization. There were several centers of civilization in both the Old and the New Worlds. Mesopotamia, Egypt, the Indus Valley in Pakistan and India, and the Yellow River Valley in China were among the earliest centers in the Old World; Mexico, Guatemala, and Peru had the earliest centers in the New World.

In addition to allowing a considerable growth in population, farming also apparently encouraged a sharp increase in technological development. The excerpt indicates an emphasis on developing more efficient techniques for doing things (the "better mousetrap" is an example). This emphasis seems to have been characteristic of many agricultural communities, particularly during the early phases of development. In the Old World, the domestication of plants was followed fairly rapidly by new discoveries and inventions in metallurgy, pottery, fermentation and brewing of alcoholic beverages, textiles, architecture, and many other areas. Pottery itself was actually developed before plants were domesticated, and probably in a different locality entirely, but it was so thoroughly accepted and innovative improvements were so routinely made by agricultural peoples that for years archeologists and other researchers assumed pottery was an inevitable part of the complex of domestication, developed in response to the needs of these peoples. It has been only in the last decade that archeological evidence of the development of pottery independent from agriculture has reached the textbooks, and consequently the classroom (Chard 1969:204).

DOMESTICATION OF ANIMALS: NEW LIFE STYLES

The domestication of grazing animals apparently followed the domestication of plants, although it has not yet been determined precisely where or why animals were first domesticated. It has been generally assumed that the dog was the first, but this assumption has recently been challenged. Archeological evidence in the Near East indicates that sheep and goats were domesticated there before dogs (Chard 1969:200–201). The case for dogs is still good, however, in spite of the challenge. Since dogs are carnivores and scavengers, they can easily survive on the scraps around a hunting camp. If the ancestors of dogs did begin to hang around a hunting camp, there are a number of reasons why their presence might have been tolerated. First, the domestic dog tends to bark at the approach of strangers. We do not know whether his wild predecessor did so, but if he did, notification of the approach of an outsider could have given a survival advantage where relationships between hunting groups were hostile. Second, domestic dogs are scavengers—and this might well also have been true of their immediate ancestors. As scavengers, they help to keep a camp clean. Hunters might not be esthetically concerned with cleanliness, but since dogs eat human excrement as well as garbage that draws flies, the health of groups with dogs might well have been better than that of groups without them. If true, this was another survival advantage for the hunters. Third, dogs are a handy food source in times of emergency. Their presence around a camp would have added still another survival advantage. Later, the advantages of dogs for hunting, transport, sheepherding, hair for textiles, and so on made them even more popular. Another reason for considering them the earliest of the domesticates is their almost universal association with man. There are few—if any—human groups that lack dogs. Dogs accompanied man into the New World and probably into Australia, both populated long before any grazing animals were domesticated, so the case for the primacy of dogs still seems strong.

Grazing animals, since they do not eat bones, hide, meat, refuse, or similar items available in hunting camps, were not domesticated until man had supplies of forage to maintain them. It has been suggested that the first animals were kept by farmers for the purpose of having sacrifices for the gods available at short notice (Chard 1969:201). Since wild grazing animals do not have the surplus milk, woolly coats, or other useful characteristics that evolved under domestication, it is difficult to suggest a motive for their domestication other than that of having meat easily available. Since man *can* survive without meat, certainly long enough to hunt for it or trade for it if hunting is impractical, there are not many conditions that would require the immediate availability of meat other than the demands of gods or rulers, both of which are notoriously impatient. It is also possible, of course, that the human tendency to save effort led the farmer to keep animals around so that he would not have to hunt for them when he or his family wanted meat. The only difficulty with this suggestion is that farmers frequently seem to regard hunting as an enjoyable activity. It is also questionable whether raising animals is really easier than hunting them, and farmers seem rather reluctant to kill their domestic animals (particularly when they do not have many) except on special occasions.

Large herds of animals are not common among farming peoples. Instead, a farmer is likely to have only a few animals of several different types. The excerpt illustrates this pattern. Chickens, kept for both eggs and meat; a horse or two; some pigs; a few cows (for

Reindeer herding in Lappland. *Werner Bischof/Magnum*

milk and meat); some sheep, which were given up because the farm
was not large enough to move them around as much as the author
felt was necessary; a pony; a goat; and fish are mentioned. Middle
Eastern farmers often have chickens, sheep, and goats, with perhaps
a donkey or a mule in addition; Southeast Asian peoples often have
chickens, water buffalo, and pigs. When there are enough of the
larger animals, such as cows or water buffalo, in a community, they
may be placed in a single herd in the charge of the children of the
village, or the community may hire a herder (Beals 1964:5, 15; Kipling 1936:102).

In areas where environmental conditions demand that animals
be moved seasonally to better pasture, there are several possible al-

ternatives open to the community. The village may hire specialists to herd; families may take turns sending members away to herd for periods of a few weeks at a time; or the whole community may move with the animals—a pattern called transhumance.° Farming cannot be practiced with transhumance unless the seasons and the environment are unusually cooperative, so that the herds can be brought to the agricultural area at about the same time the planting needs to be done and removed only after the harvest. When the environment is not suitable for this, the people must make a choice between splitting up the community for long periods of time or giving up either farming or large-scale herding. Nomadic herdsmen do little or no farming and depend almost entirely on the animals they herd. These people are not truly the "wanderers" their name suggests— few groups are. Instead, they travel within a specific range over fairly specific routes, on a more or less regular schedule. Their movements are quite predictable to anyone who knows them well.

Although this pattern is similar to many hunting patterns in amount of mobility, it is apparently a secondary development following the domestication of plants and animals, and not a direct evolution from hunting. The values of hunters and herdsmen tend to be quite different in regard to the animals they depend on. As mentioned in Chapter 1, hunters seem to prefer to kill young animals and cows when they can because the meat is tenderer. Herdsmen prefer to kill old, barren, unproductive animals. Herdsmen also care for their animals physically, carrying and protecting the young and weak, feeding the motherless animals (the frequent biblical references to the concern and care of the shepherd for his flock illustrate this attitude). This behavior is alien to hunters, who do not know the proper techniques and usually lack both the skill and the inclination to perform necessary tasks (such as aiding in difficult births and castrating the male animals). Attempts to convert hunting peoples into herdsmen have generally been unsuccessful, so the possibility of the shift being a "natural" evolutionary development seems unlikely. Hunters have been known to convert to herding under outside stimulus, but even with this encouragement the transition seems difficult (Lantis 1952:127ff.).

Nomadic herdsmen tend to concentrate on only one or two types of animal, the particular one chosen varying from one environment to another. Northern peoples such as Lapps or Tungus base their economy on the reindeer (Service 1971:91–111). People on the Asian steppes raise horses (Forde 1968:299–309). Desert peoples, relying mainly on small animals such as sheep and goats, use both horses and camels for riding and for transport (Richardson and Batal 1949:496). People in the Himalayas depend heavily on the yak

(Ekvall 1968:11). The nomadic herdsman pattern apparently never developed in the New World, where the only domesticated animals were the llama, the alpaca, the guinea pig, and (possibly) the turkey—none of which are suitable for riding, hauling, or transporting heavy loads. Although the llama was and still is used as a pack animal, most cannot carry more than sixty pounds. Consequently, they are not as useful for hauling or transport as are Old World animals that can carry far heavier loads. No animals suitable for these purposes existed in the New World centers of plant domestication (the bison lived north of the main centers).

The nomadic herdsman's life style never has been one of the most popular, and today it is limited to a relatively few peoples in isolated parts of the world. It has rarely, if ever, been a completely independent way of life, since its members are normally in a symbiotic relationship with some farmers. But the herdsmen, who are as mobile as hunters and gatherers, have had an influence on Old World history quite out of proportion to their numbers. With the horse and the camel giving them a great advantage over peoples on foot, nomads were in a position to raid villages and cities, and did so with some regularity. They were frequently the "barbarians" so familiar in history books. Villagers sometimes bought them off with "gifts" of grain or local artifacts, a practice that often developed into mutually beneficial trade relationships, the herders contributing meat and animal products in return for the villagers' grain.

Some of the herders collecting tribute from cities yielded to temptation and lived a luxurious life on the riches they milked from their conquests. In a generation or two, these conquerors were apt to become a ruling class, virtually indistinguishable from their former enemies as they lost their distinctive cultural characteristics. For many years, it was assumed that this was the process by which all nation-states and empires were established (conquest from the outside), and it may be true for some of them (Hoebel 1964:154). Not all villages and cities were conquered, however. Some apparently fought back. The Great Wall of China was constructed to keep out mounted barbarians. Some nation-states apparently had their beginnings in organizations formed to combat the incursions of these invaders (Cohen 1968:237). (Other factors involved in the formation of nation-states and empires are discussed in Chapter 4.)

In the Old World, the discovery of the technique of castrating male animals to make them docile enabled even people who were

FACING PAGE: The Great Wall of China, constructed to keep out mounted barbarians. *René Burri/Magnum*

not specialist herdsmen to use some of the larger animals—geldings and oxen, for example—to haul loads and to plow. The development of the wheel (and subsequently the cart and the chariot) revolutionized both transportation and warfare, just as the invention of the plow radically altered agriculture. Again, the lack of suitable large domesticated animals in the New World prevented these innovations from developing there. Even though archeological evidence shows that the concept of the wheel was present in the New World (Ekholm 1964:493–495), it was never applied. For the wheel to be accepted during its early development, apparently a combination of factors was necessary, only one of which was the concept of the wheel itself. Some others were the need to move heavy loads over land; large expanses of firm, flat land to support the clumsy early wheels; easy access to wood from which to make wheels; and large, strong domestic animals to pull the heavy carts (Chard 1969:222). This combination of factors simply never occurred in the New World.

Evolution of animals under domestication led to increased milk supplies and changes in the nature of the coat of certain of them (wool appeared on domesticated sheep, for example). In the western part of the Old World, these changes were utilized: techniques for making butter and cheese were invented, and textiles using wool were developed. If you had been given no information about the source of the excerpt at the beginning of the chapter, you would still be able to tell that the farming system described had its origins in the western part of the Old World by the mention of wool bedding and cloth and cheese making, because none of these were used to any significant extent in Asia (except by nomadic herdsmen). Animal power and meat have been and remain the primary uses for animals in most of the Orient. In India, cows are sacred, and meat is not eaten by pious Hindus. Clarified butter is extensively used, however, both for cooking and for religious purposes. Pigs, which were a late domesticate and are notoriously hard to herd, were not acceptable animals for all peoples; they were rejected in several places in the Middle East. However, they form a mainstay in parts of Asia and in the Pacific Islands (Oliver 1971:62; Hogbin 1971:27).

FOOD-PRODUCING TECHNIQUES

At present, we do not know much about the techniques used by the early domesticators of plants. Modern Middle Eastern villagers

FACING PAGE: An ox used to plow a field in the Red River delta of Vietnam. *Werner Bischof/Magnum*

usually scatter seed broadcast on plowed ground (Pierce 1964:27).
Archeological finds in early civilizations indicate that in Mesopotamia a seed funnel was attached to the plow so that the grain was
deposited in the furrow (Frankfort 1964:353; Barnouw 1971:224).
Both techniques are relatively late, since they obviously developed
after the domestication of animals and the invention of the plow.
The only archeological evidence from earlier periods consists of harvesting tools, rather than planting implements. In other parts of
the world, people domesticated different kinds of crops, and therefore developed different techniques of cultivation. Root crops, for
example, are typically grown by placing a piece of an old root in the
ground; seeds are seldom used. The root pieces are usually placed
either in individual mounds or in rows; they are never just scattered
over a field. Maize—the staple crop in the New World, known to
most people in the United States as corn—was traditionally planted
by seed in individual mounds, never scattered. Today it is usually
planted in rows. In the Valley of Mexico, farmers developed a
unique type of agriculture called *chinampa*. Working in the shallow
lakes, they dredged rich bottom silt and aquatic plants into artificial
islands, often called floating gardens, although they did not float.
These permitted intensive agriculture with high yields (Armillas
1964:321).

In some parts of the world, fields are devoted to a single crop.
This is typical of the cereal grains, such as wheat and barley, and of
rice. In other parts of the world, fields contain several crops. This
is particularly true of root crops such as potatoes, yams, and man-
ioc, which are often grown with other vegetables. A traditional combination in the New World was maize, beans, and squash, the bean
climbing the corn stalk, and the squash sheltering in its shade. The
system of small fields containing multiple crops planted and tended
entirely by hand is usually called horticulture ° or gardening, to distinguish it from the system of large fields containing a single crop,
where animal or mechanical power is used at various stages of the
production process, which is called plow agriculture or simply agriculture.

The two systems frequently have a different division of labor.
The excerpt describes a division fairly typical of plow agriculture.
Women worked in and around the house (although as children the
girls sometimes participated in rounding up or herding the few cows
the family had). Men were responsible for work in the fields. In
plow agriculture societies in which women do help in the fields, their
work is generally secondary, and the men are normally responsible
for the work using animals or machinery. Although some variation

is permitted to allow for the exigencies of life, when the pattern is broken—even in an emergency—it may be a subject for scorn or amusement. For example, in the comic strip Barney Google and Snuffy Smith, when Snuffy's wife Loweezy does the plowing, this is both a source of amusement and additional evidence of the bad character of her husband (Laswell n.d.). Similarly, in the 1860s, Mary Livermore expressed her shock and disgust at women working in the fields, until she realized that the Civil War had made it necessary by taking so many men from the fields (Livermore 1890:146–147). In horticultural systems, on the other hand, women normally work in the fields, either with the men or alone. Both sexes often perform the same tasks, although in some societies men do the heavier work of clearing the fields. In a few places, the women are entirely responsible for the plant produce, while the men concentrate on cattle herding or some other prestigious activities (Gatheru 1965: 17; LeVine and LeVine 1966:12).

If we compare the division of labor between hunters on the one hand and agricultural peoples on the other, some similarities are

Kikuyu women working in a field of pyrethrum flowers north of Nairobi. *Marc and Evelyne Bernheim/Rapho Guillumette*

apparent.   In both, the activities of women seem to be concentrated near the home.   Horticultural peoples may differ somewhat in this regard, yet the gardens are not too far away to take children to, and women can still keep an eye on them as they work.   In this sense horticulturists are similar to gatherers whose women range rather widely, with their children, collecting plant foods, and who often travel farther from the home base during the day than women in societies that depend primarily on large game hunting.

ATTITUDES AND VALUES

In both hunting and agricultural societies, major decisions are made by adult males, and the influence of women is often slight and indirect.   Women tend to be somewhat more influential in horticultural societies, but actually the weight given to the opinion of women varies sharply from one society to another regardless of subsistence base, and even within the same society there are considerable variations depending on the individual personalities involved. No society known (except for mythical or legendary ones) relegates men to a secondary position in regard to decision making.   The occasional presence of a female ruler does not invalidate this statement, since all of those known to history have been surrounded and guided by male advisors who made or influenced most of the decisions.   In any case, the pattern of decision making in the society at large was not appreciably altered to any great extent by the existence of a female ruler.   (This subject is discussed further in Chapter 4.)

One difference in value orientation can be discerned at the very outset of plant domestication.   Some societies—for what reasons we do not know at present—came to look on nature as an enemy, the environment as a foe to be conquered, subdued, and forced to cooperate with man.   Other societies seem to have conceived of nature as a friendly or beneficent force that would provide man with abundance if treated properly.   The concept of nature as a hostile—or at best indifferent—force seems almost to be limited to societies with plow agriculture; it is rare among horticulturists.

Probably as a result of the difference in attitudes, technology in various parts of the world has taken divergent paths.   The desire to protect stores of grain, for example, which is universal among agricultural peoples, led in some areas to the development and improvement of means for trapping or killing animal thieves.   In other areas, people concentrated on building better and stronger storage facilities.

In the section on the rat massacres, the excerpt indicates an orientation toward the destruction of rodent pests. The father's pessimism regarding the weather, his lack of interest in nonproductive plants such as flowers (which were "traps for weeds"), and his refusal to sympathize with his son's sufferings from cold confirm the existence of the concept that nature is an enemy man must be strong and vigilant to overcome. The author of the excerpt, however, seems to show a more positive attitude toward nature. The book has several passages that reveal a love and respect for nature. In the excerpt, the author demonstrates his awareness of natural forces and his willingness to work with rather than against them by his approach to the swimming pond. Instead of replacing each washed-out barrier with a newer and stronger one, trying unsuccessfully over and over to dominate the stream as his father had done, the author dug the swimming pond off to one side of the main stream after the first washout. The two concepts—conquer or cooperate—are both present in the United States, but only recently has the cooperative concept begun to influence the thinking of significant segments of the population, primarily as a result of the excesses to which the "conquer" notion has led.

The apparently universal human tendency to save time and effort has led to the development of labor-saving devices in almost all areas of the world, although strongly held values have sometimes kept this trend from developing very far. The excerpt illustrates one effect of values on technological innovations. When the author bought his father a spring-tooth harrow with a seat, his father removed the seat and stored it before using the harrow, because it was "lazy" to sit while harrowing. The father was also apparently unwilling to install a pump in the kitchen for the drinking water (which would have saved the labor of the women and children who had to haul it upstairs in buckets), although he had installed a pump for washing water—presumably in the interests of efficiency. (The author indicates his different attitude by reporting that with the first money he earned, he installed a pump for his mother.) Values rejecting labor-saving devices are often imbedded in a religious system. The Amish, for example, reject mechanical devices in general for religious reasons (Clark 1937:235). Various inventions have been denounced as "the work of the devil" (Taylor 1962:75).

Religion is another aspect of man's life that changed as a result of the domestication of plants and animals. Like all peoples, hunters and gatherers are concerned with the supernatural (see Chapter 7), but the focus of their concern differs from that of farmers. For example, the hunter is not so preoccupied with weather. His food supply is not likely to be destroyed by an early frost, a violent storm, or even a flood. Although different foods are available at different times, the hunter usually does not depend on the abundance of a single brief season for most of his year's supply of food. When he does (as is the case with the sedentary hunters of the Northwest coast of the United States), his life pattern tends to resemble that of the village farmer.

Weather is a central concern of the farmer, however. After all his labor, an unforeseen weather disaster can wipe out his crop and leave him in danger of starvation, if it does not kill him immediately. The disaster in Pakistan in 1969 indicates that farmers are not exempt from these problems even in this time of advanced technology. Farmers in all parts of the world have tried to predict and control the weather, often turning to the supernatural to do so.

Attitudes toward time may also be related to the form of subsistence. To the hunter, one day is much like another, seasonal differences come slowly and gradually, and he tends to measure time in large units—"moons" or seasons. The farmer in many parts of the world, however, must plant at just the right time, or the crop will not ripen before the weather becomes adverse. The desire to know the best time to plant is widespread and may be responsible for the development of sophisticated calendars by such widely separated agricultural peoples as the Sumerians of Mesopotamia and the Mayans of Guatemala.

Farmers are also more accustomed to wait for deferred rewards than are hunters. Even though a hunter is sometimes unsuccessful, he more frequently returns home with game that is consumed immediately. Hunting people are famous (or notorious) for the tremendous quantities of food they are able to eat when it is available. Frequently, no matter how large the kill, people in the camp eat continuously (with brief periods for sleep or other essential activities) until it is all gone. More than one observer has wondered why the hunters do not preserve some of the kill to provide for the inevitable (to the observer) days of shortage to come (and of course some do, as the excerpt in Chapter 1 shows). Hunters do not seem to have the same sense of the inevitability of hunger as do the observers, although they have usually experienced meatless days. Hunting people are also famous for their lack of anxiety about the future.

The farmer, on the other hand, *must* plan ahead. He cannot have immediate rewards for his labor, since it takes time for crops to grow and ripen. He cannot gorge on the harvest until it is all gone, or he will have neither seed nor food for the future. A farmer in most of the world (everywhere that crops cannot be grown on a year-round basis) must engage in heavy work for several months to a year before he has any edible reward—and then he may lose it at the last minute because of some human or natural disaster. In the light of this difference in the demands of the subsistence methods, one could predict that in values, as reflected in child training, religion, and other areas of life, hunters and gatherers would probably most often stress immediate rewards and have only a shadowy concern for the future (or an afterlife). Farmers, in contrast, would be more likely to stress future rewards. It would be surprising to find a hunting and gathering people whose values were focused on future rewards, or an agricultural people whose main concern was with the immediate present.

The excerpt indicates an emphasis on deferred rewards in child training. A great deal of effort was invested in a variety of tasks whose reward was expected in the future. The emphasis on education is an illustration. Education is rarely immediately useful, yet the parents of the author stressed it to such an extent that he felt "it was not strange that Closson and I should turn our attention to teaching." (He was fortunate that his education began to "pay off" in terms of a job when he was only sixteen, and barely one jump ahead of his students. Today, because of the requirements of certification, teachers have to invest much more time and effort before they are able to reap even meager rewards from their education.) The elder Gilbert's emphasis on education is surprising compared with his attitude toward such things as flowers, birds, and other "useless" items. Obviously, he did not consider education useless, in spite of its lack of immediate visible benefits and the fact that it deprived him of farm labor for a major part of the day and the year. From this, one may conclude that he was looking toward future rewards.

Another consequence of domestication is increasing specialization. Yet in spite of the development of technology that accompanies domestication, the excerpt indicates that specialization is associated more with urbanization than with domestication itself. The children in the excerpt used scraps to build play equipment, the women in the family made cheese, the father built a rat trap, the boys churned butter, a grandfather made shoes, the family made mattresses of corn husks and "bedsprings" of rope, woodchuck grease was rendered out of animals family members had probably killed. When the author had his own farm, he raised pigs, slaughtered them, and prepared hams and bacon; the women canned beef from the family's own cattle; and for a while the family used wool from their own sheep for bedding and clothing—but notice, they did

Senutu tribe weavers of the Ivory Coast. *Marc and Evelyne Bernheim/Rapho Guillumette*

send the wool out to be made into cloth. In many societies, the women (or men) would have spun the wool into yarn or thread and either woven it into cloth or knit it into a variety of items.

In a modern, industrial, urbanized society, almost all these goods and services are purchased from specialists. This is a recent development, however, as the excerpt indicates. The early farm village was nearly as self-sufficient as a hunting and gathering band. Most individuals in the farm village were full-time farmers. Specialists—if any—worked at their specialties only part of the time. The great upsurge of full-time specialization appears along with cities and urbanization.

FACTORS IN URBANIZATION

Since human population increased rapidly after the domestication of plants and animals, why did all the early farm villages not develop specialists and grow into cities? Some did, but for a city to develop out of a farm village, most of the farmers would have to leave, or else give up farming, since one of the characteristics of a city is that it is a concentration of nonfood-producing specialists who exchange their specialties for food produced outside its boundaries. All cities are symbiotic with their hinterlands. No city population produces enough food to feed itself. Instead of a farm village growing gradually into a city, it is more likely that a concentration of specialists served as a nucleus.

Another problem about urbanization was suggested earlier. Even with a concentration of specialists, as a community grew in size, its people had to develop new methods of social control to settle the inevitable disputes and conflicts of interest. If the villagers were not able to make successful innovations in this area, the community could never grow into a city, since after a certain point it would lose population as individuals and families were forced out, voluntarily went in search of a more satisfactory location, or were killed in quarrels and feuds. Only villages successful at social control were able to grow.

Why would specialists gather and settle in a single location? What groups were likely to develop new forms of social control, so that a city could grow? What kinds of specialists were likely to congregate? Was there only one category or were there several? We do not yet know the answers with any certainty, but archeological evidence increasingly indicates that certain religious systems played an important part in the urbanization process. In Mesopotamia (the cradle of civilization in the Old World), the earliest monumental structure of the earliest civilization so far discovered is a religious shrine. The earliest city-states in Mesopotamia were centered around a temple, which was the focus of economic, scientific, and governmental, as well as religious, activity. Religious specialists organized and managed agriculture, trade, and manufacturing, as well as religion. The temple building was a workshop, a storehouse, a market center, an employment agency, an inn, and a dining hall, as well as a place of worship (Frankfort 1964:350–356). In the New World, the earliest monumental structures are located in what were clearly ceremonial centers. As in the Old World, art and science developed in the service of the gods. The prevalence of priest-kings and divine or semidivine rulers in the early civilizations should be so well known as to need no further comment.

Obviously, not all religious systems, even among agricultural peoples, acted as catalysts for urbanization. What did religions that encouraged urbanization and civilization have in common? We do not yet know. The mounting evidence of the significance of religion in the development of civilization is so recent that this question has not been investigated and so remains unanswered for the moment.

The domestication of plants provided humanity with an alternative life style for the first time in its history. Now people could live either as hunter-gatherers or in rural villages as food producers. The domestication of animals added still another life style—that of the nomadic herdsman. The development of the city provided a fourth alternative—that of the urbanite. For the first time, we have a large group of people whose life style was not directly involved in the food quest. This group did not become a majority in any society until the last few decades in some of the modern industrial states. The four alternatives were the only ones for thousands of years, but recently, under pressure of increasing industrialization, the differences in life styles have continued to increase. At some point, a quantitative change becomes a qualitative one. Surely the contemporary "urbanite" who does not live in the city—the commuter whose social and business lives are almost completely separated; the executive who directs a vast economic empire without having any physical contact with it, yet who can communicate directly with almost any member of it at a moment's notice; the internationalist, who maintains homes in several countries and commutes between them regularly, traveling thousands of miles a year—deserves to be categorized separately from the "urbanite" of a few centuries ago. The tremendous increase in speed and distance of communication combined with an almost unimaginable increase in technological complexity have created new opportunities for life styles as different from the first urbanite's as his was from the hunter-gatherer's (Toffler 1970:12).

SUMMARY

The survival of individual members is an essential condition any group must meet if the group itself is to survive. One basic need for individual survival is food, along with air, water, clothing, and shelter. Chapter 1 dealt with one means of satisfying the basic need for food—hunting and gathering. This chapter deals with other alternatives that developed after the domestication of plants and animals.

Another way of looking at the means for satisfying the survival need for food is in terms of the demands the various subsistence methods make on individuals. The two major alternatives (farming versus hunting-gathering) have varieties within them that make similar demands on people—for example, the demands on the sedentary hunter (whose subsistence is based on fishing) are not so different from the demands on the small village farmer. The life of the nomadic herdsman and the nomadic hunter are similar in many ways. On the other hand, the demands made on the hunter-gatherer are far different from the demands made on the commercial farmer in a modern industrial state. The urbanite, past or present, has still a different set of demands to cope with.

The city is a recent development in the history of man, more recent than domestication, of course. It has posed problems to human survival that man was only beginning to solve at the start of the twentieth century. Now, even as we are still trying to solve the problems of the city, it may be that modern technological developments have made the city obsolete (Hoebel 1966:530). One question that is often asked today is whether cities as we know them are really essential to contemporary society. With modern transportation and communication, do people have to be physically concentrated in one place? Perhaps cultural centers, trade centers, manufacturing centers, industrial parks, and living centers—all separated from each other but linked by efficient mass transportation and sophisticated communications of all sorts—are the trend of the future (Toffler 1970:401–403). We live in an exciting time, a transitional time, and a difficult time, possibly equivalent to the early days of agriculture and civilization (Toffler 1970:12). It is not easy to predict the trends of the future, but it is profitable (and fun) to try.

3 Distribution of Needed Goods and Services

In addition to solving the problems of how to obtain the basic necessities for biological survival, a society must also ensure that individual members have sufficient access to them. The distribution of goods and services is essential in all societies because all human groups have some division of labor. As a result, no one individual obtains all the basic necessities of life for himself. Even in the simplest societies, where the division of labor is based only on sex and age, some individuals do or have something that other individuals need. Society is made up of interdependent people, and to ensure the survival of these individuals—and consequently of the society itself—the necessities must be distributed among the members.

Goods and services are produced; they are distributed; they are used. Throughout this process choices of various kinds are made. This chapter focuses on what some of the choices and alternatives are. It is particularly concerned with the ways in which different societies have faced the problem of distribution, one all societies must solve successfully if they are to survive. In reading the excerpts in this chapter, concentrate on answers to the questions of who gives what to whom, and under what circumstances.

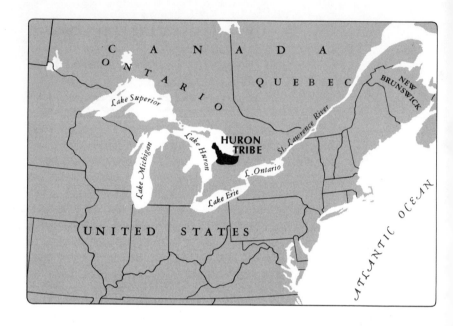

Huron Indian Life: Dreams, Cures, and Reparations

In addition to the desires that we generally have that are free—or, at least, voluntary in us, . . . the Hurons believe that our souls have other desires, which are, as it were, inborn and concealed. . . .*

Now they believe that our soul makes these natural desires known by means of dreams, which are its language. Accordingly, when these desires are accomplished, it is satisfied; but, on the contrary, if it be not granted what it desires, it becomes angry, and not only does not give its body the good and the happiness that it wished to procure for it, but often it also revolts against the body, causing various diseases, and even death.

· · ·

In consequence of these . . . ideas, most of the Hurons are very careful to note their dreams, and to provide the soul with what it has pictured

---

* Abridged from "Relation of What Occurred in the Country of the Hurons . . . in the Years 1647 & 1648" by Father Paul Ragueneau, in Ruben G. Thwaites (ed.), *The Jesuit Relations & Allied Documents* (Cleveland: Burrows Bros., 1898), Vol. 33, pp. 189–195, 199, 203–209, 229–235, 239–249. Odd-numbered pages are in English; even-numbered, in French. The writer was a French Jesuit who lived for several years with the Huron Indians in Canada.

to them during their sleep. If, for instance, they have seen a javelin in a dream, they try to get it; if they have dreamed that they gave a feast, they will give one on awakening, if they have the wherewithal; and so on with other things. And they call this *Ondinnonk,*—a secret desire of the soul manifested by a dream.

Nevertheless,—just as, although we did not always declare our thoughts and our inclinations by means of speech, those who by means of supernatural vision could see into the depths of our hearts would not fail to have a knowledge of them,—in the same manner, the Hurons believe that there are certain persons, more enlightened than the common, whose sight penetrates, as it were, into the depths of the soul. These see the natural and hidden desires that it has, though the soul has declared nothing by dreams, or though he who may have had the dreams has completely forgotten them. It is thus that their Medicine-men . . . whom they call *Saokata,* acquire credit, and make the most of their art by saying that a child in the cradle, who has neither discernment nor knowledge, will have . . . a natural and hidden desire for such or such a thing; and that a sick person will have similar desires for various things of which he has never had any knowledge, or anything approaching it. For . . . the Hurons believe that one of the most efficacious remedies for rapidly restoring health is to grant the soul of the sick person these natural desires.

. . .

Now the ways in which those Medicine-men . . . claim to see the hidden desires in the soul of the sick person are different. Some look into a basin full of water, and say that they see various things pass over it, as over the surface of a mirror—a fine collar of Porcelain; ° a robe of black squirrel skins, which are here considered the most valuable; the skin of a wild ass, richly painted in the fashion of the country; and similar objects, which they say are the desires of the sick person's soul. Some seem to fall into a frenzy, . . . and, after exciting themselves by singing in an astounding voice, they say that they see those things as if they were before their eyes. The others keep themselves concealed in a kind of tabernacle, and in the midst of the darkness pretend that they see around them the images of the objects for which they say that the sick person's soul has desires, which are frequently unknown to him.

But to return to ordinary dreams, not only do most of the Hurons try to gratify their souls' pretended desires for the things that are pictured to them in their dreams; but they also have a habit of giving a feast when they have had a propitious dream. For instance, if any one has dreamed that he captured an enemy in combat, and split his head with a war-hatchet, he will give a feast, at which he will tell his guests of his dream, and will ask that he be given a present of a war-hatchet.

And it never fails that some one among the guests will offer him one; for on such occasions they make it a point of honor to appear liberal and munificent.

They say that these feasts are given to compel the soul to keep its word, because they believe that it is pleased at seeing this expression of satisfaction for the propitious dream, and that, consequently, it will set to work sooner to accomplish it. And, if they failed to do so, they think that that might be sufficient to prevent such a result, as if the indignant soul withdrew its word.

. . .

The Hurons recognize three kinds of diseases. Some are natural, and they cure these with natural remedies. Others, they believe, are caused by the soul of the sick person, which desires something; these they cure by obtaining for the soul what it desires. Finally, the others are diseases caused by a spell that some sorcerer has cast upon the sick person; these diseases are cured by withdrawing from the patient's body the spell that causes his sickness.

. . .

. . . When a person falls ill, his relatives call in the Medicine-man . . . who is to decide as to the nature of the disease. If he says that the sickness is natural, they make use of potions, of emetics, of certain waters which they apply to the diseased part, and sometimes of scarifications or of poultices. . . .

But, as a rule, these Medicine-men go further, and assert that it is a disease caused by desires . . . And sometimes, without much ceremony, they will mention to the patient four or five things which they tell him his soul desires—that is to say that he must try to find them, if he would recover his health. . . .

. . . when they see that the patient is a person of note, they usually . . . give a medical prescription that will arouse the entire public to activity. They will say that the sick person's soul has fifteen or sixteen desires,—some of which will be for very expensive and valuable objects; others for the most diverting dances in the country, for feasts . . . and for all sorts of pastimes.

When the prescription is given, the Captains of the village hold a council, as in a matter of public importance, and deliberate whether they will exert themselves for the patient. And, if there be a number of sick who are persons of note, it is impossible to conceive the ambition and intrigue displayed by their relatives and friends to obtain the preference for them, because the public cannot pay those honors to all.

When the Captains have decided in favor of one of these, they send a deputation to the sick man to learn from his lips what his desires are. The patient knows very well how to play his part on those occasions, for, though very often the illnesses are very slight, . . . he will reply in a dying voice that he is exhausted; that his involuntary desires are causing his death, and that they are for such and such a thing.

This is repeated to the Captains, and they set about procuring for the sick man the fulfillment of his desires; to that end they hold a public meeting, at which they exhort all to contribute. And private individuals take a pride in showing themselves munificent on such occasions, for all this is done by sound of trumpet, each one striving to outvie his companion; so that, frequently, in less than an hour the patient will be provided with more than twenty valuable things which he has desired; and they remain to him when he recovers his health, or go to his relatives if he happen to die. Thus a man becomes wealthy in a day, and is provided with all that he needs; for, besides the things that are prescribed by the Medicine-man, the patient never fails to add many others, which, he says, have been shown to him in dreams,—and whereon, consequently, the preservation of his life depends.

Afterward, the dances are announced that are to be performed in the cabin, and under the eyes of the patient, during three or four consecutive days, and on which, it is also said, his health depends. . . .

It is the duty of the Captains to see that all is done in an orderly manner, and with much display. They go into the cabins to exhort thereto the men and women, but especially the élite of the young people; each one tries to make his appearance there dressed in his best, to keep up his importance, and to see and be seen.

Afterward, the relatives of the sick person give very splendid feasts, to which large crowds are invited; the choicest morsels fall to the lot of the most notable persons, and of those who have made the best show during those days of public magnificence.

After that, the patient never fails to say that he is cured, although he sometimes dies a day after the solemnity. But, as these illnesses are usually . . . slight passing ailments, the sick man is often really cured; and that is what gives those remedies so great a reputation.

Such is the occupation of our Savages throughout the Winter; and most of the products of their hunting, their fishing, and their trading, and their wealth, are expended in these public recreations, and moreover, in dancing the sick are cured.

. . .

Since we have given the finishing touches to our Relation, Our Lord has caused such various accidents to happen to us . . . that we had enough material for a new Relation. But I shall leave for another season what cannot be said in a few words, and I shall speak only of a murder committed on the person of one of our servants, named Jacques Douart. That young man, who was twenty-two years of age, wandered a short distance from the house on the evening of the twenty-eighth of April, and was killed by a blow from a hatchet . . .

We could not doubt that the murder had been committed by some Hurons, and we have since obtained positive information of it. . . .

. . .

The whole country was in commotion, and the most notable persons among the nations who dwell in it were summoned to attend a general meeting on the matter. . . .

. . .

. . . it was publicly decided that reparation should be made to us in the name of the whole country for the murder. . . .

. . .

. . . Here, therefore, is what occurred.

When the Captains had come to their decision, we were summoned to their general meeting. An elder spoke on behalf of all, and, addressing himself to me as the chief of the French, he delivered a harangue to us . . .

"My brother," the Captain said to me, "here are all the nations assembled. . . . A bolt from the Heavens has fallen in the midst of our land, and has rent it open; . . . Have pity on us. We come here to weep for our loss, as much as for thine, . . .

. . .

". . . Speak now, and ask whatever satisfaction thou wishest, for our lives and our property belong to thee. And, when we strip our children to bring thee the satisfaction that thou desirest, we shall tell them that it is not thee whom they must blame, but him who has made us criminals by striking so evil a blow. Against him shall our indignation be turned . . ."

After replying to that harangue, we placed in their hands a bundle of small sticks, a little larger and thicker than matches, tied together; these indicated the number of presents that we desired as satisfaction for the murder. Our Christians had informed us of all their customs, and had strongly urged us to be firm if we did not wish completely to spoil matters . . .

The Captains at once divided the sticks among themselves, so that, as each Nation provided a portion of the presents demanded, reparation was made to us according to the custom of the country. But it was necessary for each one to return to his own village, to gather all his people together, and to exhort them to provide that number of presents. No one is compelled to do so; but those who are willing bring publicly what they wish to contribute, and they seem to vie with one another in proportion as their wealth, and the desire for glory or for appearing solicitous for the public weal, animate them on such occasions.

When the day designated for the ceremony had arrived, crowds flocked to it from all parts. The meeting was held outside our house.

In the evening, four Captains were deputed by the general council to come and speak to me . . . They presented themselves at the door. Here not a word is said, nor a thing done, except by presents; these are formalities that must be strictly observed, and without which no business can be considered as properly transacted.

The first present of those Captains was given in order that the door might be opened to them; a second present that they might be permitted to enter. We could have exacted as many presents as there were doors to be passed before reaching the place where I awaited them.

When they had entered, they commenced to speak to me by means of a present which they call "the wiping away of tears." . . . Then came the present that they call "a beverage." . . . "to restore thy voice which thou has lost, so that it may speak kindly." A third present was to calm the agitated mind; a fourth, to soothe the feelings of a justly irritated heart. Most of these gifts consist of porcelain beads, of shells, and of other things that here constitute the riches of the country, but which in France would be considered very poor.

Then followed nine other presents, to erect a sepulchre for the deceased,—for each gift has its name; four presents, for the four columns that are to support the sepulchre; four others, for the cross-pieces on which the bed of the deceased is to rest; and a ninth present, to serve him as a bolster.

After that, eight Captains, from the eight nations that constitute the Huron country, brought each a present for the eight principal bones in the frame of the human body,—the feet, the thighs, the arms.

Here their custom compelled me to speak, and to give a present of about three thousand porcelain beads,—telling them that this was to make their land level, so that it might receive them more gently when they should be overthrown by the violence of the reproaches that I was to address to them for having committed so foul a murder.

On the following day, they erected a kind of stage in a public place; on this they suspended fifty presents, which are the principal part of the reparation and which bear that name. What precedes and what follows are only accessories.

For a Huron killed by a Huron, they are generally content with thirty presents; for a woman, forty are demanded,—because, they say, women cannot so easily defend themselves; and, moreover, as it is they who people the country, their lives should be more valuable to the public, and their weakness should find a powerful protection in justice. For a stranger, still more are exacted; because they say that otherwise murders would be too frequent, trade would be prevented, and wars would too easily arise between different nations.

Those to whom reparation is made carefully examine all those presents and reject such as do not please them; these have to be replaced by others which satisfy them.

That is not all. The body for which a sepulchre is erected must not lie naked therein; it must be clothed from head to foot,—that is to say, as many presents must be given as there are articles of clothing required to dress it, according to its condition. To that end they gave three presents that bear only the names of the things that they represent, a shirt, a doublet, trunk-hose, shoes, and a hat; and an arquebus, powder, and lead.

After that, it was necessary to draw out from the wound the hatchet with which the blow had been struck,—that is, they gave a present bearing that name. As many presents are needed as there have been blows received by the deceased, to close all the wounds.

Then came three other presents,—the first, to close the earth, which had gaped in horror at the crime; a second, to trample it down; and, thereupon, it is customary for all the young men, and even for the oldest, to commence dancing, to manifest their joy that the earth no longer yawns to swallow them in its womb. The third present is for the purpose of throwing a stone upon it, so that the abyss may be more inviolably closed, and may not reopen.

After that, they gave seven other presents,—the first, to restore the voice of all our Missionaries; the second, to exhort our servants not to turn their arms against the murderer, but rather against the Hiroquois, the enemies of the country; the third, to appease Monsieur the Governor when he should hear of the murder; the fourth, to rekindle the fire that we always kept up to warm passers-by; the fifth to reopen the door of our hospice ° to our Christians; the sixth, to replace in the water the boat in which they cross the river when they come to visit us; the seventh, to replace the paddle in the hands of a young boy, who has charge of that ferry. We could have exacted two other similar presents to rebuild our house, to erect again our Church, and to set up again four large Crosses, which stand at the four corners of our enclosure, but we contented ourselves with those.

Finally, they concluded the whole with three presents given by the three principal Captains of the country, to calm our minds, and to beg us to love those people always. All the presents that they gave us amounted to about one hundred.

We also gave some, in return, to all the eight nations individually, to strengthen our alliance with them; to the whole country in common, to exhort them to remain united together, that they might, with the French, better resist their enemies. . . . We also gave them some presents to console them for the loss they had recently suffered through the killing of some persons by the enemy. Finally we ended with a present which assured them that Monsieur the Governor and all the French of Quebec, of Montreal, and of Three Rivers, would have nothing but love for them, and would forget the murder, since they had made reparation for it.

. . .

. . . The whole matter was concluded on the eleventh of May.

Murder was an expensive business among the Hurons! The French Jesuits did not agree with Huron concepts of justice, but their leader, Ragueneau, was wise enough to recognize that it would be futile and foolish to try to impose French concepts of justice in this situation.

Gift-giving to settle conflicts within a group and between groups is widespread. Its *manifest function* ° (the one explicitly intended by members of the society) is to compose the differences between individuals or groups, and thus restore social tranquillity. But a *latent function* ° (real, but unintended and sometimes unrecognized by members of the society) is to distribute wealth.

CONCEPTS: WEALTH, PROPERTY, OWNERSHIP

What constituted wealth in the Huron culture? In any society, according to economic theory, things are valuable if they are scarce in relation to the demand for them. In most of the Western world, the last part of this sentence is taken for granted because there is a great deal of similarity in the things regarded as desirable among various Western cultures. Westerners therefore usually assume an item is valuable simply because it is scarce. The clause "in relation to demand" must always be kept in mind when dealing with non-Western societies, however, since items that may not be at all desirable in Western eyes may be in great demand in other societies, and vice versa. Many of the Indians of the northeastern United States were so uninterested in gold and silver, for example, that they unintentionally misled Europeans. Asked to show them deposits of gold or silver, the Indians guided them to deposits of lead, copper, or (in one case) even salt (Clinton 1817:7; Quinn 1955:820–821). The only metals these Indians used before contact with Europeans were copper and occasionally meteoric iron. After contact they were avid for objects of iron and steel, but still relatively uninterested in gold or silver. The Indians also desired glass beads, another item that was novel to their culture.

Because the Europeans were *ethnocentric* ° and culture-bound ° (thought solely in terms of their own society's values), they assumed the Indians were stupid, since they would give valuable furs for cheap knives, kettles, and beads. But from the Indian point of view, these stupid Europeans gave precious knives, kettles, and beads (which the Indians could not produce themselves, but which were more durable, useful, unique, and attractive—to Indians—than the stone, clay, and shell items they replaced) for cheap furs anyone could get with a little effort—at least during the early years of contact. This point of view was, of course, as ethnocentric as the European one, but the Western world has no monopoly on ethnocentrism. Who was exploiting whom? At this point in time, it was probably even. Both Europeans and Indians felt they were getting a good bargain. Later, of course, when unscrupulous traders resorted to trickery (getting Indians drunk and cheating them out of goods they had paid for, or just outright robbing them of their furs), the exploitation was obvious, and led to a great deal of bitterness and violence.

All known societies have some items that are regarded as more desirable than others. When these are scarce in relation to the demand for them, they constitute the wealth of the society. Ragueneau mentioned some things Hurons regarded as valuable—fine porcelain collars, robes of black squirrel skin. All societies seem to have some concept of property. Property consists of both the valuable thing itself (whether it be tangible or intangible) and the network of rights and obligations people have toward one another in regard to the thing. Property rights ° usually include rights to control, exploit, use, enjoy, or dispose of the valuable thing (Hoebel 1964: 58). All societies recognize the individual's rights over some things, but no society leaves such rights absolutely unrestricted. That is, all societies recognize private property, but all societies also limit it.

Societies differ considerably in what members regard as properly subject to individual control and what things they consider more appropriately controlled by the group. Even in the United States, where society is considered to place great emphasis on private property, there are numerous restrictions on individual property rights. Real estate can be taken away from its private owner if the public need for it is great (the right of eminent domain °) or if the owner fails to pay the public regularly for the privilege of ownership rights (taxes), and the owner is often restricted in the use he may make of the property (zoning laws). An author or composer with a copyright ° (rights over a certain organization of sounds or words) can benefit from it only for a certain period of time; then that particular organization becomes part of the public domain and can be freely copied by anyone.

Other societies may regard land as something not subject to individual control, or may restrict the sale of salt, matches, or some other useful commodity to a government monopoly. Conversely, some societies permit private currency, or private ownership of highways and rivers (*Encyclopaedia Britannica* 1970, 3:101; 1966, 22: 400). Most societies, even simple ones, recognize the principle of individual effort. That is, if a person invests time and effort in something, most societies grant him certain rights over it. (In industrial societies, paying a worker extinguishes his rights over the items he works on.)

It is clear that the Huron recognized private ownership and also that they placed some restrictions on it. People who owned things were expected to give them away under certain circumstances—for the public good, or for the assistance of other individuals. In one situation (described elsewhere in *Jesuit Relations*) a Huron family was forced to share its grain during a famine on the threat of having its storehouse and living quarters burned down. Obligatory sharing of game was mentioned in Chapter 1 and another example is given in Chapter 4.

REDISTRIBUTION

The problem of who gets what in a society began early in man's history—began, in fact, as soon as there were fewer indivisible items available than there were people who wanted them. Human societies, like all other groups, have a dominance structure °—that is, certain individuals have preferential access to the "good things" of life, usually food, space, and mates. Dominance certainly plays a part in determining who gets what in the society (the methods by which the dominant individual is decided upon are considered in more detail in the next chapter). Here, our concern is with the problem of distribution itself. If five hunters cooperate to kill a mammoth, who gets the tusks? If three help kill a bear, who gets the skull? If they kill a deer and share the hoofs (to make rattles), who gets the extra one? Some way of deciding such questions also had to be developed in response to the division of labor. If men kill the animal, how do women get any meat? If women cook the food, how do men get any? There must be some method of distribution, and from the Huron example, it obviously does not have to be based on an exchange system ° in the market.° It does not even have to involve exchange.

The Huron excerpt illustrates two methods of distribution or redistribution of wealth. The first method was through reparations.° The excerpt deals with reparations between societies, but Ragueneau reported that murders within Huron society were settled the same way. He even mentioned the specific value the Huron placed on human lives. In spite of the relatively precise economic evaluation of different victims, however, the function of reparations as a means of distributing wealth apparently went unnoticed, even by Ragueneau. Therefore, this function was latent rather than manifest among the Huron.

It is difficult to determine just how large a proportion of wealth was distributed by reparations in Huron society. Other parts of *Jesuit Relations* indicate the amount was larger than one might expect from the excerpt alone, since reparations were not limited to cases of murder. A variety of crimes and social offenses were settled in the same manner. In the case of theft, for example, the victim had the right to confiscate the possessions not only of the robber, but also of his *extended family.*° (The extended family among the Hurons included parents, brothers, sisters, all the sisters' offspring, plus maternal aunts, uncles, and distant cousins.) For most offenses, the entire family of the culprit was considered responsible, just as all Hurons were considered responsible for the intertribal conflict described by Ragueneau. If it proved impossible to determine precisely who the culprit was, residents of the village nearest the scene of the crime were collectively held responsible and had to pay reparations (*Jesuit Relations* 1898, 19:85). If a crime took place within a village and the culprit could not be determined, presumably all the people not related to the victim would be held responsible. No such case was reported in *Jesuit Relations*. When a crime took place within a single village, there was apparently never any doubt about the identity of the guilty party.

Note that when collective responsibility was accepted, the cost was theoretically borne by everyone except people related to the victim, but actually, since the contributions were voluntary, those who were wealthy or who were trying to increase their status in the society contributed most. Contributions were made publicly, and, according to Ragueneau, people "seem to vie with one another in proportion as their wealth, and the desire for glory or for appearing solicitous for the public weal, animate them on such occasions." The same motivation can be seen at work in the United

States when moderators of telethons for charitable causes publicly announce the names of contributors along with the amount each has given or when donors challenge others to match their contribution. War Bonds were sold at public auction during World War II to encourage people to compete publicly for prestige. The method presumably resulted in people contributing more than they would have had their contribution been private, for there are apparently many societies in which people do not want to appear stingy or selfish in front of their fellow citizens.

However frequent and significant reparations may have been, they certainly did not account for so large a proportion of wealth transfer as did the distributions that occurred as a result of illness. Ragueneau stated that this was the major occupation of the Huron during the winters and that "most of the products of their hunting, their fishing, and their trading, and their wealth, are expended in these public recreations." There is little real evidence that the Huron recognized the distributive function of the activity, although Ragueneau assumed they did. In several places in the excerpt, he implied that the invalids were faking, that they took advantage of the occasion to ask for more than even the medicine man had suggested, or that they exaggerated the seriousness of their condition in order to get more goods. It is difficult to know whether Ragueneau was making an accurate inference, or whether he was misled by knowledge of the motivation that could have been correctly attributed to a Frenchman in the same situation.

Since Ragueneau did not believe that desires of the soul could cause illness (not having read modern psychological literature), he apparently assumed that the Huron did not really believe it either and used it to their own advantage. (Although if *no one* believed it, the trick could not have worked.) Studies of other societies, however, show that most people really do believe concepts of their culture regarding the cause and cure of diseases. It is only after alternative explanations are persuasively presented to them that a few doubters appear. Even then, the experience of doctors and missionaries has demonstrated that it is quite difficult to shake people's beliefs in this area. So it is probable that the Huron did not recognize the latent distributive function of the ceremony, but were aware only of the manifest function of healing the sick.

The same assumption of collective responsibility that appeared in cases of crime also held in cases of sickness. Illness resulting from desires of the soul was beyond the individual's conscious control, so he could not be blamed for wanting something that belonged to someone else. If he did not receive what his soul wanted he might die, and the blame for his death would rest on the shoulders of those who had denied him. This can easily be inferred from statements in the excerpt, and the inference is supported by other Jesuit reports. Most Jesuits agreed with Ragueneau and believed the sick were lying to get something for nothing, or, if they did believe the individual was telling the truth about his dream, assumed the dream was inspired by the devil. In either case, Jesuits usually refused to contribute anything in response to dreams or soul desires. The Huron, naturally, interpreted the refusal as malicious and accused the Jesuits of trying to kill them off. Since epidemics were brought into Huron country either directly or indirectly by Europeans (even though Europeans were often unaware of it), the charge was not totally irrational. This belief was a factor in the martyrdom of several Jesuits (Talbot 1956:207). Possibly the large amount of ceremonial distribution reported by Ragueneau was due to the increased incidence of illness. Such distribution patterns may have been less significant in the precontact period.

Other redistributive methods are used in various cultures. Taxation is one method common in highly industrialized societies. Another method is the giving of gifts to a leader, king, or priest, who then redistributes the gifts to other members of the society. In a redistributive pattern, the donor normally does not expect an immediate direct material return for his gift. A major difference between this and distribution through a market system therefore seems obvious: redistribution ° does not involve profit. If the word "reward" is substituted for the word "profit," however, the difference largely disappears, since most ceremonial or redistributive gift-giving does involve some kind of reward. The giver in Huron society anticipated and usually received increased respect from other members of the society. He might increase his prestige, gain more power, and also improve his relationship with the supernatural. The excerpt states that "private individuals take a pride in showing themselves munificent." At the return feasts given by the sick person's relatives, ". . . the choicest morsels fall to the lot . . . of those who have made the best show." The generous person therefore was ranked among the "notables" of the country. This was clearly reward enough to inspire the Huron to considerable effort. The excerpt says that each one tried to outdo his companion, and within less than an hour, the patient received more than twenty valuable items he had asked for. Monetary profit, therefore, is not the only motivation that inspires competition; competition can and does occur in redistributive systems.

Systems that require individuals to give heavily to their leaders or to supernatural specialists (taxes, tithes) may create a different

An ancient Egyptian rendering of a ceremonial offering. *Brown Brothers*

motivation. Even though expensive gifts to priests may inspire esteem or improve relations with the supernatural, a primary motivation (especially in paying taxes) is often to escape punishment. (Nonetheless, the taxpayer has his reward in escaping penalties.) This motivation exists in the Huron situation too, but it is secondary.

Redistributive systems often exist alongside market systems in complex societies. The United States has both taxation and ceremonial distribution. Gifts are given to individuals on Christmas, Easter, birthdays, and other significant anniversaries; contributions are made to charitable, research, and religious organizations. Some financial profit may be involved in the latter cases because of tax savings, yet many individuals would contribute to such organizations even if the contributions were not deductible. The cost of personal gift-giving is not usually deductible in any case.

Even when financial profit is not involved, Americans and people in other societies make precise (if unconscious) calculations of the value of gifts. There is a good reason for this. The culture prescribes what is an appropriate gift for a particular situation. Almost anyone can recall a time when he was embarrassed by either giving or receiving a gift that was too expensive (or too cheap) for the occasion. A certain delicate precision of calculation is required to determine just how much should be spent on a gift to impress or please the recipient without embarrassing him. Occasionally, someone deliberately sets out to humiliate another person (usually a rival) by giving an overly expensive gift, or to insult him by a gift that is obviously too cheap. If the rivalry is over a girl, a gift may be given to her instead of to the rival. In that case, the calculation must be even more precise, since the gift should humiliate the rival but not embarrass the girl. The most significant factors involved in the calculation include the socioeconomic status of both donor and recipient, the nature of the relationship, the intensity of the relationship, and the occasion.

EXCHANGE

Technically, redistribution systems are not exchange systems because there is no immediate return. All societies have some sort of exchange system *if* there is both a demand for something and a differentiation in suppliers. That is, there will be *no* exchange if the person who wants something supplies it himself. In the New England farm excerpt in Chapter 2, the man wanted cider and made his own. In the Piegan excerpt in Chapter 1, the person who wanted buffalo went out and killed one. There was no exchange under those circumstances. Exchange can occur only when someone wants what someone else has. The Huron excerpt does not illustrate exchange, but exchange based on several different principles did occur in the Huron culture. First, there was exchange within the family, stemming from the division of labor. Men hunted and did some work in the fields. Women worked in the fields and in the home. The work organization was similar to that of the Piegan, with the exception that agriculture was added. Family units automatically exchanged the results of their labor without keeping an elaborate account of who contributed how much. Some societies *do* keep an account of what one family member owes another in regard to food, shelter, and so on (Pospisil 1964:30). Other societies keep such an account only for things that are not normally part of the family exchange pattern—for example, large loans between adult siblings in the United States. In most societies, however, even though members indignantly deny paying any attention to family exchange, if a husband or wife does not fulfill economic expectations (if the wife is lazy, a poor housekeeper, does not cook or sew for her husband; or if the man does not hunt, work in the fields, or somehow provide food), members of the society condemn him or her, and beatings or divorce may result. When this happens, it seems inaccurate to say that *no* attention is paid to the exchange process within the family.

The reciprocal nature of family exchange suggests that no one is supposed to make a profit through it. There are at least two types of reciprocal exchange, one identical and one equivalent. In identical reciprocity, the same goods or services are exchanged. For example, men may exchange work in the fields, working in each other's fields by turns, or the families involved in a wedding may exchange the same items to validate the marriage. In equivalent reciprocity, different things members of the society regard as equivalent are exchanged—fish for vegetables, food for labor. People do not interpret this exchange as producing a profit for anyone. Nevertheless, the items involved in an equivalent reciprocal exchange are often "equivalent" only in the eyes of the members of the society. Are steel knives really equivalent to furs? Are two bushels of corn really equivalent to one bushel of fish? On the other hand, if both parties to a transaction interpret it as a reciprocal exchange of equivalents, not involving profit, does it make any sense to impose the evaluations of a totally different society and claim that one party is exploiting the other? Use of the word "reward" may be helpful again. In the case of reciprocal exchanges, both parties feel the exchange has been rewarding. Each one has received something he wanted, and to get it has had to give up only something he was willing to part with—something he wanted less than what he got in exchange. Perhaps a culture-free definition of exploitation is what occurs when one party to an exchange feels he has not received an equivalent value for what he has given, but is still forced to acquiesce and continue in the same exchange process. "Exploitation" thus becomes a relative term that can be applied in situations of discontent without imposing external evaluations in terms of one culture or another.

In addition to the exchanges within the family, the Huron also engaged in exchanges between families. These were usually based on identical reciprocity of services. Reciprocal exchanges of equivalents also occurred between tribes. Hurons traded maize with other Indian groups for furs, meat, and fish; and traded both maize and furs with Europeans for European-manufactured goods. Except in cases where Europeans were involved, none of the exchange was through a market system. Even exchanges with Europeans were sometimes made on the basis of fixed trade arrangements with the tribe, rather than by individual sales based on market principles (Hamilton 1951:389–391).

In reciprocal "gift" exchanges (reciprocal gift-giving °), the recipient has an obligation to return the gift. When a gift is given to someone specifically to create this feeling of social obligation, the process is called prestation.° Prestation is the driving force behind some economic systems. As with ceremonial gift-giving, there may be no direct or immediate return for the gift, but the reward expected is usually explicit and may involve profit in deferred form. In a prestation system, the donor often expects to be repaid by services of some sort (political support, preferential treatment), rather than by a return gift. Other members of the society also expect the recipient to repay the donor, and there is usually a consensus on both the proper amount and the nature of the repayment. In such societies, if the recipient does not perform as expected, he loses respect in the eyes of his fellows and is not trusted in future dealings.

Prestation, like ceremonial distribution, can and does occur in societies with market systems. Its presence in the United States is indicated by the reaction people have when they learn that some influential political figure has accepted an expensive automobile or other expensive gift. The public is not concerned about possible repayment in kind; it fears that the gift will be repaid by preferential treatment. (When money is given, it is called a bribe, rather than a gift.) There is a general reluctance in the United States to accept expensive gifts from people to whom one does not want to feel obligated. Parents, particularly mothers, are apt to act distressed on learning that their daughter has accepted an expensive gift (other than an engagement ring) from a man. They tend to worry about how the obligation might be repaid.

THE PROBLEM OF BIAS

Notice that the terms used and the interpretations given by members of a society may not coincide with those of the analyst. The Huron interpreted gift-giving as a healing process; Ragueneau interpreted it as ignorant people succumbing to deception; and here we interpret it as a form of wealth distribution. Which interpretation is "correct"? The answer depends on the point of reference. For the Huron, a man who gave away a black squirrel robe was being morally responsible and helping heal a fellow citizen. For Ragueneau and other Jesuits, he was either deceived or in league with the devil. Classification of the characteristics of the society based on the members' viewpoint is called *emic* ° (Price-Williams 1968: 307). When the classification is made according to some external system of analysis, it is called *etic*.° Anthropologists are currently arguing over which method is valid, or more valid.

Comparisons between societies almost always involve etic classifications, and without cross-cultural comparisons, there is no way to discern general patterns (if any exist). Without generalizations, there is no "science" of man, there is only the history of individual groups of men. The study of man then becomes limited to description and anecdote. Needless to say, anthropologists who are attempting to arrive at theories of human behavior reject the argument that each man and each society is unique, without any common patterns, processes, or characteristics. On the other hand, particularly in the areas of knowledge and thought processes, gross errors have been made by attempting to force the categorizations of one culture into the categories of another. Emic-oriented studies add a great deal to the body of information about man's thought processes and psychology. Ethnobotany, for example, deals with the way in which different societies classify their botanical knowledge; ethnomusicology is the study of the musical idiom of different societies. Emic-oriented studies can provide new insights and can be highly productive of increased understanding of the subject matter itself. We know more about music in general after learning non-Western ways of arranging and producing musical sounds. Such knowledge can enrich our own musical idioms. Both emic and etic approaches can be useful, but for different purposes.

Highly industrialized societies may be complex, but in some respects they parallel simpler ones. One of the goals of anthropology is to be able to understand complex societies better through the use of insights gained from the study of simpler societies. As you read the following excerpt from an industrial society, try to identify similarities with and differences from the Huron society.

Captaining an Industry

. . . I was the eldest of five; four boys and a girl.* There was excitement for us all in the fact that I had a job in the mechanical field, so that my education would count. From the time I was eleven and began attending Brooklyn Polytechnic Institute I had been interested in mechanics, in engineering.

· · ·

. . . Father certainly was not rich, but he had always managed to keep us in comfortable circumstances. As a rule, there was a cook in our kitchen, but if there were not, my mother well knew how to cook. She was the daughter of a Methodist Episcopal minister. Father was the son of a private-school master. Neither had any business forebears.

Well, I am bound to admit the first sight of my opportunity was disappointing. It was a gloomy, machinery-cluttered loft in a building in Market Street in Newark . . . I worked there as a draftsman for

* Abridged from *Adventures of a White-Collar Man* by Alfred P. Sloan, Jr., in collaboration with Boyden Sparkes (New York: Doubleday, Doran & Co., 1941), pp. 7–12, 18, 21–22, 24–27, 32–40, 43–44, 48–49, 57–59, 72–75, 77–78, 83–84, 86–87, 94, 98, 100, 102, 107, 133–135, 143–147. Reprinted by permission. The adventures begin in 1895.

several months, pending removal of the business to near-by Harrison. But that was even more disappointing. . . . Not far from a city dump on a weed-grown, marshy plain was an old weather-worn building, like an overgrown barn. . . . Once the factory had been painted brown. Only one word describes it: "dirty." Smoke from the dump carried an acrid odor. Eventually across the wall nearest the railroad track there was lettered in black this legend: HYATT ROLLER BEARING COMPANY.

• • •

The antifriction bearing put at the disposal of engineers a workable instrumentality of priceless value. Hyatt was a gifted, practical, hard-working inventor in a period when inventors were able to work with reasonable hope of producing something as individuals rather than as cogs of great research organizations.

. . . Today John Wesley Hyatt—and many inventors of his time—with all his accomplishments would find himself regarded as scientifically illiterate. As a matter of fact, he would be. The modern research laboratories of industry demand men having years of training in some form of science, whose talents can be coordinated on a specific problem. . . .

• • •

I soon began to wonder how secure my job was. Literally, the business was being operated from week to week. Each payday was a crisis. . . . For months the gross business of the company had totaled only a few thousand dollars, but the pay roll and the other charges, for raw materials, freight and other things, had amounted to much more. The difference had always been supplied by Mr. Searles out of his own pocket. But Mr. Searles was becoming grumpier by the week, according to Pete [the paymaster]. Consequently all of us . . . were relieved each time Pete returned, bearing another check drawn aganst the Searles bank account.

• • •

The business was being operated badly. We seemed to capitalize only a fraction of our opportunities. Both Pete Steenstrup and I saw that plainly, but we could do little. . . .

• • •

Mr. Searles . . . decided that he would put no more money into Hyatt. . . . Unless some new backer could be found, it would be necessary to close down the works.

Because of the friendship of my father and Mr. Searles, they had discussed the situation . . . My father and a man named Donner, an associate of Mr. Searles in the American Sugar Refining Company, . . . bought into the company. I think Mr. Donner and my father each put up $2500. That was as far as Mr. Donner would go, but my father said he would advance more if the business showed any promise. Thereafter Pete, instead of going with the pay roll to Mr. Searles, went to my father. Pete and I had become partners.

. . . my salary was $175.00 a month. . . . We had six months to put the business on its feet, and we made good. With Pete selling and with me handling the production end, in our first six months we made a profit of $12,000. I'm not likely to forget that. Pete was given the title of sales manager. I was general manager.

· · ·

But for a long time after we had shown we could make money the business faced a crisis each Saturday. Pay-roll worry has whitened a lot of hair in this country, mine included. . . . When a business is making money and expanding, it is to be expected that it will always be short of capital, simply because it is too successful in relation to its resources.

· · ·

One day in our mail we found a letter from Kokomo, Indiana. A man named Elwood Haynes wanted to know about our bearings. He was making gasoline-powered road cars—automobiles. This inquiry came to us in 1899 and he had been making his gasoline-engine machines since 1894, never more than a few each year. . . .

. . . That was the beginning of our real adventures. It woke us up. If one automobile manufacturer wanted something better than ordinary greased wagon axles, why not sell all of them? . . .

· · ·

On the first big order he got in Detroit, Pete recklessly called me on the long-distance telephone. . . . he had a trial order from the Olds Motor Works. They wanted 120 bearings, four for each rear axle on thirty automobiles. Pete was beside himself, and so was I.

· · ·

A wildfire of experimenting in machine shops and barns was becoming a boom almost like a gold rush. In 1896, when Ransom E. Olds turned away from steam and made his first gasoline car, probably there were no more than thirty self-propelled carriages in America. But three years later, when we got our first order from Elwood Haynes, at least eighty separate business projects for making horseless carriages were under way. . . .

Speed! That was the most important word of all to Ransom E. Olds. He was a pioneer in the field of quantity production. . . . But to Henry M. Leland [general manager of Cadillac Motor Car Company] the most important word was not speed; it was precision. . . .

· · ·

I remember how this was brought home to me. The white beard of Henry M. Leland seemed to wag at me, he spoke with such long-faced emphasis. . . .

"Mr. Sloan, Cadillacs are made to run, not just to sell."

. . .

"Your Mr. Steenstrup told me these bearings would be accurate, one like another, to within one thousandth of an inch. But look here!" I heard the click of his ridged fingernail as he tapped against a guilty bearing. "There is nothing like that uniformity.

. . . "Mr. Sloan, do you know why your firm received this order?"

. . . He pointed into the factory yard, where a lot of axles were piled like cordwood.

"The bearings in those axles out there did not stand up under the Cadillac load. . . . We canceled the order . . . Unless you can give me what I want, I'm going to put five-hundred Weston-Mott axles out there beside those other rejects."

That was a terrible threat. We'd lose the business of the Weston-Mott Axle Company. They'd have to change the design of their axle to use another bearing, which might end forever the relationship between Weston-Mott and Hyatt Roller Bearings. To Mr. Leland I spoke as softly as I could. . . .

. . .

But Mr. Leland interrupted, "You must grind your bearings. Even though you make thousands, the first and the last should be precisely alike." We discussed interchangeability of parts. A genuine conception of what mass production should mean really grew in me with that conversation.

I was an engineer and a manufacturer, and I considered myself conscientious. But after I had said good-by to Mr. Leland, I began to see things differently. I was determined to be as fanatical as he in obtaining precision in our work. An entirely different standard had been established for Hyatt Roller Bearings.

. . .

This may seem inconsequential, but truly it is of great importance, because the ability to produce large quantities of parts, each one just like the other or sufficiently alike, within a predetermined allowance of inaccuracy, is the foundation of mass production, as we understand that term today. . . .

. . .

In 1905 a considerable part of our bearings were shipped to Utica, New York, and one day I learned that one of our biggest customers was considering an important change. . . . The Weston-Mott Company, of Utica, was being tempted to move its axle plant out to Flint, a small town in Michigan. . . .

. . .

. . . The men trying to effect this change were William C. Durant and his partner, J. Dallas Dort. They were carriage manufacturers who had refinanced Buick.

That was a trivial incident of itself, but I believe it marks the first step in the integration of the automobile industry. Thereafter, bit by bit, we were to see a constant evolution bringing the manufacture of the motorcar itself and the manufacture of its component parts into a closer corporate relationship. . . .

• • •

Why had Durant and Dort been so anxious to get Weston-Mott's axle plant established next door to the new Buick factory in Flint? Every piece of the motorcar is essential in the sense that the automobile is not complete unless every part is available. Delay in delivery of any part stops the work. A dependable supply of parts might well make the difference between success and failure. Distance added uncertainty. It was natural, therefore, for the industry to correlate all its manufacturing within a rather narrow geographical area. . . .

• • •

The Hyatt Roller Bearing Company was dependable. We had to be in order to survive in the automobile-parts business. Literally, it was a capital offense to hold up a production line. . . .

Too much, too many jobs depended on keeping the schedule of deliveries. . . .

No excuse was any good if you failed to deliver. Often in the caboose of a freight train that carried a carload of Hyatt roller bearings you might find a Hyatt man who would cajole, bribe or fight, as the occasion demanded, to keep our bearings moving toward their destination. Eventually we kept two men in Buffalo, just to make absolutely sure no cars of Hyatt freight could go astray.

• • •

The confidence of the Ford organization in our roller bearings and in our ability to deliver was a most important factor in making Hyatt what it ultimately turned out to be.

• • •

Naturally, we had an indifferent product in our beginning at Hyatt. Our costs were necessarily high. But all that was true of . . . the automobile itself. To start out for a ride was an adventure; to return with no parts missing, and all parts functioning, was a miracle. . . .

Then the public seemed to be willing to pay a big price for an indifferent piece of apparatus—and like it. They forgot its shortcomings because it provided a new thrill. Fortunately before people's patience wore out, the cars improved.

As the parts of the motorcar became better, we continued to improve the standards of our Hyatt roller bearings. . . .

. . . Mr. Ford had determined that he had to have better steel in order to make stronger cars, at the same time avoiding the tendency to make them heavier and heavier. As a result of Mr. Wills' [C. Harold Wills] efforts, the answer was found in vanadium steel. When Mr. Ford prepared to introduce this new material into his Model T, I did the same at Hyatt.

. . .

. . . I had been so busy trying to make more and better Hyatt roller bearings that I had had little time to consider the economics of Hyatt's position. . . . my first realization of the importance of price as affecting volume was taught to me by Henry Ford. He had the vision to see that lower prices would increase volume up to the point that would justify such lower prices through reduced costs. . . .

. . .

. . . Ford was growing as no industrial enterprise had ever grown before. Hyatt Roller Bearing Company was obliged to grow with Ford, or else give way to some other supplier who would keep pace. The whole trick of that growth was to keep improving the technique of manufacture

An early automobile assembly line. *Courtesy of General Motors Corporation*

and to keep lowering the price of the car to reach an even bigger market. However, an even more amazing thing was the discovery that as the price of the car was reduced, wages could be raised. I well remember the consternation that spread through the industry when Mr. Ford made the dramatic announcement of a five-dollar-a-day minimum wage for his workmen. Many thought cars could not be sold on that basis. Who would pay the price?

At that time industry's practice was to set wages low, the lower the better. Reduce when you could, increase when you must. The power of an economic wage rate to stimulate consumption had not been realized. The five-dollar rate made good, but only because the Ford worker was enabled to produce more. From 1909–10 to 1916–17 the price of Ford's Model T was lowered year by year as follows: $950, $780, $690, $600, $550, $490, $360. The magical result of that was a volume which overwhelmingly justified the cost of the factory changes which preceded each cut in price. In those same years his production schedule grew as follows: 18,664; 34,528; 78,440; 168,220; 248,307; 308,213; 533,921; 785,432. . . .

. . .

. . . Closer integration was inevitable as the automobile industry passed out of the pioneering stage. But few had sufficient daring for the accomplishment of such vast trades as were even then in the making. William C. Durant was one. Ben Briscoe for a time was another.

. . .

Every deal made by William C. Durant for another automobile company after he organized the General Motors Company touched the interests of many parts manufacturers. Repeatedly I was to discover that Durant had taken over a Hyatt customer. . . .

. . .

. . . We were pouring profits into new buildings, new machines. It was a time of terrific growth in the industry. . . .

. . .

However, I was not altogether happy about the increase in our business. The process of integration was raising a problem for me. Actually, we had two gigantic customers. One was Ford, and one was General Motors. Suppose one or the other or both decided to make their own bearings? The Hyatt Roller Bearing Company might find itself with a plant far bigger than it could use and nowhere to go for new business. I had put my whole life's energy into Hyatt. Everything I had earned was there in bricks, machinery and materials. I was, I feared, out on a limb. But I was not alone. Other parts makers were out there, too.

. . .

. . . The same uncertainties that troubled makers of parts were valid worries of those who bought our parts. Suppose Buick or Willys-Over-land or Ford suddenly got the idea it might be cut off from an important source of supply? Lack of one tiny part might hold up their assembly line. That fear was the nightmare of the business.

. . . In my heart I felt I would be acting soundly for our business if I made a deal with Durant.

. . .

. . . What they were forming was United Motors Corporation, destined to become an affiliate of General Motors.

. . .

They made me its president. . . . There were to be 1,000,000 shares of United Motors, and in 1916 there was a wild sound to that alone. I think we were about the first ever to issue so many shares. Today the practice of having sufficient shares to keep units of ownership small is generally approved. . . .

. . .

. . . in 1918 United Motors was consolidated with General Motors Corporation and later on was liquidated. I became a director of General Motors on November 7, 1918, and six weeks later, a vice-president. . . .

. . .

In bringing General Motors into existence, Mr. Durant had operated as a dictator. But such an institution could not grow into a successful organization under a dictatorship. Dictatorship is the most effective way of administration, provided the dictator knows the complete answers to all questions. But he never does and never will. . . . If General Motors were to capitalize its wonderful opportunity, it would have to be guided by an organization of intellects. A great industrial organization requires the best of many minds. . . .

. . .

Up to the time Mr. Durant left I had not had any direct responsibility for the manufacture of automobiles. My activities had been confined to the accessory group of operations. But I now began to have a broader scope as a sort of principal assistant to the president. Mr. du Pont . . . gave us his time and the benefit of his great ability without limit until he resigned as president in May 1923, when I succeeded him.

The prime responsibility of General Motors now became mine. . . .
. . . In the two years that Mr. du Pont had been president, much time had to be consumed in meeting the daily administrative problems. . . . At the same time we had to give thought to a fundamental plan upon which we could build . . . The prime consideration in that problem was a definite concept of management. The first step was to determine whether we would operate under a centralized or decentralized form of administration. . . . We realized that in an institution as big as General Motors was even then . . . any plan that involved too great a concentra-

tion of problems upon a limited number of executives would limit initiative, would involve delay, would increase expense, and would reduce efficiency and development. . . . After forty years of experience in American industry, I would say that my concept of the management scheme of a great industrial organization, simply expressed, is to divide it into as many parts as consistently can be done, place in charge of each part the most capable executive that can be found, develop a system of co-ordination so that each part may strengthen and support each other part; thus not only welding all parts together in the common interests of a joint enterprise, but importantly developing ability and initiative through the instrumentalities of responsibility and ambition—developing men and giving them an opportunity to exercise their talents, both in their own interests as well as in that of the business.

· · ·

My responsibilities had expanded enormously. At Hyatt, big as it was, I had been obliged to consider the interests of only a few stockholders, a few customers and three or four thousand workers. But as president of General Motors, I realized our thinking affected the lives of hundreds of thousands directly and influenced the economic welfare of many important communities, in some of which we were almost the sole provider. In some way, visible or invisible, as we expanded, the economic welfare of millions was becoming linked with the welfare of General Motors. . . .

· · ·

Bigness is essential in many branches of business and industry if the community is to be served on the best economic basis, and without bigness in some ways it cannot be served at all. . . . On the other hand, some see danger in bigness. They fear the concentration of economic power that it brings with it. That is in a degree true. It simply means, however, that industrial management must expand its horizon of responsibility. . . .

. . . An advancing standard of living means that more workers are becoming bigger and better consumers. Therefore industry's wage level is an important factor in this broader responsibility of industry because it involves the matter of purchasing power. . . . Many believe the wage level is wholly at the discretion of management. That is not so . . . Because, other things being equal, as we raise wages we increase costs and selling prices. . . . Higher prices mean reduction in consumption, less employment. . . . I wish most sincerely that there could be a broader recognition of the fundamental economic fact that the wage level depends on the amount of the productivity of the workers. Entirely so. Also the productivity of the worker depends upon the tools that the employer gives him to work with. The more efficient the tools, the more the worker produces and the higher wages he will inevitably receive. . . . the only true answer to the great question of more things for more people everywhere is more work efficiently performed. . . .

THE HURON AND THE AUTOMOBILE INDUSTRY: COMPARISONS

The last sentence of the Sloan excerpt contains a major part of the credo of the modern industrialized world. While it is basically true, there is some controversy over whether it is *desirable.* Modern methods of mass production are infinitely more efficient in producing *things* than the old handicraft techniques. If everything in industrial societies had to be made by hand, we would have a world in which the very few live in luxury while the majority lack almost all material comforts—a situation that in fact currently exists in many parts of the world, and that was characteristic of all nations and empires until less than a century ago.

In most highly industrialized nations today, although there may be wide gaps between rich and poor, the average citizen has comforts his ancestors could not have dreamt of. Some of these did not exist a hundred years ago, of course—electric lights, television, washing machines, refrigerators, indoor plumbing, central heating. But others—privately owned homes with several rooms; oranges, melons, and fresh vegetables in winter; fashionable, easily cleaned clothes; private transportation—are the results of a technological revolution that has brought incredible material prosperity to the majority of people in the United States and a few other high-technology societies. An ordinary working man in the United States lives in luxury hardly surpassed by members of the elite in some underdeveloped countries.

None of this material affluence could exist without techniques that make it possible to produce an enormous quantity and variety of goods quickly and cheaply. Such production strains the environment; the United States consumes a highly disproportionate share of the world's resources. Partly because of this, people in other countries (and in the United States itself) have become highly critical of America, which is called a selfish and ruthless exploiter of poorer nations. Unfortunately, however, the population of the rest of the world is not really interested in decreasing American consumption so much as it is in raising its own living standard to the level of that of the United States. No country seems about to dedicate its citizenry to remaining forever without the material luxuries commonplace in the United States. Instead, communist, socialist, and capitalist countries *all* seem to be making every effort to industrialize so that they too can produce more goods more cheaply for their citizens. The main argument dividing countries today is not so much what they are trying to do as how they are trying to do it. All of them at least give lip service to the goal of increasing production, but argue about the "best" (both most efficient and most ethical) way of attaining that goal.

The excerpt from Alfred Sloan's autobiography provides a first-hand account of some of the events that took place during the expansionist phase of the automobile industry, certainly one of the prime examples of American industrial organization. Comparison of this excerpt with the one on the Huron reveals both similarities and differences. Both the Huron and Sloan were apparently motivated by the desire to succeed, to attain prestige in the eyes of their fellows, and to avoid failure. The cultures (including the values) of the societies determined how members could acceptably go about reaching their goals. In Huron society, esteem was gained by giving away quantities of goods in response to the pleas of the sick, or to aid the society as a whole. Of course, a Huron had to have wealth before he could give it away, so one might infer that the desire to gain prestige motivated not only generosity, but also the accumulation of goods in the first place. Sloan was certainly motivated to acquire wealth, although his drive as expressed in the excerpt was not so much to have personal possessions as to expand his business. Particularly during the early years, he returned most of the profits to the business instead of using them to improve his own living standard.

American culture, in contrast to that of the Huron, did not strongly pressure Sloan to be generous or to consider public welfare before his own, yet this pressure was not entirely absent. The book from which the excerpt was taken shows a strong awareness of responsibility to the public and consideration for the common good (even if not sincere, these attitudes would not be expressed unless the writer felt they would draw approval from his readers). The extent of the contributions made by rich businessmen to various organizations that benefit the general public testifies to the existence of some social pressure. If the *only* motivation for charitable contributions were to avoid taxes, they could be made anonymously. The fact that individuals usually want their name associated with large contributions indicates that they expect to receive some public approval for their act.

MONEY

In detail, of course, the differences between the Huron and the United States economies are considerable. Sloan operated in a cash economy; the Huron did not at the time of the excerpt, although in later years porcelain (glass) beads assumed many of the functions of money. Shell beads made into belts or collars had been in use prior to contact with Europeans, but apparently had not served as money in any sense. The belts and collars had many of the characteristics of money,° however. They could be broken down into individual beads—small change, as it were; the shells were relatively standardized and were durable and portable. Having most of the characteristics of money, wampum (beads) could and did quickly assume the functions of money under the impetus of European contact. Wampum was legal tender in some parts of the frontier. The value of the beads was relatively stable in the colonies; it was even put into church poor boxes, and was occasionally stolen (Munsell 1850:8–10, 90–91; Orchard 1929:63). It was used as a standard of value, a store of wealth, a source of ready capital,° and a medium of exchange. Insofar as it fulfilled these functions, it was equivalent to money. Shells, cacao beans, and various other items have served the same purposes in other parts of the world.

Money makes it possible to have a more complex and also a more impersonal exchange system. Under a barter ° system, exchange can get cumbersome, since an individual has to bring the things he has to trade to market and has to take home the items he has traded for. Exchange usually takes place on a face-to-face basis. Exceptions such as dumb or silent barter ° are possible, but rare. (In this form of barter, one party leaves in a particular place the items to be traded and goes away. The other party either removes the items, leaves others in their place, and then also goes away, or leaves its items with the others so both may be examined by the first group. The first party returns and either gets the traded items or chooses what it regards as fair and leaves. Then the second group returns and completes the trade. There is no direct contact.)

Exchanges can either be reciprocal fixed exchanges between trading partners (particularistic exchanges,° in which the emphasis is on the social relationship between the two rather than on the economic exchange), or they can be exchanges in a market situation where there are a number of buyers and sellers and the price asked and received by each depends on the decisions of the others (universalistic exchanges,° in which decisions are made on the basis of technical factors such as cost and quality, with emphasis on the exchange rather than on social factors) (Belshaw 1965:79–80, 114). Even in a market-like situation, barter remains more personal because of the face-to-face contact of the participants.

OCCUPATIONAL SPECIALIZATION

In barter, the same individual is simultaneously a buyer and a seller. As he exchanges his chickens for potatoes, he is simultaneously selling chickens and buying potatoes. Consequently, there is less specialization. The presence of cash makes greater specialization and greater impersonality easier. Comparison of the Ragueneau and Sloan excerpts illustrates this. Among the Huron, a man was normally a producer, a distributor, and a consumer, sometimes almost at the same time. A few people engaged in trade with other Indians and with Europeans. In most cases, however, the individual

A meat market in Peking, where exchange is based on the personal relationship between buyer and seller. *Marc Riboud/Magnum*

The New York Stock Exchange, an impersonal exchange system where buyer never meets seller. *Cornell Capa/Magnum*

doing the trading had obtained or made the things he was trading with—he had killed the animals, worked in the fields, or made the artifacts, or his wife may have tanned the skins. Occupational specialization was minimal.

The Sloan excerpt provides a tremendous contrast. Here occupational specialization was extensive. Sloan's original company, Hyatt, did not make a car or even a major part of a car. It made only bearings, some of which were used in axles, most of which were put into cars. Sloan himself did not sell, design, or even make the bearings personally. What he did was to organize their production. Hyatt invented and designed bearings, unnamed workers made them, and Pete Steenstrup sold them. Other individuals packed them for

111

shipping, transported them to the railroad, and loaded them on trucks. Just getting them to their destination was the work of hundreds of men Sloan did not even know. Although the company employed people to help get the shipments through on time, Sloan never had any personal or direct contact with the railroad workers who also had a part in the delivery.

The Huron system was simple: there were relatively few different things for people to do, and fairly direct contact between the producer, the distributor, and the consumer. Sloan's society supported a highly complex system with hundreds of different specializations and a tight interdependence between people who never knew or even saw one another. Such a society is heavily dependent on blind trust. Unless Durant could trust Sloan to deliver on time, for example, he could not be sure he could produce and sell cars, or (ultimately) pay his workers. Sloan was dependent on the reliable performance of the railroad workers. The factory workers at Ford, Weston-Mott, and Cadillac were equally dependent on Sloan and his workers. How could anyone be sure that all these unknown individuals would perform as required? Obviously, since most of the interdependent people did not even know each other, no one could rely on the informal social pressure and the direct influence on their fellow citizens that was available to the Huron. Hurons who did not do what they were supposed to could be beaten, could have their possessions confiscated, or their property burned by the people they injured. Sloan, Durant, Leland, and all the unnamed workers involved in the production of automobiles had no such recourse.

Sloan explains one of the levers available in a complex society. Leland threatened to cancel his order if Sloan did not make the axle bearings to precise specifications. If Weston-Mott lost Cadillac business, Hyatt would lose Weston-Mott's business, would not be able to meet its payroll, and would probably be forced out of business entirely. Sloan acted to preserve his business, but he did more. He accepted the reasoning of Leland about the need for standardization and incorporated it into his own thinking. He passed it along to his workers by insisting they follow the specifications exactly. If they did not, his lever was to fire them. How much of Leland's reasoning Sloan's employees accepted (or even knew about) is not certain. Studies of factories show that quite a few workers regard the demand for precision as an annoyance to be evaded when possible (Selekman 1947:120–121), which would seem to indicate that they either do not know or reject the rationale behind precision manufacture (or are hostile to their bosses and indifferent to the quality of the product).

COMPETITION

The threat by Leland and the consolidation process initiated by Durant are characteristic of a universalistic system. Leland and Durant were making economic decisions on the basis of technical factors such as quality, convenience, and cost. They were not influenced by personal, social factors. The Huron on the other hand operated on a particularistic basis. Economic decisions were made on the basis of social and personal factors—for example, what their relationship was with the individual or what the individual's relationship was with the community.

The threat that he would lose business could not have been used against Sloan if he had not known there were other businesses ready to take his place. In other words, Sloan could have ignored Leland's demands if Hyatt had been the only source of axle bearings and if Weston-Mott had been the only source of axles. Economic competition, rather than social pressure, served to ensure the necessary levels of performance in Sloan's society. In Huron society, where individuals had to provide required gifts or lose status, competition was social as well as economic. Emulative competition °—exerting oneself to do better than a competitor—can be used to great advantage by a society, since it harnesses individual energies that can then be channeled to produce social benefits. Competition is not always guided constructively, of course; it can be destructive.

In addition, competition can take the form of attempting to pull down rather than to outdo a competitor—suppressive competition.° The resulting battles can stall any attempts at change or improvement. In some societies, the individuals who move out ahead of the majority in any way are faced with strong social condemnation. Individuals and group members are ridiculed, scorned, and ostracized until they give up the new behavior. If new possessions are acquired or made, they may be damaged by those who do not have them (Madsen 1964: 21–23). On one American Indian reservation, a woman was afraid to have plumbing put into her house because "people would say I stole the money" (Richards, C. 1957: 24). In a Latin American community, a European immigrant was forced to give up her varied diet of vegetables and subsist almost entirely on rice because her in-laws accused her of trying to copy the upper classes. Since alienating her in-laws might have resulted in losing her husband, she was forced to modify her diet. There was no question of the in-laws trying to outdo their new daughter-in-law by providing an even better diet—they just forced her to give up hers. In suppressive competition, the reaction of the group is to destroy any advantage obtained by others and thus restore the status quo.

The two forms of competition are different in their results for individuals and for societies. In the United States, the first type of competition is regarded by the middle-class majority as "healthy," and the second type as counterproductive and harmful. Several different minority groups, however, either do not distinguish between the two kinds of competition or are familiar only with the suppressive type, and consequently condemn all competition as destructive. By not encouraging the first type, they *de facto* practice the second; the result is resistance to change and the preservation of the status quo.

Competition also takes a cooperative form. Sloan touches on it only lightly in the excerpt, but describes various examples in the book. In cooperative competition,° individuals work with others in a group, but compete in trying to outdo other groups. Team sports are often examples of cooperative competition. The rivalry of Ford and General Motors is an example Sloan describes; nationalism and warfare might be examples on a larger scale. Cooperative competition can take both the emulative and the suppressive forms described above with the same results for groups as for individuals. Competitive cooperation ° is still another form; one example would be an old-fashioned husking bee or barn raising in which people work together to get a task done (husking someone's corn, or building someone's barn), but individuals try to outdo each other at certain tasks. The one who husks the most corn, or hauls the most lumber, or splits the most shingles gets a prize. Individuals compete while they are cooperating. Thus competition and cooperation are not necessarily mutually exclusive behaviors or values; they can coexist.

CONCEPTS EXCLUSIVE TO INDUSTRIALIZED SOCIETY

The Sloan excerpt reveals several concepts characteristic of highly industrialized societies, but not of hunting and gathering or agriculturally oriented ones. One of the most important is the concept of high turnover—low unit profit leading to increased total profits. Ford was able to increase wages to his workers and at the

FACING PAGE: An Amish barn raising in Pennsylvania. *David S. Strickler/Monkmeyer*

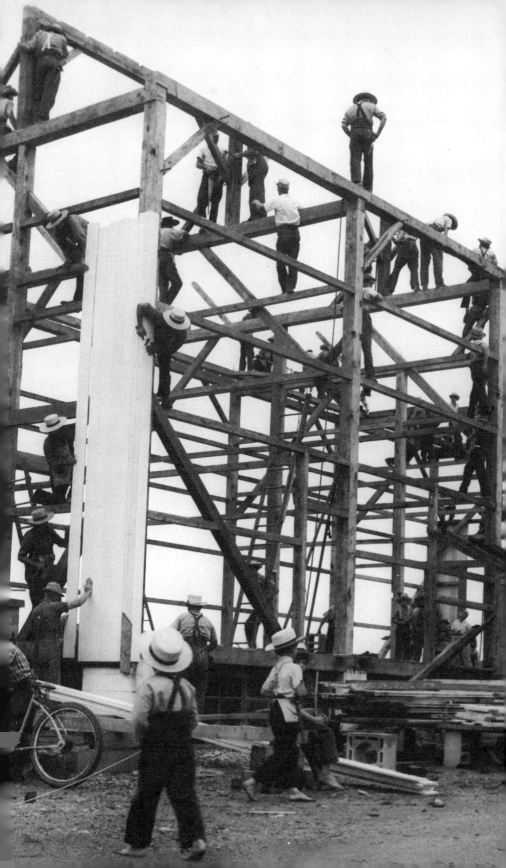

same time lower prices. He did this through lowered costs of production, made possible by more efficient (not more expensive) production and by increased sales, which brought in a greater total profit although the profit on each car might have been smaller. (As an illustration: an item priced at $100 makes a $50 profit, but only 10 are sold each week. This provides $500 a week profit. The same profit can be made if 100 a week are sold at $55, and twice as much profit if 1,000 are sold at $51. Since there are usually more people who can pay $51 than $100, the potential market is greater and so is the potential profit at lower prices. If, in addition, the cost of production drops to $25, the advantages of the lower price are even more obvious.)

In an agricultural society, unless new land can be brought under cultivation or new technology increases crop yield, the only way one person can get more is at the expense of someone else. Ford demonstrated clearly that in an industrialized society, under certain circumstances, *everyone*—workers, consumers, and managers—can get more. The significance of this has not spread to all societies, particularly to those recently emerging from an agricultural economy; people in such societies tend to retain the traditional orientation of an agricultural culture. (Even in the United States it is occasionally forgotten.)

The Sloan excerpt indicates another trend of American industry, consolidation combined with limited autonomy. First, the automobile industry physically and economically consolidated the manufacture of various parts in order to ensure the economic safety of the main manufacturer. Sloan felt Durant had shown insight and wisdom in consolidating the different companies in one area and under one control. He felt Durant was a dictator, however, and dictatorship an effective form of administration "only so long as the dictator knows all the answers." Such omniscience was impossible in an organization as complex as General Motors became. Sloan's philosophy of organization was quite different. He felt that the best individuals should be selected on the basis of technical factors (knowledge, skill, and competence) and then placed in charge of a department and given the freedom and authority to run it, so long as each maintained the necessary coordination with other departments. This particular philosophy has been widely followed in American industrial organization and has led to a success that has aroused envy and admiration all over the world (Servan-Schreiber 1968:203). More recently, the philosophy has led to the development of special "problem-oriented" production teams, planning boards, consultant firms, and other variously named groups created or employed for a specific task, given considerable autonomy for the duration, and then disbanded or dismissed when the task is finished. These temporary, high-powered groups form the basis of what Alvin Toffler calls "Ad-hocracy" and regards as the inevitable successor to bureaucracy in the super-industrialized state (Toffler 1970:109).

The Sloan excerpt illustrates another innovation that has had a profound effect on the American economy. In 1916 United Motors issued a million shares of stock, an amount almost unheard of at the time. There is no space to discuss this development in detail, but issuing large quantities of low-priced shares has made it possible for millions of relatively poor people to take part in the development of and profit from American industry. In 1916 this was a risky game, because the small stockholder was (and still is in many countries) ignorant, powerless, and unprotected. The development of the Securities Exchange Commission, the passage of laws requiring disclosure of financial matters, the demands that companies trading large amounts of stock maintain certain standards of business procedure, and so on have provided a measure of protection to the small stockholder that is unequaled in other parts of the world. It has made investment of small amounts of money both safer and more profitable, with the result that industry has been able to tap a generally unavailable source of development capital. In other parts of the world, people will put any surplus cash into land or hoard it, rather than invest it in industry. There are always more poor people than rich, so a small amount of money from many poor people often adds up to a larger total amount than any rich man can (or dares) to risk. The American economic system has resulted in a much wider sharing of both risks and profits than occurs in other areas of the industrialized world. For example, statistics show that one out of every six adults in the United States owns stock. In 1968 almost 55 percent of the individual shareholders had incomes under $10,000, and large corporate or institutional holdings amounted to 22.4 percent of the total value of stocks (New York Stock Exchange 1969: 43–45).

There are problems and drawbacks, of course. Ownership of large businesses has become so diffuse that the "owners" often exert little real control over the direction and procedures of the company they "own." Management of the business, far from being controlled by the founder or by a man vitally interested in it financially, often is controlled by paid employees who may own little stock in the company. Even when they own large blocks of shares, people in management are apt to be more concerned with ensuring the profits of stockholders than in making risky innovations or costly but socially responsible changes. Management of large business is less susceptible to public pressure (except from a significant number of stockholders) than is the individual owner. The consequences of this are obvious in the areas of minority relations and environmental pollution, for example. Some people are now attempting to correct this situation by trying to persuade the owners of large amounts of stock to make their position known on matters that affect the public welfare. People such as Ralph Nader attempt to make large concerns more responsive to public opinion. In the book (although not in the excerpt), Sloan points out the need for this kind of responsibility on the part of big business, and implies that if large companies like General Motors do not develop some form of responsibility, the public will force it on them. His words have a prophetic ring.

SUMMARY

The division of labor, common to all human societies, has two obvious consequences. First, it makes humans dependent on one another and thus contributes to group solidarity. Second, it makes it necessary for some kind of distribution to occur to ensure individual and consequently group survival. Rules for distribution also become necessary when cooperative endeavor produces some indivisible but desirable product. Rules are necessary to settle the question, for example, of who gets the trophy skull if five hunters cooperated to kill the animal.

There are a number of ways in which distribution may occur. A simple society may have only one or two ways, whereas a complex society may have several. In small, simple societies where most contacts are direct and face-to-face, distribution is usually highly personal. Goods and services often travel exclusively along kinship (real, fictitious, or *affinal* °) lines. The guiding principle may be one of equivalent or identical reciprocity, wherein no individual is expected to gain at the expense of another and both must be satisfied. In this situation, goods and services are usually exchanged directly without the use of a neutral medium such as money. Acceptance of a gift usually places the recipient under obligation to repay it either in kind or with some service. Distribution may occur without exchange; that is, in ceremonial distribution, where the donor expects to get his reward from someone or something other than the recipient (he expects prestige from society, esteem from his fellows, or good fortune from the supernatural).

Distribution in highly complex societies may include these patterns as well as market distribution, a method that is rare but not entirely absent in simple societies (Pospisil 1964:18). This form of distribution or something similar to it may be almost inevitable in large societies with a great deal of specialization. Distribution and exchange in the market are frequently impersonal, and in large complex societies there usually is no direct face-to-face contact between producer and consumer. Economic decisions are made on the basis of price, quality, and other technical factors, rather than on the basis of personal relationships between people. There is usually some medium of exchange (money) in terms of which all goods and services are valued.

Studies of a society with a market system tend to be complicated by the fact that systems of reciprocal exchange and ceremonial or redistributive distribution coexist with it. Personal and social factors are almost never entirely absent in economic decisions, and this also complicates the study of a system that is theoretically supposed to be impersonal.

The values of a society largely determine the way in which its distribution system works. The goals toward which people strive and the manner in which they try to attain those goals are determined by what members of the society agree are "good" and "proper" goals and methods. In the next chapter, social goals are discussed—how they are developed, and how a society deals with people who do not use the approved means for attaining goals.

4 Maintaining Order and Organization

One of the characteristics that distinguishes a group or a society from a simple collection of people is interdependence. When people are interdependent, individuals must behave predictably, or the society cannot run smoothly. Since all societies have a division of labor, tasks performed by some are essential to the survival of others; they therefore must be done and the results—if any—distributed. A society in which everyone did exactly as he pleased could exist only if each individual were so indoctrinated or programmed that he wanted to do just what had to be done precisely when it was needed. This can happen only when social behavior is entirely controlled by instinct (as in insect societies), or by effective thought control that fortunately is still beyond man's technological capabilities.

In the first three chapters, we have dealt with various ways in which different societies satisfied the functional prerequisites of providing and distributing nourishment, shelter, the "good things" of life, and necessary services. In this chapter we focus on the division of labor and the ways members of different societies keep behavior within tolerable limits of variation. In the excerpts, pay particular attention to what is expected of whom and what happens if those expectations are not met.

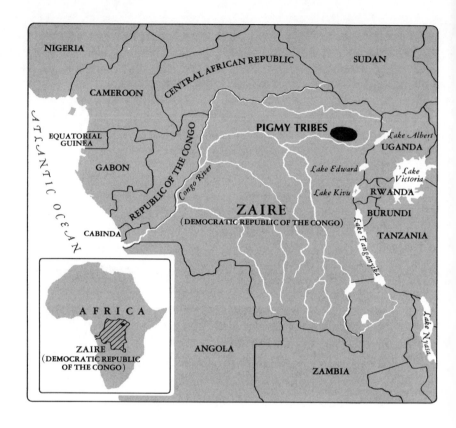

Pygmy Life: Cooperation and Castigation

I remember one morning in particular when we went to kindle the Fire of the Hunt outside the camp, because it was the day that old Cephu committed one of the greatest sins possible in the forest.*

I doubt if any of us had managed to snatch more than two hours' sleep, and we were all quiet while preparing for the hunt. In a Pygmy camp this is the surest danger signal of all, for usually everyone is talking and laughing and shouting rude remarks from one end of the camp to the other. It was not only that we were tired, but of late Cephu had refused to contribute to the molimo ° [both a ceremony and the instrument used in it] basket, and that morning he had been heard to call out, in his loudest voice, that he was fed up with the molimo of "that camp over

* Abridged from *The Forest People* by Colin M. Turnbull, pp. 95–107. Copyright © 1961 by Colin M. Turnbull. Reprinted by permission of Simon and Schuster and Chatto and Windus Ltd. Colin Turnbull has lived and traveled more closely with the Pygmy people than any other non-Pygmy.

there." Even though he always made his camp a short distance off it was close enough to be thought of as the same camp, and whether or not we appreciated his presence we thought of his camp and ours as being the same. Even his unwillingness to take part in the molimo was accepted, to maintain some semblance of unity; but this sudden statement made it impossible to ignore Cephu's feeling of rivalry any longer. Rather than cause an open breach, everyone in the main camp kept his thoughts to himself and was silent.

About an hour after dawn, four or five youths with their nets and spears went off to light the hunting fire. I went with them . . . Shortly afterward we were joined by half a dozen of the younger married men, the most active hunters, and we lit the fire at the top of the hill. Leaves and twigs were piled around the base of a young tree, and an ember brought from the camp set them ablaze. More leaves were thrown on so that dense clouds of smoke went billowing up to the invisible sky, until finally the flames burst through with a great roar of victory. There was no great ritual or ceremonial, but somehow this act put the hunters in harmony with the forest and secured its blessing and assistance for the day's hunt. The Pygmies regard fire as the most precious gift of the forest, and by offering it back to the forest they are acknowledging their debt and their dependence.

As we sat around waiting for the others, one or two couples passed by. They were going ahead so they would have extra time for gathering mushrooms on the way. They paused to chat and then walked on, lightly, swiftly, and gaily. Before long the main body of hunters arrived and asked where Cephu was. We had not seen him. It seemed that he had left the camp shortly after us but instead of passing by the hunting fire had followed a different path. Someone suggested that he was building a fire of his own. This brought cries of protest that not even Cephu would do such a thing. There was much shaking of heads, and when Ekianga arrived and was told what had happened he stood still for a moment, then turned around, looking in all directions to see if there was any sign of smoke from another fire. He said just one word, "Cephu," and spat on the ground.

By the time we got to the place where we were to make our first cast of the nets everyone was more silent and miserable than ever. It did not make matters any better to find Cephu there already, contentedly sitting over a fire eating roast plantains. He looked up and greeted us in a friendly way, and when asked why he had followed his own path he opened his eyes wide and softly said that he had misunderstood and taken the wrong trail. There were angry remarks, but Cephu ignored them all and went on munching at his plantain, smiling at everyone in his kind, gentle way.

Ekianga and a few others made a brief reconnaissance, and when they came back they gave instructions as to the best direction for setting up the nets. The womenfolk, who had been foraging around for mushrooms and nuts, picked up their baskets and went ahead with the small children. They trod lightly and made no noise beyond an occasional crunch of a rotten branch, buried deep beneath the carpet of leaves. We all spread out in a long semicircle, each man knowing exactly who should be to his right and who to his left. I went with Maipe, who had been sent by Njobo with his net. We soon lost sight and sound of the others, but Maipe knew just where he would be expected to set up his net, and he took a short cut. I lost all sense of direction and could not even tell on which side of us the women were waiting for the signal to beat in toward our nets. We followed a little stream and paused by an enormous outcrop of huge stone boulders, almost perfectly square in shape, some of them eight feet across each face. Maipe looked around, then sat down to wait. After a few minutes, Moke's nephew appeared to our left, stringing his net out through the undergrowth as he came.

The end of the net stopped a few feet short of the boulders, and Maipe deftly joined it to his net; then, slipping each coil off his shoulder in turn, he hung his own net, fastening it to low branches and saplings. It stretched for about three hundred feet, so that one end was completely out of sight from the other. It stood about four feet high, and Maipe walked the length of it, silently adjusting it so that it touched the ground all the way along and was securely fastened above. If he found the net drooping where there was no support, he cut a sapling, stuck it in the ground and hung the net on it, bending the top sharply back, twisting it around and through the mesh so that the net could not slip. When this was done he took up his spear and casually sharpened it with a stone picked off the ground.

It was about another five minutes before he suddenly stood up and beckoned me to do the same. He stood absolutely motionless, his head slightly on one side, listening; his spear was raised just a few inches from the ground. I listened too, but could hear nothing. The forest had become silent; even the crickets had stopped their almost incessant chirping. Maipe raised his spear higher, and then at some signal that I did not even notice there was a burst of shouting, yelling, hooting and clapping, as the women and children started the beat. They must have been about half a mile away, and as they came closer the noise was deafening. We saw one antelope, a large red sondu,° ears back, leaping toward the boulders as though it were heading straight for our net, but at the last moment it saw us and veered away to the left. Maipe could probably have killed it with his spear, but he said, "That is not for us. It will probably fall into Ekianga's net." Just then there was a lot of yelling from Moke's nephew. Maipe vaulted over the net and ran swiftly, leaping and bounding like the sondu to avoid obstacles. I followed as best I could, but was passed by several youngsters from farther down the line before I reached the others. The sondu had gone into Ekianga's net, just as Maipe had said, but while all the attention was in that direction a water chevrotain, the *sindula*,° had tried to fight its way through Moke's net.

The sindula is one of the most prized animals; it is not much larger than a small dog but is dangerous and vicious. Moke's nephew had been left all by himself to deal with it, as the others in that area were helping Ekianga with the sondu. The youngster, probably not much more than thirteen years old, had speared it with his first thrust, pinning the animal to the ground through the fleshy part of the stomach. But the animal was still very much alive, fighting for freedom. It had already bitten its way through the net, and now it was doubled up, gashing the spear shaft with its sharp teeth. Maipe put another spear into its neck, but it still writhed and fought. Not until a third spear pierced its heart did it give up the struggle.

Pygmy nets strung for the hunt in a forest of the Belgian Congo. *Courtesy of the American Museum of Natural History*

It was at times like this that I found myself furthest removed from the Pygmies. They stood around in an excited group, pointing at the dying animal and laughing. One boy, about nine years old, threw himself on the ground and curled up in a grotesque heap and imitated the sindula's last convulsions. The men pulled their spears out and joked with one another about being afraid of a little animal like that, and to emphasize his point one of them kicked the torn and bleeding body. Then Maipe's mother came and swept the blood-streaked animal up by its hind legs and threw it over her shoulder into the basket on her back.

At other times I have seen Pygmies singeing feathers off birds that were still alive, explaining that the meat is more tender if death comes slowly. And the hunting dogs, valuable as they are, get kicked around mercilessly from the day they are born to the day they die. I have never seen any attempt at the domestication of any animal or bird apart from the hunting dog. . . .

Ekianga was busy cutting up the sondu by the time I reached his net, for it was too large an animal to fit in his wife's basket. Usually game is brought back to camp before it is divided, and in some groups the dead antelope would have been sent back to camp immediately, around the neck and shoulders of one of the youngsters. But here the womenfolk crowded around as Ekianga hacked away, each claiming her share for her family. "My husband lent you his spear. . . ." "We gave your third wife some liver when she was hungry and you were away. . . ." "My father and yours always hunted side by side. . . ." These were all typical arguments, but for the most part they were not needed. Everyone knew who was entitled to a share, and by and large they stuck to the rules.

Above all the clamor, and in the process of re-coiling the nets and assembling for the next cast, a disgruntled Cephu appeared and complained that he had had no luck. He looked enviously at the sondu and the sindula, but nobody offered him a share. Maipe's mother hurriedly covered the chevrotain with leaves to avoid argument. She worked efficiently, not bothering to take the basket off but using her hands behind her back, and bouncing the basket on her buttocks until the dead animal was completely hidden by the leaves.

We went on for a mile or two and made another cast. Once more Cephu was unlucky, and this time he complained even more loudly, accusing the women of deliberately driving the animals away from his nets. They retorted that he had enough of his own womenfolk there, to which he replied rather ungallantly, "That makes no difference; they are a bunch of lazy empty-heads."

They were still arguing when they set off for the third cast. I had caught sight of old Moke and stayed behind to talk to him. He had not left with the hunt but had gone off on his own, as he usually did, with his bow and arrows. I was surprised to see him. He said, "Don't follow them any longer; they will deafen you with their noise. Cephu will spoil the hunt completely—you'll see." He added that he had happened to be nearby, waiting for the animals either to break through the nets or to escape around the edges. He picked up a large civet cat, the skin slightly stained where it had been pierced by an arrow. "Not very good for eating," Moke commented, "but it will make a beautiful hat. Cephu won't get even that—he is too busy watching other people's nets to watch his own. His is a good net to stand behind with bow and arrow!" He chuckled to himself and swung the cat high in the air.

We ambled back slowly, Moke talking away, sometimes to himself and sometimes to me. On the way he stopped to examine some tracks that were fresh . . . He announced that they were made by a large male leopard, and that it was probably watching us . . .

Back in the camp I was surprised to find that some of the hunters were back already, including Maipe. They had taken a short cut, and traveled twice as fast as Moke and myself. Some of them said it was because rain had threatened, but others, more bluntly, said it was because they did not like the noise Cephu was making. There were a number of women in the camp, and they seemed anxious to change the subject, so Moke told them about the leopard tracks. They laughed and said what a shock the hunters might get if they came back along that trail. One of them started miming the leopard lying in wait, its eyes staring from that side to this. The others formed a line and pretended to be the hunters. Every few steps the "leopard" turned around and jumped up in the air, growling fiercely, sending its pursuers flying to the protection of the trees.

This dance was still in progress when the main body of the hunters returned. They strode into camp with glowering faces and threw their nets on the ground outside their huts. Then they sat down, with their chins in their hands, staring into space and saying nothing. The women followed, mostly with empty baskets, but they were by no means silent. They swore at each other, they swore at their husbands, and most of all they swore at Cephu. Moke looked across at me and smiled. He was skinning the civet.

I tried to find out what had happened but nobody would say. . . .

. . .

The rest of the hunters came in shortly afterward, with Cephu leading. He strode across the camp and into his own little clearing without a word. Ekianga and Manyalibo, who brought up the rear, sat down at the kumamolimo ° and announced to the world at large that Cephu had disgraced them all and that they were going to tear down the kumamolimo and abandon the camp and end the molimo. Manyalibo shouted

A celebration dance in a Pygmy camp. The hooded figure in the center is the witch doctor. *Pickett/Monkmeyer*

that he wanted everyone to come to the kumamolimo at once, even Cephu. This was a great matter and had to be settled immediately. . . .

Trying not to walk too quickly, yet afraid to dawdle too deliberately, he made an awkward entrance. For as good an actor as Cephu it was surprising. By the time he got to the kumamolimo everyone was doing something to occupy himself—staring into the fire or up at the tree tops, roasting plantains, smoking, or whittling away at arrow shafts. Only Ekianga and Manyalibo looked impatient, but they said nothing. Cephu walked into the group, and still nobody spoke. He went up to where a youth was sitting in a chair. Usually he would have been offered a seat without his having to ask, and now he did not dare ask, and the youth continued to sit there in as nonchalant a manner as he could muster. Cephu went to another chair where Amabosu was sitting. He shook it violently when Amabosu ignored him, at which he was told, "Animals lie on the ground."

This was too much for Cephu, and he went into a long diatribe about how he was one of the oldest hunters in the group, and one of the best hunters, and that he thought it was very wrong for everyone to treat him like an animal. . . .

Manyalibo stood up and began a rather pompous statement of how everyone wanted this camp to be a good camp, and how everyone wanted the molimo to be a good molimo, with lots of singing, lots of eating, and lots of smoking. But Cephu never took part in the molimo, he pointed out, and Cephu's little group never contributed to the molimo basket. . . .

Cephu tried to interject that the molimo was really none of his business. At this Masisi, who had befriended him over the chair incident, and who had relatives in his camp, rounded on him sharply. He reminded Cephu that he had been glad enough to accept help and food and song when his daughter had died; now that his "mother" had died, why did he reject her? Cephu replied that Balekimito was not his mother. This was what everyone was waiting for. Not only did he name the dead woman, an unheard-of offense, but he denied that she was his mother. Even though there was only the most distant relationship, and that by marriage, it was equivalent to asserting that he did not belong to the same group as Ekianga and Manyalibo and the rest.

Ekianga leaped to his feet and brandished his hairy fist across the fire. He said that he hoped Cephu would fall on his spear and kill himself like the animal he was. Who but an animal would steal meat from others? There were cries of rage from everyone, and Cephu burst into tears. Apparently, during the last cast of the nets, Cephu, who had not trapped a single animal the whole day long, had slipped away from the others and set up his net in front of them. In this way he caught the first of the animals fleeing from the beaters, but he had not been able to retreat before he was discovered.

I had never heard of this happening before, and it was obviously a serious offense. . . .

Cephu tried very weakly to say that he had lost touch with the others and was still waiting when he heard the beating begin. It was only then that he had set up his net, where he was. Knowing that nobody believed him, he added that in any case he felt he deserved a better place in the line of nets. After all, was he not an important man, a chief, in fact, of his own band? Manyalibo tugged at Ekianga to sit down, and sitting down himself he said there was obviously no use prolonging the discussion. Cephu was a big chief, and a chief was a villager, for the BaMbuti never have chiefs. And Cephu had his own band, of which he was chief, so let him go with it and hunt elsewhere and be a chief elsewhere. Manyalibo ended a very eloquent speech with . . . "Pass me the tobacco."

Cephu knew he was defeated and humiliated. Alone, his band of four or five families was too small to make an efficient hunting unit. He apologized profusely, reiterated that he really did not know he had set up his net in front of the others, and said that in any case he would hand over all the meat. This settled the matter, and accompanied by most of the group he returned to his little camp and brusquely ordered his wife to hand over the spoils. She had little chance to refuse, as hands were already reaching into her basket and under the leaves of the roof where she had hidden some liver in anticipation of just such a contingency. Even her cooking pot was emptied. Then each of the other huts was searched and all the meat taken. Cephu's family protested loudly and Cephu tried hard to cry, but this time it was forced and everyone laughed at him. He clutched his stomach and said he would die; die because he was hungry and his brothers had taken away all his food; die because he was not respected.

The kumamolimo was festive once again, and the camp seemed restored to good spirits. An hour later, when it was dark and fires were flickering outside every hut . . . From Cephu's camp came the sound of the old man, still trying hard to cry . . . From our camp came the jeers of the women, ridiculing him and imitating his moans.

When Masisi had finished his meal he took a pot full of meat with mushroom sauce, cooked by his wife, and quietly slipped away into the shadows in the direction of his unhappy kinsman. The moaning stopped, and when the evening molimo singing was at its height I saw Cephu in our midst. Like most of us he was sitting on the ground, in the manner of an animal. But he was singing, and that meant that he was just as much a BaMbuti as anyone else.

Even a simple hunting and gathering society makes demands on its members. Cephu did not do what was expected of him. Men of the society hunt cooperatively by setting up nets alongside one another, and Cephu set his in front of the rest. He had already violated a series of social norms,° group consensus as to what should or should not be done, before the net episode (Greer 1965:24). He refused to contribute to the molimo, or even to participate in it. He failed to pass by the hunting fire the morning of the hunt. Although the other members of the society were annoyed, no concerted action was taken against him until he set up his net ahead of the others. Why did this act cause a strong social reaction? Perhaps because it was the last in a series of actions that were progressively less and less acceptable? The author seems to feel the act would have called forth the same reaction even if it had occurred without any previous offenses. He called it "one of the greatest sins possible in the forest." (Actually, it is better called a crime°—an offense against people. The term *sin°* is usually restricted to offenses against the supernatural.)

KEEPING VARIATION WITHIN LIMITS: LAWS

The dependence of the group on cooperative hunting makes the offense a grave one. If any hunter could set up his nets where he pleased, the hunt would become a contest for the best location. Men who got their nets set out in front would have an advantage over those in the rear, and there would be gaps in the line through which animals could escape. Instead of an effective hunting technique, the process would turn into an exercise in futility: it would produce more rivalry and hostility than meat for the group. Cephu simply could not be allowed to get away with his behavior because it would imperil the method by which the whole group survived. By "doing his thing" he threatened everyone's survival. There was a confrontation, and Cephu was threatened with exile. In the Pygmy environment, this was equivalent to a death sentence unless he and his group could associate with another band, because they were too few to survive alone. Cephu gave up in the face of this threat and offered an alternative—surrender of the meat he had illegally obtained. The alternative was accepted, and Cephu was restored to the good graces of the community.

Even the punishment of confiscating his food was alleviated by one of his relatives, who carried food to the camp so no one really had to go hungry. Clearly, the BaMbuti were not bent on revenge. Once Cephu's behavior was again within tolerable limits, members of the society were satisfied. Cephu began participating in the molimo once more, so the system worked even though the BaMbuti had no specialized law enforcement personnel nor a formal legal code. These devices are not necessary in a small society where everyone interacts on a face-to-face basis. In such societies, everyone knows what is expected, which variations will be tolerated and which ones will not be. Crime of the sort that occurs in larger societies tends to be rare in small groups, where there is seldom any doubt as to the identity of the guilty party. The whole paraphernalia necessary for the protection of the individual in complex societies is superfluous.

Note that even though members of the society eased the punish-

ment and welcomed Cephu back without any apparent recrimina-
tions, they did not allow him to profit from breaking the rule. The
"stolen" food was taken from him, and although he got some food
later from a relative, this normally would have happened anyway if
he had been unsuccessful in the hunt. The message from the society
was unmistakable: "Abide by the rules and you are one of us, so we
will take care of you. Violate them and we will cast you out, for
you are no longer a BaMbuti." When Cephu heeded the message,
he was reintegrated into the group.

When violation of a norm is met by a severe punishment (or the
threat of one) imposed with the approval of society, the norm may
be called a law ° (or a legal norm). "You must not set your net in
front of others" is a legal norm among the BaMbuti. The other
norms Cephu broke, such as "a man should contribute to the molimo
basket" or "a man should pass by the hunting fire before a hunt,"
were apparently only social norms, not legal ones (legal norms are
a special kind of social norm).

Whenever *any* norm is broken, members of a society usually
have a negative reaction at first. If the reaction is mild (indicated
by expressed irritation, angry remarks, gossip, and so on), the norm
is called social, which roughly corresponds to the sociologist Sumner's term *folkways.*° If the reaction is severe, however, the norm is
more likely to be called a law, corresponding—more or less—to
Sumner's term *mores* ° (the singular is *mos* not *more*) (Sumner
1911:23, 30).

Cephu was judged by the adult males acting together, and
punishment was administered by most of the group, who went together to his camp to get the meat. Small societies often handle
trouble this way. Among the Huron, a larger and more complex society, judgment was passed by a council of elders, and leaders in the
society took an active part in enforcing the decisions (part of this
process is reported in the excerpt in Chapter 3). Punishment and
judgment may also be carried out by individuals or small groups
especially assigned to the task.

More complex societies have full-time specialists, although they
may also have part-time specialists selected for a specific situation,
like jurors. Simpler societies rarely have full-time specialists.
Some—the Pygmies, for example—may lack specialists entirely, or
may appoint people for specific occasions. The Cheyenne Indians
appointed members of one of the military societies to act as police
for the period of a communal buffalo hunt. Members of the appointed group had the right and duty to apprehend and punish anyone violating the legal norm: "There will be no individual hunting

until the group hunt is over." After the hunt ended, the military society gave up its task (Hoebel 1960:53, 54). Note that the functions of apprehension, judgment, and punishment were performed by one group, not by separate individuals or groups as in the modern United States. Here police are supposed to apprehend, but not judge or punish; members of the court judge, but do not punish or apprehend; and jailers (or others) punish, but do not judge or apprehend.

If punishment for a violation is explicit, known in advance, and impersonally applied to all violators, it is called a formal sanction,° whereas if it is spontaneous and varied according to both the circumstances and the individuals involved, it is usually called an informal sanction.° (Sanction° is a rather unusual word in English, since it can mean both punishment and reward. The double meaning can occasionally cause confusion. For example, the sentence "The Z—— society sanctions polygamy" does not really make clear whether the society punishes polygamy or encourages it.)

Small societies of under 1,000 people usually have informal sanctions, whereas in large, complex societies formal sanctions are needed to cope with large numbers of people. The figure 1,000 appears to be the maximum with which informal controls work, and even this number may be too high. In a recent symposium on hunters and gatherers, the typical size of human groups was discussed. Although the participants could not agree on the reason for it, they noted that 25 was the average size of the local group or band, although actual groups ranged in size from 18 to over 50. The tribe, a loose association of local bands with a similar language and culture and recognizing a common group identity, was normally limited to about 500 people. The range was from about 100 to slightly over 2,000, but the upper levels were somewhat exceptional. When the population reached about 1,000 the tribe usually showed signs of beginning to split (Lee and DeVore 1968:155, 156, 245–248). Some societies tend to fission even sooner, when the population is under 300 people. When the number grows larger than this, the groups tend to split up—violently in the case of the Yanomamo (a tribe on the border of Venezuela and Brazil), and peacefully in the case of the Hutterites (a religious sect whose communities are located in Canada and the northern United States) (Chagnon 1968:120; Hostetler and Huntington 1967:105–108).

Another difference between simple and complex societies is in the proportion of public to private law. In small societies, the injured party is usually granted the right to revenge himself on the offender, if he can. This is called private law.° If the wronged individual does nothing, the society also does nothing. If the wronged individual takes revenge, the society passively approves, unless he goes so far that he exceeds the consensus of what is proper revenge. Cephu's offense was clearly against the group, and the group acted in response to it. If he had robbed a specific individual, however, what would the group have done? Since the society is small, group members probably would have allowed the wronged individual to take his own revenge. Among the Huron, when a man was robbed he could loot the robber's cabin and confiscate all his goods with society's approval (*Jesuit Relations* 1898, 13:11, 13). In such a case, the individual is the authorized agent of the society for the moment. He is *enforcing* the law, not committing another offense. In private law, the individual "takes the law into his own hands," but with the approval of society, not against it. When one party does not accept the right of the other to revenge, however, private law can get out of control. In the most common situation, group A gets revenge in retaliation for the murder of one of their own members by killing a member of group B. Instead of accepting the retaliation as legitimate, members of group B may feel that the original killing was justified, or that the choice of the revenge victim was inappropriate (he may have been of a much higher status than the original victim, for example). Consequently, group B members feel that now *they* are the injured parties and entitled to revenge. They kill another member of group A. This is the beginning of a feud, which is likely to continue until one group is exterminated or both groups decide the scales are balanced and that neither group is entitled to any more revenge. Without some overriding authority to make such a judgment and enforce it, however, the latter solution is unlikely, and disruptive violence will probably continue for generations. The need of society to reduce or prevent such violence can lead to public law,° where the society as a whole takes the part of the injured person and regards the wrong done him as a wrong done the entire society. Then the society as a whole or some specialized members of it apprehend, judge, and punish the offending individual (Hoebel 1964:27, 28). This happens occasionally even if the so-called victim does not feel wronged and does not want revenge. Cases of prosecution of prostitution, abortion, drug abuse, gambling, and so on are examples (Schur 1965:169).

Some aspects of law are easier to see in a complex society. In a simple one, so much of the social control is informal that it is difficult to state with certainty what would happen if a norm were broken, because certain ones almost never are. Suppose Cephu had simply ignored everyone's reaction; what would the BaMbuti have done? If a norm is never broken, how can you tell whether it is law or only habit?

In the following excerpt, norms are broken more often, and there are a variety of different reactions, both on the part of the lawbreaker and of the society. Note particularly what some of the norms are, whether there are any specialized positions for dealing with norm violations, and what the reactions of the violators are under different circumstances.

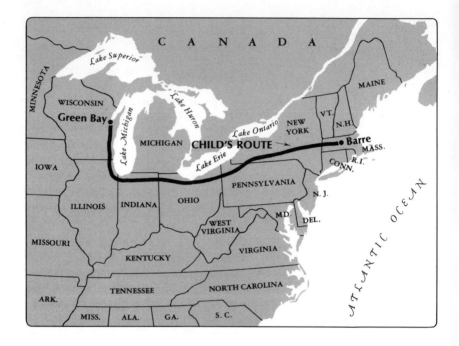

Authority and the Frontiersman

I was born in the town of Barre, Worcester County, Massachusetts, April 3rd, 1797.* At the age of ten, I was left an orphan, and never inherited a cent from any person. I was turned loose upon the wide world without anyone to advise or protect me, and had to struggle through poverty.

I remained in my native state until 1816. I was then nineteen years of age, and was hard at work at fifty cents per day, when the Town Collector called on me for a minister tax. The amount was one dollar and seventy-five cents, which appeared to me like a large sum to pay a minister, who performed no manual labor. I told the collector I had no money and inquired what would be the consequence if I failed to pay the tax? *"Pay or go to jail,"* was the reply; I didn't like the jail alternative, so I told the collector he must wait until I could get some money. He consented, and called again in a few days; but I was still moneyless. . . . It began to be close times with me—I must pay, go to jail, or

* Abridged from "Recollections of Wisconsin since 1820" by Colonel Ebenezer Childs, in Lyman C. Draper (ed.), *Collections of the State Historical Society of Wisconsin* (Madison: The State Historical Society of Wisconsin, 1906), Vol. 4, pp. 153–154, 165–167, 175–181. Reprinted by permission of the State Historical Society. Col. Childs was one of the early settlers in Wisconsin and a respected citizen at the time L. C. Draper recorded his recollections.

run away. I determined on the latter course, settled with my employer on Saturday night, who paid me for my services, and made the necessary preparations for a quiet departure.

With a fine pony, and a few articles of clothing, which I packed into an old pair of saddle-bags, I started on Sunday morning after the people had gone to church. I went as much as I could across lots, and along unfrequented roads, in order to get past the church without being discovered. . . . I finally got safely beyond the limits of the town; but in passing through another town, I had necessarily to go close to the church, in passing which I was hailed from the front door. I cast a furtive glance in that direction, and saw a long-spliced Yankee coming towards me. I spurred up the pony, and kept out of Yankee's reach. Soon finding that his long legs could not overtake my nimble horse, he went back, and mounted a fine horse in the church shed, and gave me chase. . . . Had the tithing-man been a good rider, he would have overtaken me; as it was, after pursuing about two miles, he gave up the chase and returned. . . . I arrived at my sister's that night, and left early the next morning for the State of New York. My business took me off the main travelled road from Boston to Albany and when I regained it, I learned that a tithing-man and several assistants had passed in hot pursuit, but I was too smart for them, and evaded them all. It was at that time a violation of law for a traveller to journey on the Sabbath in Massachusetts, and if he could not be arrested on that day by the tithing-man, he could be followed and apprehended anywhere within the State. When I crossed the State line, and got into New York, I felt greatly relieved. I was then in the land of freedom, and out of reach of oppression. [He continued to travel and moved slowly west until, about 1821, he reached Green Bay, Wisconsin.]

. . .

Old Judge Charles Reaume lived about two years after I settled in the country. He was a man of great importance when I first came to the Bay, and for a long time previously. He had been appointed a sort of Justice, I think by General Harrison, when he was Governor of Indiana Territory. When Reaume held his courts, he would dress in his British uniform red coat, and cocked hat, and put on an air of pompous dignity. There was a noted case brought before him by a young lady for seduction and breach of marriage promise. After hearing the testimony, the honorable court rendered judgment in this wise—the seducer was sentenced to purchase a calico dress for the injured lady, and two dresses for the baby, and the constable to pay the costs by splitting a thousand rails for the Judge. This decision of the Court was complied with, though the constable was not well pleased with the part assigned him—not being able exactly to comprehend why he should be mulcted ° in damages; but at length agreed to split the rails on condition that the Judge should board him while doing so. This was paying pretty roundly for the honors of office.

The first jury trial held at Green Bay before Robert Irwin, I was the plaintiff. . . . I gained my suit. The defendant in the case was a Frenchman. He and his friends were outrageous in their denunciations of the d——d Yankee court and jury. The next trial which was brought before Squire Irwin, was one in which a colored man claimed pay for labor done for L. Grignon. A jury was impanelled, when Grignon, the defendant, brought in his account as an offset against the negro's claim; and in the account, tobacco was charged at four dollars per pound, common clay pipes at fifty cents each, common calico for the Indian trade at one dollar and fifty cents per yard. The jury took the responsibility to reduce Grignon's account one half, and striking a balance, returned a verdict in the darkey's favor, at which he was greatly rejoiced, while his opponent was not a little restive . . .

. . . In 1824, Hon. James D. Doty was appointed Judge for the North-Western district of Michigan Territory . . . The first term of Judge Doty's court was held at Green Bay, when he charged the grand jury to

A courtroom scene at the turn of the century. *Brown Brothers*

inquire particularly in relation to persons living with women to whom they were not legally married. The grand jury found thirty-six bills of indictment against inhabitants of Green Bay for fornication, and two bills for adultery. I was a witness before the grand jury in eighteen cases, and I was also one of the jury. . . . The court was . . . very lenient towards those who had been indicted; the Judge informing them that if they would get married within ten days, and produce a certificate of the fact, they would not be fined. They all complied with this requirement, except two, who stood their trial. Their plea was, that they were legally married, had lived a great many years with their wives, and had large families of children—that their marriages had been solemnized according to the customs of the Indians. The court took a different view of the legality of those marriages, and fined those two men fifty dollars each and costs. We all thought at the time that Judge Doty was rather hard in breaking in rough shod, as he did, upon our arrangements, but we had to submit, and make the best we could of the matter.

. . .

In the winter of 1827–28, Daniel Whitney obtained permission of the Winnebagoes to make shingles on the Upper Wisconsin. He employed twenty-two Stockbridge Indians, and one white man to superintend the party; and he engaged me to take the party up the Wisconsin, and supply them with provisions. . . . When I reached Fort Winnebago on my return, Major Twiggs, the commanding officer of that garrison, informed me, that Whitney's men must be sent out of the country; that he expected the Indian Agent that day from Prairie du Chien, who would go up and conduct the whole party off from the Wisconsin; that Whitney had no right there, and if the Indian Agent needed any assistance in putting a speedy check to this trespass upon the Indian lands he should furnish the necessary quota of soldiers to effect it.

Major Twiggs then advised me not to attempt to go up where the men were making shingles; that if I did, I might get into trouble. I told him that I was employed by Whitney to supply his men with provisions; and that all the Indian Agents and soldiers combined could not prevent me from fulfilling my engagements. I told him furthermore, that this difficulty had all been brought about by false representations to the Agent; that I delivered provisions to the Winnebagoes for Whitney's men, and that they were all satisfied that Whitney should make as many shingles as he pleased. He flew into a violent passion, and told me that I would be sorry for my course, and for what I had said. I told him that I disregarded all his threats, and then left him.

I then went up to where the men were at work. They had made about two hundred thousand shingles. I delivered my provisions to the party, and was about leaving camp, when a Frenchman came on a clean jump. He told me that there was a great lot of soldiers and officers at Grignon's Trading Post a short distance below; that Mr. Grignon had sent him to inform me that the soldiers were after me, and that I had better go back into the woods, and keep out of the way. I told my men to take their teams a short distance down the river, and remain there until I should call for them; and with my own team I went down to Grignon's, where I found the Agent, one officer and twelve soldiers. The Agent informed me that he had come up to take all of Whitney's men out of the country. I asked him if he proposed to take me? He replied that he should take all he should find committing trespass on the camp. I went with them. When we arrived, the men were all out in the woods. I started to where they were at work, and I went to work shaving shingles. The Agent soon arrived with his party. I told the shingle-makers that they must quit work, which they did; but I kept on until all left, hoping they would attempt to arrest me, but they did not. After awhile I went to the shanty, where they were all assembled. The overseer asked me to go out of doors with him, that he wished to speak with me. When we got to the door, I asked him what he wanted of me; he replied that he wanted my advice as to what course he should pursue. I told him that if that was what he wanted, I would give him the best advice I had, in the house, before the whole party, Agent, soldiers and all; that if I were in his place, and had charge of the men, I would not surrender alive, but that he might do as he pleased. The overseer consulted with his men, and they finally concluded to surrender.

At this juncture, I called on my eight stout Frenchmen who speedily came up with their teams. I told them that as the foreman and Indians were prisoners, that we would take charge of the shanty and property belonging to Whitney; upon which we all spread down our blankets, and turned in for the night. The next morning the overseer called to his men to get breakfast. I jumped up and told them, that as they were prisoners, they were out of Whitney's employ, and forbade them touching a single thing in or about the shanty. I called my men, and told them to get breakfast. That opened the eyes of the Agent and officer; and the latter remarked, that the commissary at the Fort had sent his compliments to me, requesting me to let him and his men and the prisoners have provisions enough to last them back to the Fort. I told him that he should not have a pound of anything—that they might starve first. Soon after the Agent came to me, and coaxed me until I concluded to let them have a supply; I sold them pork at fifty cents per pound, flour twenty-five cents, corn fifteen dollars per bushel, and let them have a horse and train ° [a wooden sled with plank runners, drawn by a single horse] to return with for ten dollars. They took breakfast and left. I collected all of the tools, provisions, and other articles, and took them down to

Grignon's, and stored them. The next day I started for the Portage, and encamped where Portage City is now located. That night a sergeant came to my camp to inform me that I had better not proceed by way of the Fort as Major Twiggs was in a high rage, swearing that if I should come nigh the Fort, he would have me arrested, put in irons, and sent to Prairie du Chien; that I was as much a trespasser on the Indian lands as any of the party of the shingle-makers, as the officer an soldiers of the detachment . . . had seen me making shingles. The sergeant advised me to go across the country, and keep entirely clear of the Fort. I kindly thanked him for his good wishes, but told him that I had business with the sutler ° at the Fort, and should go that way to see him; and that I was not in the habit of dodging any mortal man or set of men. The Agent sent me word, that I had better not go near the Fort; that he had heard what Twiggs had said, and it would be prudent to avoid coming in contact with him. Still I was determined to go by way of the Fort, while my teamsters were averse to it. I simply told them, if they were cowards they could go any way they pleased.

On the ensuing morning I got ready, and started for the Fort, my men all following. Nearing the garrison, I discovered all of the officers down at the river near the crossing place. The soldiers were getting out ice. When they saw me, Twiggs left, and went to the Fort. I crossed the river, and drove up to the sutler's store. I had not been there long, when a soldier came in and informed me that Capt. Gwin, the commissary, wanted to see me at the Fort. I told the soldier that I would endeavor to be more polite than the Captain had been—that he might give my compliments to him, and tell him if he wished to see me more than I did him, then he would find me at or near the store. The clerk was very uneasy, and requested me to leave the store, as he was fearful of trouble. I went out of doors. Soon after a number of officers came near where I stood—Capt. Gwin among them. The Captain asked me if I had really refused to let the officer and soldiers have provisions when they were up the Wisconsin? I frankly told them that I did; and if it had not been for the Agent, I certainly should not have let them have any, and that I was sorry that I had yielded to the Agent's urgent solicitations. Capt. Gwin was very indignant, and said that the officers had hitherto thought a great deal of me, but now I had forfeited all of their respect and confidence. I expressed my regret at losing their confidence; that I had my own views of duty, in doing which I could not consult their wishes. I got on my train and started; and in passing the Fort, I gave three cheers, and went on my way rejoicing. I did not see Twiggs again.

• • •

As early as June, 1825, Hon. John P. Arndt obtained a license to maintain a ferry across Fox River, a short distance above Fort Howard. Soon

Fort Howard in Green Bay, Wisconsin, ca. 1850. *The State Historical Society of Wisconsin*

after, the commanding officer placed a guard on the west side of the river, to prevent the ferry-boat from landing—contending that no one had a right to cross without first obtaining leave of him. I was at this time boarding with Arndt, and took one of his boats, with one man with me, to try and see what the guard would do with me. As I approached near the opposite shore, the guard came down to seize the boat; I directed the man to turn the boat around, and throw the stern to the shore. He did so, and as I jumped out, the boat received an impetus which pushed it into the stream, when the man returned unmolested. I was arrested, went to the Fort, and laughed at the officers, and told them that I thought I was in a free country; and so believing, that I should go and come when and where I pleased, that they might all go to ——.

Soon after, Judge Arndt thought that he would try the experiment of crossing and landing on the western bank of the river. But as soon as they landed, he and his companion were arrested, and taken to the Fort. Arndt was a little mulish, and refused to go, but was overcome by numbers, and dragged to the Fort by brute force. He was finally discharged with an admonition not to attempt to cross again without permission from the commanding officer. The court sat a short time after, and Arndt commenced a suit against the commanding officer for false imprisonment; the officer was fined fifty dollars and costs, and the court decided that Fox River was a public highway, and that any person had a right to obtain a license for a ferry at any point across the river, and the military had no right to interfere. The guard was withdrawn, and we had no further trouble about crossing and re-crossing Fox River.

SETTLING CONFLICTS

Laws are really effective only when the people in general support them. The failure of prohibition in the United States and the present difficulty in enforcing laws against marijuana use, abortion, and segregation illustrate the problem. Punishment is usually thought of as a deterrent to further misbehavior. Yet for it to be effective—if it is—it must be a probable consequence of norm violation. A $10 fine may be a more effective deterrent than twenty years in prison if there is a 99 percent chance that the lawbreaker will have to pay the $10 and a 99 percent chance that he will not have to serve twenty years. In addition, whatever happens must be regarded by the lawbreaker as a punishment. A Navajo complained to me about jailing a man for public drunkenness. He said the drunk was put into a nice warm jail where he didn't have to do anything but lie around, and he was fed three good meals a day. Meanwhile, his family was suffering out in the hills. His family should be jailed, the Navajo said, and the man condemned to shift for himself (Richards, C. n.d.: field notes). This is a perfectly sensible suggestion when jail itself is not regarded as a shameful, humiliating experience.

Furthermore, punishment must be imposed by individuals or groups that are in some way accepted as having the right to do so by the person being punished. Consider the resistance fighters in France during World War II. If one was caught, he was subjected to imprisonment, torture, and even death—all more severe punishments than we normally inflict on norm violators. Yet the threat of this treatment did not stop acts of sabotage and espionage. Resistance fighters regarded the danger as an occupational hazard, one of the risks they had to run to carry out a dangerous mission, not as a punishment for breaking a norm. Germans were not felt to have any "right" to make laws. They were the enemy, the outsiders, people to be defied and fought by any means available.

Much the same situation occurs in any counterculture group° in any society. Members of these groups, whose culture is opposed to that of the mainstream of the society, are not likely to be deterred by what *other* people (the enemy) regard as punishment. It is necessary to ask: "Does this person regard what we are doing as a punishment?" and "Does this person think the people punishing him have the right to do so?" If the answer to both questions is "No," then the proposed "punishment" will probably not be effective in bringing about any desired change in behavior. It will not even be satisfactory revenge.

Childs, in the Wisconsin excerpt, was completely unmoved by the army threats. He *tried* to get arrested. In the shingle incident, when the foreman asked him for advice, Childs said he would die before surrendering. Note that Childs makes a distinction between an order he regarded as illegitimate and one he disliked but accepted because it emanated from legitimate authority. He obeyed the latter, but the former he gleefully defied and dared the bogus authority to do its worst. Childs was not exceptional; others on the frontier acted in a similar way. The parallel with the modern situation should be apparent. Militants are often acting in the good old American tradition of the Boston Tea Party. The justice—or lack of it—of a cause is not at issue. The point is that this behavior is apt to occur in any society when the norms and the legitimacy of its authorities are called into question.

Wisconsin prior to 1860 was not nearly so complex as Wisconsin is today, of course, but it was considerably more complex than the Pygmy society described in the first excerpt. In Wisconsin, for example, there were several specialized statuses° (positions in society) whose roles° (behavior expected of someone in a particular status) were primarily concerned with law, whereas in the Pygmy society there were none. The Wisconsin excerpt mentions judges, jurors, a town collector, and a tithing-man. The town collector and tithing-man tried to enforce laws; the judges and jurors were responsible for investigation of possible law violations, decisions on whether norms were violated, whether the accused violated them, the punishment to be imposed if he did, and settling conflicts of interest. Settling cases of trouble is a main function of law. Law also defines relationships between members of the society and distributes power within the society (Hoebel 1964:275).

Some norms are regarded as important to the supernatural, not just to secular society. Individuals who break such norms may expect misfortune, illness, madness, or death—all of which are regarded as supernatural punishments in various societies. So long as the supernatural is expected to punish sins, and so long as the punishment is limited to the guilty individual, society takes no action. Sometimes, however, an offense by one individual is believed to expose the entire group to supernatural vengeance. Remember in Chapter 3, all members of the Huron society were held responsible for the actions of one individual. This occurs in many societies around the world. In such cases, members of the community usually attempt to detect the guilty individual to punish him, and thus avert the wrath of the supernatural. A case of this type is reported in the Old Testament. The Israelites were badly defeated in battle. Their leader, Joshua, asked the supernatural for the reason and was informed that someone had disobeyed the strict command of God not to keep booty from Jericho. Joshua asked the supernatural to reveal the guilty party. (This is also a common practice in many societies.) First, Joshua cast lots to determine the tribe of the sinner, then the family, then the household, and finally the specific individual. When he was confronted with the results of the divination,° the man confessed, and the booty was found in his tent. Then members of the society killed him and his children, and destroyed his possessions. After they had thus removed the sinner from their midst, Joshua and his men again attacked the people who had defeated them, and this time the Israelites won. Of course, that convinced them that the divination and the punishment had been correct (Joshua 7:1–26; 8:1–27).

There are several other ways in which the supernatural may be involved in determining guilt or innocence. One means is the ordeal. The accused is given poison, asked to put his hand into boiling water, touch his tongue to a hot iron, and so on. In these cases, the supernatural is expected to protect the innocent and cause the guilty to suffer. During the witch trials of the Middle Ages, there was a slightly different approach. Suspects were tied up and thrown into rivers or lakes. If they floated, it was assumed they had the devil's help, and so they were usually taken out and burned. If they drowned, however, it was regarded as proof that God had accepted the innocent soul, so all was well. A case of "heads I win, tails you lose" for the accused. Trial by combat was another method for determining guilt or innocence. Either the accused himself or a champion willing to fight for him battled the accuser (or *his* champion). It was assumed that the supernatural would ensure the triumph of right (Leach 1949:829).

Trial by jury (jurors are supposedly ordinary citizens with no special legal training selected from a random group without any connections to either defendant or plaintiff, and free from special biases) is a recent and unique institution confined to the English-speaking world (and some former colonies). The presumption that the burden of proof is on the accuser is also unusual. In most legal systems, the accused is responsible for proving his innocence. (It is much easier to disprove something than to prove it; a system in which one must prove his innocence is biased against him, whereas one in which the plaintiff has to prove the accused's guilt is biased in the accused's favor.) Even in systems in which there is some form of court and trial, the participants (other than the accused and witnesses) are usually members of the legal establishment rather than ordinary citizens. Such systems tend to be biased against the accused and *may* be more susceptible to corruption. On the other hand, if such a court and legal system is staffed with dedicated, altruistic, incorruptible individuals, it may render a more objective judgment than a jury. (Only the naive expect this to happen most of the time, however. Dedicated, altruistic, incorruptible people are seldom in the majority in any society. A system that depends on staffing all, or even most, key positions with such individuals is bound to function erratically.)

The jury system is by no means perfect, of course. The selection process for jurors may be arranged in such a way that representatives of minorities or certain special groups are systematically excluded. A lawyer who knows how to play on the emotions of the jurors may win his cases even though his evidence is weak. Such things pervert the whole concept of a jury trial, in which the objectivity of the jurors is a major goal. Some people assume that jurors should favor the accused, but that does not necessarily result in justice any more than having jurors biased for the prosecution. Objectivity, dispassionate neutrality, and a willingness to decide either way according to the strength of the evidence presented is the ideal behind the jury system. Bias in favor of the accused is already built into the system through the expressed statement that the accused is presumed innocent unless the prosecution can convince the jurors that he is not. In most other legal systems, the guilt of the accused is assumed and the purpose of a trial is simply to determine the degree of punishment that should be imposed.

The conflicting underlying assumptions of different legal systems have led to a great deal of misunderstanding between societies, since most people tend to believe other legal systems are like their own. If they feel their own system is unfair, they either assume the other society has an equally unfair system or (if they admire the other society) assume the other system is better. To some people in South America, the jury system sounds like a radical but fair process in contrast to their own (which even some members of the upper class regard as corrupt). Students in a Peruvian school insisted they would not have supported the cause of Chessman (a robber sentenced to death by California courts whose case became a *cause célèbre* in the late 1950s) if they had known he had had a jury trial. Castro was roundly criticized in the United States for condemning political prisoners without a jury trial—although Spanish justice and its New World descendants have never included such a thing. In both cases, ignorance of the other system was partly the cause of the misunderstanding.

Complex methods for determining guilt and innocence—whether they involve the supernatural or secular institutions such as police and jury—are usually limited to large, complex societies. The Huron, for example, did not need to determine the specific guilty individual because the entire community was held responsible even when the criminal was known. In the case of the Pygmies, there was never any question of who was guilty. In small, face-to-face societies, there is seldom any doubt about the identity of the guilty person (except in the case of witchcraft, which may require some supernatural assistance to detect). Detectives, police, judges, and juries are necessary only when a society grows so large that victims are unacquainted with the criminal and cannot easily identify or find him.

Punishment imposed after a norm is broken may be either psychological or physical, but it should be regarded as severe in the eyes of members of the society for the norm to qualify as a legal one. There is disagreement among anthropologists over whether this distinction is adequate. Some (E. A. Hoebel, for example) feel that the use of force or threat of force by an authorized agent of society as part of the response to the infraction is essential for distinguishing legal from ordinary social norms (Hoebel 1964:28). By this definition, not all societies have law. Other anthropologists (Leopold Pospisil, for example) think that the definition need not mention the use of force at all. Pospisil feels that law has certain attributes, such as authority (it must be accepted by all parties to the dispute), the intention of universal application, *obligatio* ° (both rights *and* duties), and sanctions that can be either psychological or physical. Since his definition is broader, Pospisil says that all societies have some form of law (Pospisil 1967:27ff.).

Whatever definition of law is chosen, some form of social control is universal, even if it is only intense indoctrination so that the punishment for norm violation is guilt inflicted by the individual on himself. The anthropological controversy is mainly a semantic one over what characteristics the social controls should have in order to be labeled "legal." Insisting on certain characteristics—for example, that law must be written and supported by specialized agencies—limits the number of societies that can be said to have *law*, but it does not change the reality that every society attempts to regulate the behavior of its members in some way to ensure that they perform predictably. Societies differ considerably in the amount of variation they can or will tolerate. The higher the level of interdependence (which increases with complexity), the greater the outward conformity demanded. Of course, in a complex society there are more varieties of acceptable ways to behave, which mitigates the demand for conformity to some extent. That is, in an industrial society a man does not have to limit his choice to being either a hunter or a transvestite ° (a person who dresses—and often acts—like a member of the opposite sex), since there are thousands of possible occupations open to him.

The increase in the demand for outward conformity seems directly correlated with the amount of specialization in the society. There may actually be a need for conformity in such cases to reduce anxiety. For example, in the United States, it is next to impossible for the average individual to determine directly the competence of the people on whom he depends. Our survival is constantly at the mercy of individuals we do not know who must promptly and accurately perform tasks we know nothing about. The food we eat and the water we drink can kill us if it is not properly cleaned, processed, and purified. Yet we usually do not know the farmer who produces the food, the employees who process it, or the workers who purify the water. Even if we *do* know an individual who plays some part in the complex chain, we usually do not understand his job and so cannot tell when he is doing it properly. (This uncertainty with our lives at stake would probably produce unbearable anxiety if we thought much about it.)

When we do have some direct contact with people on whom our lives depend (such as doctors, police, pharmacists, or others), we tend to evaluate them by superficial visible characteristics. These may not be the best to use, but they are all we have. For example, suppose you are in a strange town and suddenly have a severe pain in your chest. Your left arm begins to go numb. You see a doctor's office and, terrified, you go inside. There you find a man in leopard-skin trunks and high leather boots, striding back and forth, cracking a whip and singing an operatic aria. A receptionist nods toward him and says, "The doctor will be with you in a moment." If you are a normal individual, you will probably go right back out the door in spite of your chest pain. On the other hand, if the man had come out of an office door wearing a white smock over long pants, with a stethoscope around his neck, and if he spoke in a quiet, assured manner, you would probably relax, confident that this man could help you.   Actually, the first one might be the best heart specialist in a hundred-mile radius and the second one a fraud.   You have no way of knowing and so you judge—in your urgent need—by outward conformity to the behavior expected of a physician in our society.   You have neither the time nor the qualifications to make any valid check of the man's actual competence.

DEFINING RELATIONSHIPS

A man's position in society is called his status.   Sociologists and anthropologists differ somewhat in the way they use the term. Sociologists tend to concentrate on the individual's overall position, which is usually referred to as his socioeconomic status.   People with high status are powerful and wealthy; low status individuals are neither.   This is an example of scalar status,° status depending on rank or access to wealth and power.   Anthropologists are usually more interested in functional status,° status based on what one does in the society (Greer 1965:23; Linton 1936:113–114).   It is apparent

One of the functional statuses this individual occupies in his society is that of a cab driver.   *Constantine Manos/Magnum*

25¢ 1ST ⅕ MILE
5¢ EACH 1 MILE

that any individual occupies several functional statuses in a society. According to the excerpt, Cephu is an elder, a husband, a hunter, and a family leader. The excerpt names fifteen functional BaMbuti statuses, and several others can be deduced. Some of the fifteen, for example, are reciprocal: where there is a nephew, it can be assumed that somewhere there is also an uncle or an aunt; a mother implies the existence of a son or daughter, and so on.

Some statuses are universal—that is, they appear in all societies. The principal ones are these: man, woman, child, adult, mother, son, daughter, brother, sister. Father is not included in the list because the American word, which refers both to the *pater*,° the sociological male parent, and the *genitor*,° the biological sire, is not always appropriate. Among the Trobriand Islanders in the South Pacific, as well as among some of the Australian tribes, for example, the word applied to those we would call father actually means "mother's husband" and does not carry the connotation of biological sire, or *genitor*, at all. This is discussed more fully in Chapter 6 (Hart and Pilling 1964:22; Malinowski 1929:5–6, 195).

Note that the universal statuses are almost entirely ascribed,° assigned to an individual whether he likes it or not. Most of us do not choose to be men or women, children or adults, we just *are* by virtue of certain characteristics we possess. In the United States, if a child lives long enough, he becomes a teenager. Then, if he continues to live a few years longer, he becomes an adult. He has no choice. Ascribed status is contrasted with achieved status,° which the individual attains through some effort of his own (Linton 1936: 115–117). Ascribed and achieved statuses are simply extreme points of a continuum; some statuses fall in between. For example, it requires effort to raise a child to an adult (although less in the United States than in societies without Western medicine, where a parent who manages to raise all his offspring is regarded as almost incredibly fortunate). Once the child is an adult in the United States, however, the additional status of husband or wife is achieved rather than ascribed, since marriage is not automatic. (Some parents regard it as a *major* achievement.) Once the person is married, his or her parents have no choice in whether they become grandparents. The status of grandfather or grandmother is therefore to some extent both achieved and ascribed.

Societies vary in the ratio of achieved to ascribed statuses. One in which most statuses are ascribed may be called closed or rigid; one in which most are achieved is open or flexible. According to the American value system, societies with a high proportion of ascribed statuses are undemocratic and limit personal freedom. Members of such societies may not feel the same way, however; they may regard an open system with great anxiety. If you cannot move up the ladder of success in a closed society, at least you cannot fall down it either. Competition and the insecurities that go with potential failure are minimized in societies where one's position is predetermined by birth or some other factor over which one has no control. On the other hand, in such societies, no one has the opportunity to actualize his potential unless he is lucky enough to be ascribed into the right status. The individual must be indoctrinated to fit his status; he cannot be allowed to strive to attain the one he wants or is best suited for.

Although there are some universal statuses, there are *no* universal roles. We will stress this point again and again. Roles must be described for each society. For example, in the first excerpt in this chapter, a hunter is expected to string his net in an assigned position, alongside the net of another hunter. Then he is supposed to kill game frightened into the net by women and children. The Piegan (in the excerpt in Chapter 1) expect a hunter to kill buffalo by riding into a herd on his horse and shooting the animals with a gun or a bow and arrow. Full participation of the Pygmy women is essential to the success of the communal hunt, since they frighten the game into the nets and carry the meat back to camp. Women among the Piegan stay in camp during the hunt, and only come out if the kill is close by in order to bring back the meat. Otherwise, the men bring it in. The roles of both men and women in hunting differ from one society to the other; all that those mentioned have in common is killing game. The same behavior may sometimes be expected from more than one status. For example, in the Pygmy excerpt, both children and women make noise to frighten game; both men and women forage for mushrooms; both men and women cook. Other items of behavior are restricted to particular statuses. Women apparently never use bows and arrows among the Pygmies, and grown men never take part in the beat to frighten game. Each of the excerpts in this book may be reexamined this way to determine statuses and roles in the society described.

The way in which an individual performs one role may affect the way in which he is accepted in others. For example, Cephu's performance as a hunter threatened his membership in the band and consequently all his other statuses and roles. There are also times when role expectations are incompatible. In the United States, for example, a man cannot always be both a good son and a good husband, because to perform one role well may require him to perform the other badly. If his wife and his mother make conflicting demands on him at the same time, he has to decide which to neglect. This is known as a role conflict ° and causes problems in any society. Normally, we escape role conflict even if the role demands are incompatible because we are only called upon to perform *one* role at a time; problems occur when two or more incompatible roles are activated simultaneously. To start a heated discussion in a group of Americans, simply pose this problem: If a man capsizes in a boat with his mother and his wife, neither of whom can swim, which one should he save (assuming he can save only one)? It is a drastic example of a role conflict for which American norms provide no solution. There is no consensus as to which should take precedence. The poor male will be condemned whatever choice he makes.

Some societies *do* provide an answer to that particular role conflict. In a traditional Chinese family, for example, a man's first loyalty was to his family of orientation,° the one into which he was born. His wife could never surpass his mother. Until she bore a son, the wife was at the bottom of the priority list in the family. (She got her turn at power later, when her son married and brought home a daughter-in-law for *her* to bully, and she therefore had a great desire for sons.) A traditional Chinese would have to save his mother and let his wife fend for herself, or he would be severely criticized (Yang 1945:54). Among the traditional Eskimo, on the other hand, the old were usually sacrificed for the young; old people were abandoned or strangled (if they did not kill themselves) to give the young a better chance at survival during emergencies. A traditional Eskimo would have to rescue his wife and let his mother save herself, if she could (Jenness 1959:207, 261).

Setting priorities is one way to minimize role conflict; another is to try make it unlikely that situations which call for simultaneous performance of different roles will occur. Mutual avoidance between a man and his mother-in-law is demanded in many societies. When this is scrupuously practiced, a girl is normally never placed in a situation where the roles of wife and of daughter can be activated simultaneously.

Conflict between certain statuses may also be inherent in a situation. For example, a foreman is expected to give orders to the workmen subordinate to him, and it can be assumed that at least some of them will occasionally resent these orders. Conflict between foreman and workers is built into the situation. A few societies try to minimize such inherent conflicts by demanding joking behavior as part of the roles of the potentially conflicting statuses. That is, people are supposed to play tricks on, joke with, or tease one another. The behavior can occasionally get rather rough, but it is not entirely left up to the initiative of the participants (Simmons 1966:39–40, 280–281). Often specific behavior is required by the society. This joking behavior is thought to head off more serious and socially disruptive conflict.

Of course, rules are seldom followed exactly. There is a difference between ideal behavior (what people think *should* be done) and reality (what people actually *do*) in all societies. The gap is almost always greater in some areas than in others, but it is present in all. It can create social tension, but only if people know what the real

FACING PAGE: Village women near Ibadan performing two of their ascribed roles —pounding and sieving palm kernels for palm oil extraction. *Marc and Evelyne Bernheim/Rapho Guillumette*

behavior is, and they rarely do. (Do you *really* know from personal observation or information what the sexual behavior of the older generation is?) Instead, people *presume* they know what other people do and act on that basis. Consequently, it is the gap between ideal and presumed behavior that is significant, rather than between ideal and real. If such a gap is large, social tension will be high and members of the society will make a considerable effort to reduce the gap. But it may even be unrealistically large: during the witchcraft hysteria of the Middle Ages, people tried to wipe out sorcery and eliminate witches; actually, there was little real sorcery going on, and there were even fewer real witches. On the other hand, if the gap between the ideal and presumed is small, there is little social tension even when the gap between the ideal and real behavior is large (Richards, C. 1969:1115–1116). Americans are much more concerned about civil rights now than they were two decades ago, in spite of the fact that there is probably a smaller gap between the ideal and the real now than there was then. But as more and more people have become aware of a gap between what they think ought to be done and what they presume *is* being done, the social tension has risen.

A society may deal with the situation by attempting to change real behavior, by changing the ideal, or by changing the presumptions about behavior. In the modern age of improved communications and increasingly sophisticated opinion-making methods, whole societies have been cleverly manipulated to alter their concepts about what members of other societies are doing. Today, militants (left, right, or whatever) are all trying to convince people that the majority of Americans, or a significant proportion of Americans, are behaving in a particular way. Since people act on the basis of what they think others are doing, whichever group manages to convince the most people comes out ahead. Reality is not relevant unless people know what it is (one reason why democracy is difficult without an *informed* electorate).

All societies expect different behavior from males than from females, although in American society recently there has been a trend toward increasingly similar sex roles. The move in that direction is not complete, so sex remains one of the universal bases (along with age and kinship) for classifying people into different groups and for determining status. The specific behavior expected of men and women varies widely from one society to another. The statement above that there are no universal roles means, of course, that there are no universal male or female roles. This is difficult to believe because a large part of many roles, particularly those associated with sex, belong to *covert* culture.° (This is discussed further in Chapter 5.) Because roles do vary, it is difficult to predict how a particular individual will behave in a given situation unless the investigator knows something about the culture of the group to which his subject belongs. But the more the anthropologist knows about an individual's culture, the more accurate his predictions become. For example, if you were asked to predict what a Botocudo man would wear to a community meeting, you would probably not even be able to make a guess (unless you already know he is a coastal Brazilian Indian), but if you were asked to predict what an American male would wear to his office in New York City in the winter, your prediction would probably be fairly accurate.

A Piegan does not seek esteem the way a New England farmer does; Sloan's methods would not be appropriate for a Huron. Even if every man seeks esteem from his fellows, the way he goes about it is determined by the values of his group. To strive for a goal that is not valued or to use despised methods to reach one are unrewarding behaviors because, as Cephu learned, an individual loses esteem instead of gaining it. One definition of society is that it is a "group of individuals competing for conventional prizes by conventional means" (Ardrey 1970:104). Among men, conventional prizes and methods are manifestations of conventional understandings—that is, of culture.

DISTRIBUTING POWER

Law has still another function besides defining relationships and settling cases of trouble. It also distributes power. When people live together and the inevitable conflicts occur, who gets his way and who has to give way? If the question of precedence had to be settled each time a conflict of interest occurred, the society would be in continual turmoil. The function of a dominance structure seems to be to cut down on the amount of physical violence within the group or species. In an established system, individual animals *know* which one takes precedence in any given situation. A challenger is met by a threat from the dominant animal, which is usually sufficient to put him "back in his place." If he persists, the dominant animal physically punishes him or drives him out of the group (Ardrey 1970:156). A successful challenge, of course, raises the challenger's status, but serious challenges to the established structure tend to be rare. When adult animals who are strangers to each other are thrust together, however, there is a high level of violent conflict that results in fatalities unless the defeated one can escape from the area. (Man is by no means the only animal that kills his own kind!) The violence continues until a stable dominance structure is established. After that, the group becomes peaceful. The weakest animals are always the ones who suffer most in a society torn by conflict. One of the functions of the dominant animal seems to be to stop quarrels; he does this by almost invariably siding with the weaker of the quarreling animals—unless the quarrel is with him, of course (Ardrey 1970:157). In cases of food shortage, the weakest members again suffer most. Unfortunately, this is probably essential for group survival, since it ensures that at least part of the group will remain strong and live through the crisis. Under normal conditions, however, the dominance structure protects and benefits the weakest member of the group, so long as he does not challenge it.

As a society grows, it either develops effective mechanisms for settling disputes and distributing power, or it splits apart. In the history of man's development, the societies that survived and grew were those that developed techniques of social control enabling greater numbers of people to live together peacefully. Techniques that work in a small band where contact is on a face-to-face basis and informal social pressure is effective (among the Pygmies, for example) do not work unmodified in a large, complex society where different groups hold different values and are not so susceptible to face-to-face pressures from those who disagree. Formal controls, laws, and governments are techniques that have come about in response to the social need for order and organization (Hoebel 1964: 154).

One definition of *government* ° calls it a network of statuses whose primary roles are political—that is, dealing with public power and decision making (Swartz, Turner, *et al.* 1966:12). By this definition, the Pygmies do not have a government. Wisconsin did, although the only clearly political status mentioned in the excerpt is that of the Governor of Indiana Territory . Yet the Pygmies make group decisions and exercise public power even though they do not have specialized roles for doing so. All men are hunters and all occasionally make or help make public decisions. The BaMbuti specifically denied the existence of any special governmental status such as that of chief (let alone a *network* of such statuses) when Cephu claimed he was one.

The opinion leaders in the Pygmy group expressed the general consensus. The judges in the Wisconsin excerpt occasionally went against group consensus, but in both cases the members of the society supported their leaders and, one assumes, were ready to use force to do so if necessary. Force may be a factor in the support for authority, but it is important to realize that *no* system of social control could possibly rely entirely on force. A king/leader/president/ dictator cannot personally beat up everyone who opposes him. If he does use force to stay in power, others apply it for him, and they, at least, must support him for some reason other than the force he commands, since they are that force. In addition, force is expensive and inefficient.

Childs expressed dissatisfaction with the judge's decisions several times, but he never suggested disregarding them. When he did have a conflict with the law in New England, he ran from the area rather than defy the officials. The excerpt makes it clear, however, that this behavior was not the result of sheeplike conformity or timidity; Childs had a strongly developed idea of what constituted legitimate authority. He never questioned the right of the tithing-man to arrest him. He simply escaped from his jurisdiction. He accepted Judge Doty's decisions and even served on the investigating jury, although he did not like the new rules and said so. However, he defied, ignored, and insulted Major Twiggs. Childs did not grant Twiggs any right to control his behavior. Later, when the commanding officer of the fort tried to prevent people from crossing the Fox River without his permission, both Childs and Arndt openly challenged his right to do this. The army officer ultimately accepted the legitimacy of the court, since he withdrew the guard once the court decided the river was a public highway.

This acceptance of authority is an important part of any system of social control. If even one of the parties to a dispute does not accept the right of an overriding authority to make binding decisions, the system of social control is threatened. If the army had refused to accept the decision of the court, what could Childs have done? He could have surrendered, and no longer attempted to cross the river without permission. He could have tried to cross without getting caught, and run the risk of arrest and punishment. He could have fought. There were not many other alternatives available. The Civil War (correctly titled the War of the Rebellion) resulted from the refusal of certain states to accept the right of the federal government to make decisions that were binding on them.

Legitimacy is an important source of support for a system (Swartz, Turner, *et al.* 1966:10). If an individual does not grant other individuals the right to obtain or use power ° (the ability to make binding decisions), he does not recognize them as legitimate authorities and will challenge their decisions. In simple societies, this causes a change in leadership; in complex societies, it leads to civil disorder or to violence either within one society or between two or more. The United Nations and the earlier League of Nations provide good examples of the ineffectiveness of organizations when the legitimacy of their authority is not accepted by all the participants in a dispute.

The "authority" that guides people's behavior may be a specific set of norms that everyone knows and adheres to most of the time; yet all societies have individuals who break rules. Every individual in every society probably breaks some rules at some time during his life. What happens then? Where are the authorities to whom one can appeal? Whose opinion is most influential? Norms also determine this. In small societies such as that of the Pygmies, some individuals seem to express the group consensus better than others; they are better hunters and regarded as wiser men; they are listened to. These are the leaders. Ekianga and Manyalibo were clearly such men among the BaMbuti. When Manyalibo said the BaMbuti did not have chiefs, he must have been referring to the status called "chief," because the whole incident clearly indicates that they had leaders.

Opinion leaders in small societies are almost never female. This is not to say that women have no influence; they do in almost all societies, large or small, and in some they have a great deal. But in making public decisions, in dealing with public power, women have not been conspicuous in the societies of the world. A few complex societies have had female rulers—the two Elizabeths and Queen Victoria of England (but they were always surrounded by male advisors). There have been other exceptions. The strongly patriarchal Hebrew society was once led by a woman (Deborah) (Judges 4:4–24) and was even ruled by a queen (Athaliah) for six years (II Kings 11:1–17). But these rare exceptions do not invalidate the generalization that public decision making and public power are almost always in the hands of men. The reason for this is still being hotly debated, but whatever it may be, the preponderance of males in this area of social organization is clear.

The leader in a simple society is not "chosen" for the position. There is no formal mechanism involved. A man leads so long as his decisions are followed. When people no longer listen to him, he is no longer a leader. There is no special means for removing him any more than there was for choosing him in the first place. You cannot remove a man from a position he does not hold. Is such a leader supported by law? There is usually no norm that states that the leader must be obeyed. In fact, such leaders cannot normally command; they can only suggest. Yet their suggestions carry weight.

When Ekianga and Manyalibo told everyone to assemble at the ku-mamolimo, the excerpt indicates that Cephu did not dare delay his arrival too long. After Manyalibo said he should go and live some-where else, Cephu apparently did not think he could continue to live with the band unless he made some concessions, which he imme-diately did. One of the problems involved in studying law and power in simple societies is that obedience often seems to be "un-derstood" and unquestioning. Because of this, many early anthro-pologists and theorists felt that man in simple societies was bound by customs he was unable to defy. Bronislaw Malinowski indicated that this image of "primitive man" is inaccurate. The laws, the vio-lations, and the punishments are there; they are simply less formal and less overt (Malinowski 1966: 9–16).

In complex societies, leadership is determined in various ways:

1. The status is sometimes ascribed to an individual on the basis of his heritage.
2. Leadership can be revealed by the supernatural. The first king of Israel—Saul—was so revealed to Samuel. The Dalai Lama is chosen on the basis of supernatural signs.
3. Kings have sometimes achieved their positions by conquest or competition.
4. A leader may be chosen by vote. Among complex societies, this method of choosing a leader is relatively recent.

Councils are almost always involved at some point in the proc-ess of government (Hoebel 1966: 459). Even the most tyrannical dictator usually has a group of especially trusted advisors. In less complex societies, the council of elders may be the leadership. To get rapid decisions in times of crisis, the council may delegate power to a single individual and then revoke it when the crisis is past. If crisis situations arise often and last long enough, the posi-tion may become permanent. It has been suggested that this is how the status of king first came about in Mesopotamia (Frankfort 1964: 356–358). Ways of distributing power, then, obviously vary widely from one society to another; yet there are a few universal charac-teristics. No society known has complete equality. There are scalar status differences in the simplest society as well as in the most com-plex. The main difference is that in small societies *everyone* has a slightly different status from everyone else, as a rule, whereas in complex societies groups of people tend to be roughly equal in status, forming a class.° One class differs from another in scalar status, but within each class there are only minor differences. (There *are* differences, however. Even within the same class, there is not complete equality; some people have more power or prestige than others.) A caste ° is almost the same as a class. The difference is that people can move—although sometimes only with great difficulty—from one class to another, but no mobility is permitted between castes. Caste membership is ascribed, and although the caste as a whole may improve its rank in relation to other castes, the individual cannot. Classes and castes are rare in small societies. Simple societies lack them by definition, since having a caste system automatically makes a society complex.

Certain things seem to be valued in all societies. Everywhere people seem to want some control over their own lives, some voice in public decisions, some prestige and esteem from their fellows. Methods of gaining these valued goals differ widely from one society to another. In several, the only way to gain public power is to avoid any appearance of seeking it. Anyone who obviously tries to gain power is apt to lose it. Thus Cephu actually lost his case when he claimed that he was an important man, a chief. The response was that if he was a chief he was not a BaMbuti, since they did not have chiefs. By openly claiming power, he lost all chance at it. In such societies, the man who actually has power tends to be one who claims there is no such thing as a chief and who always appears reluctant to push his opinions on anyone. That man is listened to, and his advice followed. He may claim not to want power, but he makes key decisions that affect the behavior of others in the society; whether he claims it or not, whether he wants it or not, he *has* power.

SUMMARY

Societies, because they are made up of interacting, interdependent people, need order and organization to exist. Since man's behavior is not fully predetermined by his genes, conflicts of interest and questions of priority continually arise. All societies have developed means of coping with these problems to ensure that: (1) what must be done gets done, (2) people can rely on each other to perform necessary services and to behave in a predictable manner, and (3) behavior beyond the tolerable limits of variation is eliminated.

All societies permit some variation, and all societies permit more in certain areas than in others. The severity, complexity, and effectiveness of the means used vary, but in all cases, if behavior goes beyond what is felt to be reasonable bounds, members of the society take some action to correct the situation. If they fail, the society fractures into groups within which the conditions of acceptable variation can be maintained.

Norm violation in any society can be handled in only a limited number of ways:

1. Violators may be forced to conform to the norms or be removed in some way from the society.
2. The norm itself may be changed so that the behavior is no longer a violation (if enough people accept the violation, it becomes a new norm).
3. The limits of toleration may be increased so that the violation is permitted even if it is not fully accepted. It does not become the new norm, but it becomes an acceptable alternative.
4. Violators may form a subgroup within the society and continue to struggle with supporters of the norm.
5. The society may split into two or more societies with different norms. In this alternative, there will no longer be any conflict over norms within each new group, but the groups may be in conflict with each other.

Members of any group *must* accept some binding authority to settle disputes. If anyone refuses to do so, he threatens the society as it is constituted and becomes the potential focus for a new society. However, in order for the new society to survive, it too must solve the problem of settling conflicts of interest. History is full of accounts of both successes and failures at this game, and it is obviously an immediate concern in the present world.

Government and law are two institutions ° that complex societies have developed to deal with questions of public power, public decision making, and norm violations. Small societies may lack these institutions (it is a matter of definition), but no society lacks ways of carrying out the functions of government (making public decisions) or the functions of law (settling disputes, defining the relationships of members of society to one another, distributing power).

Wars occur when nations refuse to accept any overriding authority and yet cannot settle their conflicts of interest. One great barrier to settlement both between and within societies is a refusal of either side to compromise. A stand in support of "nonnegotiable demands" means that one of the parties to the dispute must surrender completely. If neither will do so, violence is usually inevitable unless one side can or will leave the vicinity of the other. Another barrier to settlement is a difference in the covert culture of the groups. Actions are misinterpreted, intentions are misunderstood. Increased understanding and tolerance on both sides of the quarreling groups is essential if problems arising from this source are to be reduced.

In social living, human or nonhuman, it is impossible for each individual to have his own way immediately all the time. There are no "inalienable rights" except those that members of the society choose to grant. This is an unpopular statement, but the physical world grants no rights. Ask the avalanche about the rights of villagers in its path; talk to the flood about the rights of the farmers. Even in the social world, unless individual members of a society agree, no one has any more "right" to "life, liberty, and the pursuit of happiness" than his own strength and ferocity can provide. The Declaration of Independence says: *"We hold* these truths to be self-evident." The first two words have been italicized to emphasize that the statements that followed were those the signers of the Declaration could agree on. The American Revolution itself, as well as the behavior of countless people in thousands of societies before and since, is clear proof that the "truths" are *not* self-evident. Even after they were pointed out, not everyone agreed with them. Biologically, they are not true. Socially they *may* be, if everyone in the society agrees they are. Laws and norms spell out the rights members of a society grant to one another as well as the responsibilities they owe each other. People trying to change their own rights and obligations are automatically also altering the rights of others. Anxiety, hostility, and disruption are an inevitable consequence, at least for a time.

How does a society go about getting people to want to do what has to be done? Since laws and norms have to be obeyed willingly because force cannot compel an entire society, how does it get members to accept rules as proper and authorities as legitimate? In the next chapter we deal with the most common way this is accomplished—the process of socialization.

5 Socialization

There must be order and organization for a society to survive, but societies vary widely in their norms and structures. In addition, the members cannot all be forced to follow the rules. A society functions smoothly only when its members want to do what has to be done. How does a new member learn what he needs to know to get along in the group? How does he come to want what the group wants, and shun what it disapproves?

Most new members are born into the group; while they are growing up, they are taught openly, subtly, or unconsciously the things they must know. In the course of this teaching, the growing child also learns to depend on approval and esteem from his fellows, and to want and approve of the things the group values. This teaching process is called socialization or enculturation. It proceeds smoothly in some societies and with more difficulty or trauma in others. It is never totally effective, but it is far more so in some societies than in others.

In the following excerpt, take note of what values, behaviors, and beliefs the people try to develop in the child, and what methods they use to achieve their goal. Also note who is responsible for different phases of the socialization, as well as what differences there are in training and expectations for different statuses (such as boy, girl, servant, and so on) in the society.

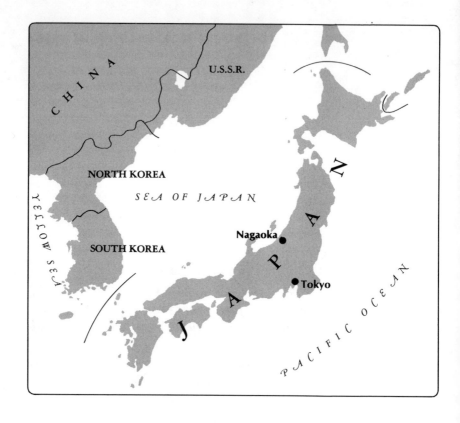

The Education of a Samurai Daughter

We did not have kindergartens when I was a child, but long before the time when I could have been admitted to the new "after-the-sixth-birth-day" school, I had acquired a goodly foundation for later study of history and literature.* My grandmother was a great reader, and during the shut-in evenings of the long, snowy winters we children spent much time around her fire-box, listening to stories. In this way I became familiar, when very young, with our mythology, with the lives of Japan's greatest historical personages and with the outline stories of many of our best novels. Also I learned much of the old classic dramas from Grand-mother's lips. My sister received the usual education for girls, but mine was planned along different lines for the reason that I was supposed to be destined for a priestess. I had been born with the navel cord looped

*From *A Daughter of the Samurai* by Etsu Inagaki Sugimoto, pp. 17–24. Copyright 1925, 1928 by Doubleday & Company, Inc. Abridged by special arrangement with the publisher.

around the neck like a priest's rosary, and it was a common superstition in those days that this was a direct command from Buddha. Both my grandmother and my mother sincerely believed this, and since in a Japanese home the ruling of the house and children is left to the women, my father silently bowed to the earnest wish of my grandmother to have me educated for a priestess. He, however, selected for my teacher a priest whom he knew—a very scholarly man, who spent little time in teaching me the forms of temple worship, but instructed me most conscientiously in the doctrine of Confucius. This was considered the foundation of all literary culture, and was believed by my father to be the highest moral teaching of the time.

My teacher always came on the days of threes and sevens—that is, the third, seventh, thirteenth, seventeenth, twenty-third, and twenty-seventh. This was in accordance with our moon-calendar custom of dividing days into groups of tens instead of sevens, as is done by the sun calendar. I enjoyed my lessons very much. The stateliness of my teacher's appearance, the ceremony of his manner, and the rigid obedience required of me appealed to my dramatic instinct. Then the surroundings were most impressive to my childish mind. The room was always made ready with especial care the day of my lessons . . . [it] was wide and light and was separated from the garden porch by a row of sliding paper doors crossed with slender bars of wood. The black-bordered straw mats were cream-coloured with time, but immaculate in their dustlessness. Books and desk were there, and in the sacred alcove hung a roll picture of Confucius. Before this was a little teakwood stand from which rose a curling mist of incense. On one side sat my teacher, his flowing gray robes lying in straight, dignified lines about his folded knees, a band of gold brocade across his shoulder, and a crystal rosary round his left wrist. His face was always pale, and his deep earnest eyes beneath the priestly cap looked like wells of soft velvet. He was the gentlest and the saintliest man I ever saw. Years after, he proved that a holy heart and a progressive mind can climb together, for he was excommunicated from the orthodox temple for advocating a reform doctrine that united the beliefs of Buddhism and Christianity. . . .

My studies were from books intended only for boys, as it was very unusual for a girl to study Chinese classics. . . .

I was only six years old, and of course I got not one idea from this heavy reading. My mind was filled with many words in which were hidden grand thoughts, but they meant nothing to me then. Sometimes I would feel curious about a half-caught idea and ask my teacher the meaning. His reply invariably was:

"Meditation will untangle thoughts from words," or "A hundred times reading reveals the meaning." Once he said to me, "You are too young to comprehend the profoundly deep books of Confucius."

This was undoubtedly true, but I loved my lessons. There was a certain rhythmic cadence in the meaningless words that was like music, and I learned readily page after page, until I knew perfectly all the important passages of the four books and could recite them as a child rattles off the senseless jingle of a counting-out game. Yet those busy hours were not wasted. In the years since, the splendid thoughts of the grand old philosopher have gradually dawned upon me; and sometimes when a well-remembered passage has drifted into my mind, the meaning has come flashing like a sudden ray of sunshine.

My priest-teacher taught these books with the same reverence that he taught his religion—that is, with all thought of worldly comfort put away. During my lesson he was obliged, despite his humble wish, to sit on the thick silk cushion the servant brought him, for cushions were our chairs, and the position of instructor was too greatly revered for him to be allowed to sit on a level with his pupil; but throughout my two-hour lesson he never moved the slightest fraction of an inch except with his hands and his lips. And I sat before him on the matting in an equally correct and unchanging position.

Once I moved. It was in the midst of a lesson. For some reason I was restless and swayed my body slightly, allowing my folded knee to slip a trifle from the proper angle. The faintest shade of surprise crossed my instructor's face; then very quietly he closed his book, saying gently but with a stern air:

"Little Miss, it is evident that your mental attitude to-day is not suited for study. You should retire to your room and meditate."

My little heart was almost killed with shame. There was nothing I could do. I humbly bowed to the picture of Confucius and then to my teacher, and backing respectfully from the room, I slowly went to my father to report, as I always did, at the close of my lesson. Father was surprised, as the time was not yet up, and his unconscious remark, "How quickly you have done your work!" was like a death knell. The memory of that moment hurts like a bruise to this very day.

Since absence of bodily comfort while studying was the custom for priests and teachers, of course all lesser people grew to feel that hardship of body meant inspiration of mind. For this reason my studies were purposely arranged so that the hardest lessons and longest hours came during the thirty days of midwinter, which the calendar calls the coldest of the year. The ninth day is considered the most severe, so we were expected to be especially earnest in our study on that day.

. . . In those days penmanship was considered one of the most im-

FACING PAGE: A Japanese winter. For a Samurai education the coldest days were chosen for the hardest tasks. *Werner Bischof/Magnum*

portant studies for culture. This was not so much for its art—although it is true that practising Japanese penmanship holds the same intense artistic fascination as does the painting of pictures—but it was believed that the highest training in mental control came from patient practice in the complicated brush strokes of character-writing. A careless or perturbed state of mind always betrays itself in the intricate shading of ideographs, for each one requires absolute steadiness and accuracy of touch. Thus, in careful guidance of the hand were we children taught to hold in leash the mind.

With the first gleam of sunrise on this "ninth day," Ishi came to wake me. It was bitterly cold. She helped me dress, then I gathered together the materials for my work, arranging the big sheets of paper in a pile on my desk and carefully wiping every article in my ink-box with a square of silk. Reverence for learning was so strong in Japan at that time that even the tools we used were considered almost sacred. I was supposed to do everything for myself on this day, but my kind Ishi hovered around me, helping in every way she could without actually doing the work herself. Finally we went to the porch overlooking the garden. The snow was deep everywhere. . . . Once or twice a sharp crack and a great soft fluff of spurting snow against the gray sky told that a trunk had snapped under its too heavy burden. Ishi took me on her back and, pushing her feet into her snowboots, slowly waded to where I could reach the low branch of a tree, from which I lifted a handful of perfectly pure, untouched snow, just from the sky. This I melted to mix for my penmanship study. I ought to have waded to get the snow myself, but—Ishi did it.

Since the absence of bodily comfort meant inspiration of mind, of course I wrote in a room without a fire. Our architecture is of tropical origin; so the lack of the little brazier of glowing charcoal brought the temperature down to that of outside. Japanese picture-writing is slow and careful work. I froze my fingers that morning without knowing it until I looked back and saw my good nurse softly crying as she watched my purple hand. The training of children, even of my age, was strict in those days, and neither she nor I moved until I had finished my task. Then Ishi wrapped me in a big padded kimono that had been warmed and hurried me into my grandmother's room. There I found a bowl of warm, sweet rice-gruel made by my grandmother's own hands. Tucking my chilled knees beneath the soft, padded quilt that covered the sunken firebox I drank the gruel, while Ishi rubbed my stiff hand with snow.

Of course, the necessity of this rigid discipline was never questioned by any one, but I think that, because I was a delicate child, it sometimes caused my mother uneasiness. Once I came into the room where she and Father were talking.

The Japanese tea ceremony, which follows the precise dictates of etiquette.
Werner Bischof/Magnum

"Honourable Husband," she was saying, "I am sometimes so bold as to wonder if Etsu-bo's studies are not a little severe for a not-too-strong child."

My father drew me over to his cushion and rested his hand gently on my shoulder.

"We must not forget, Wife," he replied, "the teaching of a samurai home. The lioness pushes her young over the cliff and watches it climb slowly back from the valley without one sign of pity, though her heart aches for the little creature. So only can it gain strength for its life work."

. . . But my lessons were not confined to those for a boy. I also learned all the domestic accomplishments taught my sisters—sewing, weaving, embroidery, cooking, flower-arranging, and the complicated etiquette of ceremonial tea.

Nevertheless my life was not all lessons. I spent many happy hours in play. With the conventional order of old Japan, we children had certain games for each season . . . And I believe I enjoyed every game we ever played—from the simple winter-evening pastime of throwing a threaded needle at a pile of rice-cakes, to see how many each of us could gather on her string, to the exciting memory contests with our various games of poem cards.

We had boisterous games, too, in which a group—all girls, of course—would gather in some large garden or on a quiet street where the houses were hemmed in behind hedges of bamboo and evergreen. Then we would race and whirl in "The Fox Woman from the Mountain" or "Hunting for Hidden Treasure"; we would shout and scream as we tottered around on stilts in the forbidden boy-game of "Riding the High-stepping Bamboo Horse" or the hopping game of "The One-legged Cripples."

But no outdoor play of our short summers nor any indoor game of our long winters was so dear to me as were stories. The servants knew numberless priest tales and odd jingles that had come down by word of mouth from past generations, and Ishi, who had the best memory and the readiest tongue of them all, possessed an unending fund of simple old legends. I don't remember ever going to sleep without stories from her untiring lips. The dignified tales of Honourable Grandmother were wonderful, and the happy hours I spent sitting, with primly folded hands, on the mat before her—for I never used a cushion when Grandmother was talking to me—have left lasting and beautiful memories. But with Ishi's stories everything was different. I listened to them, all warm and comfortable, snuggled up crookedly in the soft cushions of my bed, giggling and interrupting and begging for "just one more" until the unwelcome time would arrive when Ishi, laughing but stern, would reach over to my night lantern, push one wick down into the oil, straighten the other, and drop the paper panel. Then, at last, surrounded by the pale, soft light of the shaded room, I had to say good-night and settle myself into the *kinoji*, which was the proper sleeping position for every samurai girl.

Samurai daughters were taught never to lose control of mind or body—even in sleep. Boys might stretch themselves into the character *dai*, carelessly outspread; but girls must curve into the modest, dignified character *kinoji*, which means "spirit of control."

Imagine having to sleep in a particular position! Most people in the United States do not believe it is even possible to teach children to do such things. But different peoples have different assumptions about the nature of man, and in many societies successful demands Americans would never even consider imposing are made on children.

People of various societies also value or despise different characteristics and attitudes. Naturally enough, adults in all societies want their children to behave in ways they admire, so in most societies adults try to teach children valued characteristics and to eliminate undesirable traits. The process of teaching the young the beliefs and traditions of the society is called "enculturation," ° and the process of teaching the young how to get along in the group is called "socialization." ° This technical distinction is usually ignored, however. Sociologists (and a few anthropologists) tend to use socialization to refer to both processes, whereas anthropologists are more prone to use enculturation in the same way. In most societies, the family is responsible for a major part of both processes.

Enculturation and socialization are vital for the maintenance of a society, since certain tasks must be performed for any society to continue to exist. To ensure the performance of these necessary tasks, people must want to do what has to be done. In order for people to want to do what must be done, they must accept the goals and values of the society. People learn these goals and values and the approved methods they may use (as well as the methods they should not use) through the process of socialization or enculturation.

TEACHING VALUES AND NORMS

Few groups require young children to display the degree of self-control that was demanded by the Japanese samurai class in the past. Not even all groups in premodern Japan expected the same amount of self-control. Ishi, the nursemaid, wept at the sight of Etsu's frozen hand. She told Etsu stories, allowed interruptions, succumbed to pleas for "just one more," and laughed even as she insisted on bedtime. She also did her best to modify the strictness of the discipline without actually disobeying orders. She waded out into the yard with Etsu on her back, so the child could actually take snow off the tree branch herself. This was within the letter but certainly not the spirit of the rule, because as Etsu points out in the excerpt, technically she should also have waded into the snow herself. One gets a sense of Ishi's informality and sympathy even from the short excerpt quoted; it is much more obvious when one reads the whole book.

What were some of the characteristics people in the samurai

class of that time regarded as admirable? What did they expect of their children? How did they go about developing the valued characteristics? The excerpt indicates that both physical and mental control were highly admired and expected; in fact, this is repeatedly emphasized. By the time she was six, Etsu had learned to sit motionless for at least two hours at a time (contrast this with the expected behavior of first-graders in the United States). She felt deeply ashamed when she moved slightly and her teacher dismissed her. She does not complain that her instructor was unjust or unfair, which indicates she had already accepted (internalized °) the values of her society to such an extent that she applied its standards to her own behavior and felt unworthy or inadequate when she failed to measure up.

In some societies, people feel unworthy and deserving of punishment even if no one else knows about their failure to live up to the standards of the society. Such a society is said to be "guilt-oriented." The individual to some extent punishes himself for actual violation or even for anticipated violation of a social norm. In other societies, people feel unworthy only when other members of the group are aware of their failure. Such a society is said to be "shame-oriented." Individuals depend on punishment from some source other than themselves. The anthropologist Melford Spiro believes this dissimilarity in societies occurs because of a difference in the number of people involved in socializing a child. When only a few people are involved in the socialization of each child, a guilt-oriented culture is likely to develop, whereas in a society where there are many agents of socialization, or where these agents threaten the child that "others" will do the punishing, a shame-oriented culture is likely to develop (Spiro 1961:120). The two types are theoretical extremes, and in any real society one would expect to find both types of individuals (through perhaps more of one type than the other) and also to find individuals who exhibit a combination of guilt and shame attitudes about different social norms.

Just reading the excerpt, one has difficulty deciding whether the samurai class in premodern Japan was primarily shame- or guilt-oriented. Other parts of the book, however, indicate that much of Etsu's behavior depended on her perception of what other people thought of her actions. When she knew others did not object or even approved (in a mission school, for example, or after she went to the United States), she was apparently able to adopt new behavior easily. Had she been heavily guilt-oriented, it is unlikely that it would have been so simple for her. (Protestant missionaries, for example, reject wife-lending practices even in societies where such behavior is not only accepted but expected. General missionary resistance to changing their own behavior has even led to martyrdom. Missionaries are notoriously guilt-oriented.)

The samurai class made the basic assumption that physical and mental control were related to the extent that one was either an indication or a cause of the other. In the excerpt Etsu points out that "in careful guidance of the hand were we children taught to hold in leash the mind"—that is, if children learned physical control, they would also attain mental control. Even more explicit is this statement: "It was believed that the highest training in mental control came from patient practice in the complicated brush strokes of character-writing." As evidence that a lack of physical control indicated a lack of mental control, we read, "A careless or perturbed state of mind always betrays itself in the intricate shading of ideographs," and the comment of the teacher when Etsu moved: "Little Miss, it is evident that your mental attitude to-day is not suited for study."

Physical control might also indicate respect. Etsu mentions the hours she sat "with primly folded hands," listening to her grandmother tell stories. Other statements in the book support the idea that casual movements (particularly of the lower body) in the presence of superiors might be regarded as insulting. (During World War II, prisoners of the Japanese learned this the hard way, but many people mistook the Japanese reaction for just another fiendish way of harassing prisoners.) The samurai class assumed that physical control could and should be maintained even in sleep. They required girls to sleep in a position that affirmed control. In the United States, people tend to assume that the individual has little or no control over his behavior while he sleeps. At the same time, we also know that sleepers do not normally fall out of bed, urinate, or defecate. As any mother with small children can testify, this is learned, not instinctive, behavior. Holding contradictory assumptions simultaneously is not unusual in cultures; provided both assumptions are part of the traditional belief system, the contradictions are generally ignored by most members of the culture.

Notice that neither samurai men nor women were supposed to *lack* emotions or feeling; they were simply expected to *control* them. One could predict that Japanese from the old samurai class would be dreadfully embarrassed or ashamed to cry openly or to show signs of fear. Anglo-Saxon and early American cultures also place a high value on control of emotion, particularly in public, and assume that such control is evidence of a strong character. Jacqueline Kennedy, for example, was lauded for her "courage" at the funeral of her husband. In other societies, control over emotions is equated with a *lack* of emotions—Latin Americans often regard North Americans as "cold" and "emotionless" people. Thus, some felt that Mrs. Kennedy's behavior revealed a lack of emotions, rather than courage. Such a difference in basic assumptions and values has led to a great deal of misunderstanding between peoples.

CHILD-RAISING TECHNIQUES AND PERSONALITY

It seems reasonable to assume that different demands placed on children in various societies will produce adults who differ. This assumption is correlated with another, that it is possible to instill attitudes and values through certain methods of child training. The excerpt indicates that the Japanese certainly held the latter assumption. The relationship of child-training practices to both the culture of a society and the personality or character of the adults in that culture has been under study for some time. The standing argument about which is more important, heredity or environment, nature or nurture, has virtually been abandoned by anthropologists. No one is born without a genetic endowment or lacking an environment. A more modern approach regards the adult personality as the result of the interaction of genetic heritage, environment (both physical and social), and idiosyncratic (individually unique) experiences. This can be represented schematically by a triangle or a square (depending on whether the environment is represented by one angle or two). See the accompanying chart.

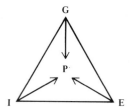

P = personality
G = genetic endowment
E = environment
I = idiosyncratic experiences

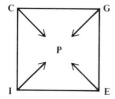

P = personality
G = genetic endowment
E = physical environment
C = culture (social environment)
I = idiosyncratic experiences

The physical environment and certain aspects of the culture are shared by all members of the society. In one of the earlier hypotheses about the relationship between culture and personality, Abram Kardiner (a psychologist) and Ralph Linton and Cora Du Bois (both anthropologists) suggested that people sharing a similar series of experiences as children tend to have similar personalities as adults— that is, they have the basic personality type of the culture. Du Bois called the cluster of characteristics that appears most frequently in a society the modal personality ° and predicted it would differ from one society to another. This statistically based concept has gained more acceptance than the basic personality type (Barnouw 1963: 106, 110). Researchers have attempted to test this hypothesis in a number of societies. Their success so far has not been spectacular, but they have uncovered some interesting and suggestive correlations (Whiting 1961:356ff.).

John W. M. Whiting and Irving L. Child have been leaders in cross-cultural research into the relationship between child rearing and individual personality. They modified the Kardiner-Linton hypothesis to include more variables, to suggest that while personality is influenced by child-raising practices these in turn are influenced by the systems the society has developed to provide for the biological needs of its members. The adult personality is then reflected in the belief systems, particularly those centering around medicine (in non-Western societies) and religion. Cross-cultural research supports a general hypothesis that harsh parental treatment during infancy is correlated with a belief in a harsh, aggressive spirit world, whereas indulgent treatment is correlated with a belief that the gods can be controlled by proper ritual and do not need to be propitiated (Whiting 1961:357).

One difficulty encountered by researchers in the area of psychological anthropology is the problem of classification. For example, was Etsu's treatment harsh or not? The demands made on her were certainly severe, but there is no indication that she was ever beaten or even struck. Shaming seems to have been a sufficient punishment even at her age. In addition, when she successfully completed her task, she was immediately rewarded with warmth, comfort, food, and approval. Using severity of demands or the strictness of expectation as a criterion, Etsu's treatment might be classified as harsh. Using frequency or type of punishment as a criterion, her treatment might be classified as moderate. Using reward for successful completion of a task as a criterion, her treatment might be classified as indulgent.

Classifying Etsu's attitude toward the spirit world creates almost as much difficulty. There is no evidence in the book that Etsu regarded the supernatural world as aggressive, although she did feel "fate" was sometimes hard and unfair. She says Buddhism has a thread of hopelessness in it that she disliked, and she became a fervent Christian as an adult (Sugimoto 1934:137–147). At what point in her life should the classification be made, and on which religion—Buddhism, Shintoism, or Christianity—should it be based? Her autobiography does not clearly confirm or refute any hypothesis, but it does illustrate some of the difficulties of research in the area of culture and personality.

One cross-cultural study found that sorcery is an important explanation for illness in societies where children are severely punished for sexual or aggressive behavior (Whiting 1961:370). Other studies have shown that aggression is most severely punished in extended households ° (where a variety of relatives live together) and in polygynous households ° (where more than one wife is present). If the suggested relationship between punishment for aggressive behavior and belief in sorcery as a cause of disease is valid, then one should find this belief especially prevalent in societies with extended or polygynous households. Studies so far show that the expected finding does occur in societies with polygynous households, especially when jealousy between wives is great (Whiting 1961:370). The studies therefore support the more general hypothesis that a basic maintenance system ° (the polygynous household) leads to certain child-raising practices (punishment of aggressive behavior) which, by producing certain personality characteristics, are reflected in a projective system ° (disease is caused by sorcery).

In some societies, the child-rearing methods are deliberately chosen to instill certain characteristics. It is clear from the excerpt that at least some of the methods used by the Japanese were of this type. In other societies, however, methods are not consciously chosen to produce a particular result. They are used simply because structural factors in the society make them almost inevitable. A woman alone for most of the day with four small children cannot possibly use the same child-rearing methods that a woman living in a large extended-family household has available to her (Minturn and Lambert 1968:551–557). In the studies mentioned above, it is unlikely that polygynous households have any intention of producing a belief in sorcery as the cause of illness when they punish aggression; it is much more likely that aggression is punished simply because living conditions in such complex households would be next to intolerable if everyone were allowed to express aggression whenever he wished. The belief in sorcery as a cause of illness is simply an unexpected byproduct of the child-rearing methods or of some other factor that produces both the punishment for aggression and the belief in sorcery.

In the United States in recent decades, changes in child-raising techniques have been introduced in response to a variety of hypotheses about the effects of certain practices (early weaning, swaddling) on adult behavior. Unfortunately, results do not seem to coincide with predictions, and it is difficult to determine whether the failure is due to faulty assumptions or to other factors in the society that override the effects of child-rearing techniques. (Both positions have supporters and detractors.) One assumption of middle-class Americans—that each child has an innate set of potentials that should be allowed to develop and which can be destroyed by interference—seems to have led to the cross-culturally unique practice of parents deliberately trying to avoid indoctrinating their children (Fischer and Fischer 1966:50). Yet there is no good evidence that the middle-class assumption is correct. In fact, anthropological data would seem to indicate that any innate potentialities are so generalized they could develop in any one of a number of directions. If a child is left without parental guidelines, his potentialities may develop in highly unexpected and unpleasant directions. He never develops without *any* guidelines, of course. If his parents fail to provide them, the child adopts those of his playmates or of individuals who impress him at school or elsewhere. The consequences of this haphazard socialization are not predictable.

Samurai in Japan certainly had no intention of leaving the socialization of their children to chance or to casual playmates. In addition to the characteristics already mentioned as desirable, they apparently regarded obedience and respect for superiors as quite important. The presence of superiors and inferiors means that Japanese society is not egalitarian,° but of course no human society ever is. Even the simplest society recognizes power differentials at some level (see Chapter 4). None gives the same power to small children that it gives to adults, for example, and it is difficult to imagine how any could. Comparison of societies on an egalitarian basis usually centers on the ways in which powerful positions are attained and maintained. A society in which such positions are ascribed on the basis of chance factors (race, age, physical appearance, family) is regarded as less egalitarian than a society in which powerful positions are awarded on the basis of individual qualification. If we look at Japanese society as pictured in the excerpt, some of the criteria for superiority and inferiority are apparent. Education, religious training, and age clearly qualified one as superior. Children, women, and servants were inferior. Some of these qualifications are chance factors (sex, age, family), but others such as education were obtained by individual effort. One might be born a samurai or a servant, but not educated or a priest.

Respect for superior individuals was expressed in a variety of ways. Avoiding unnecessary movement has already been mentioned. Etsu gives others, such as relative height or comfort. (She never sat on a cushion in her grandmother's presence, and her teacher had to sit on one in spite of his wish, because "the position of instructor was too greatly revered for him to be allowed to sit on a level with his pupil.") Bowing is mentioned several times, as is backing out of the presence of a superior (when Etsu was dismissed by her teacher). All these examples indicate that the samurai of prewar Japan had a strict and formal code of manners, detailed and precise, with little room for spontaneity or variation. Often in societies of this sort, lower-class individuals are allowed more variation in behavior; in fact, the amount of variation permitted tends to be one of the distinguishing characteristics of social class.

COVERT CULTURE

Since most socialization takes place early, certain behavior tends to become almost automatic and appears "instinctive." It is not, of course. Almost all human behavior is learned, and "proper" behavior varies so much from one group of people to another that it could not possibly be instinctive. But the automatic character of the behavior makes it difficult for someone socialized in one group to move easily into another, for such a person must unlearn accustomed behavior patterns and adopt new ones. Hardly anyone can learn the new responses as well as the people who have been trained in them from childhood. In addition, because these responses are so automatic, it is difficult for members of a class to teach them to others even if they want to. Their reactions have become part of "covert" (hidden) culture.

Covert culture refers to those concepts people take for granted, do not remember learning, and often do not realize they know at all. Behavior motivated by these concepts is assumed to be "natural," the result of "human nature" or "instinct." Yet man seems to have very few instincts. (The term *instinct* is subject to different definitions, unfortunately. Psychologists, biologists, zoologists, and others are still arguing about the "best" definitions of instinct, drives, and reflexes.) Primates—especially man—have to be taught virtually everything they need to know to survive; ants, bees, and other insects, on the other hand, are genetically programmed to do almost everything necessary for individual or group survival. Man may have some general drives (the argument over this is currently a hot one in anthropology), for companionship, aggression, esteem, or dominance; but if they exist, these drives can be satisfied in a wide variety of ways. Accepting the existence of a drive for dominance, for example, will not help an investigator predict the behavior of a specific individual in a particular situation.

Covert culture often provokes heated debates. Since people assume behavior motivated by covert culture is natural or instinctive, they are apt to be disturbed by behavior that is different, because it is "unnatural" to them. Assumptions about attributes of men and women, sexual behavior, and man's innate nature tend to be part of covert culture in most societies. Changes in these are therefore upsetting. It is also patently absurd to think of teaching instinctive behavior. After all, do bees have to go to school to learn how to make honey? The motives and intelligence of anyone who offers to teach instinctive behavior are obviously open to question.

Much of the resistance to sex education in the schools appears to be based on the belief that sexual behavior is instinctive and that early education in it will only cause children to start active practice before the society would like them to. Most of the cross-cultural evidence, however, indicates that sexual behavior is not entirely instinctive. What excites people sexually in one society may "turn them off" in another. Southern European men are excited by the bushy underarms of a woman; Americans are more often repelled by them. Trobrianders (South Pacific Melanesians) are thrilled by biting off each other's eyelashes (Malinowski 1929:334). The "normal" position for sexual intercourse varies from one society to another (Powdermaker 1933:240–241; Malinowski 1929:336; Holmberg 1969:164–165). Even American society provides some evidence that sexual behaviors are learned. Aside from the incidence of sexual problems, known to any psychiatrist, there is one experience common to almost everyone. When young people ask, "How do I know if I am in love?" most adults, relying on instinct, answer, "Don't worry, you'll know all right when it happens," or "If you have to ask, you aren't." Yet even the same adults will usually admit that they themselves were fooled at least once. It is very difficult to fool an instinct.

Temperament associated with a particular sex is also learned, at least in part. Men are not "naturally" much more aggressive than women (a doubter can watch children playing in any nursery school before cultural conditioning has had time to take full effect). Women are not "naturally" more demonstrative, emotional, affectionate, or kinder than men. It takes twelve to fourteen years of conditioning, using all the weapons at a society's command (such as scorn, ridicule, physical punishment) to teach boys that "men don't cry." If men instinctively did not cry, it would be unnecessary to indoctrinate boys. At some point in history, in Anglo-American cultures, crying came to be thought of as weak or effeminate behavior and consequently inappropriate to the male role. It would be illuminating to trace the development of this concept, since it is fairly recent (biblical personages and even knights of the Round Table wept freely), but there is neither time nor space to discuss it here (Bulfinch n.d.:377, 379, 399, 404). Any psychologist can testify to the emotional cost of the conditioning to his male patients. In short, while there may be a few differences in innate temperament associated with sex, it is still far from certain precisely what these are, and many of the differences assumed by Americans to be innate are actually learned.

Most nonverbal behavior falls into the category of covert culture. Edward T. Hall and other anthropologists have written at length about the covert aspects of such commonplace things as the use of time and space, walking, sitting, standing, and carrying burdens (Hall 1959, 1965; Birdwhistell 1970:8–9). Covert culture is not normally "taught" in the formal sense of the word, but it is learned. Children tend to imitate, and parents by their behavior and reactions tend to produce, sometimes quite unconsciously, the preferred and expected behavior from their children.

Gestures, facial expressions, posture are all learned and vary from one culture to another. Anthropological lore is full of anecdotes about the difficulties—some amusing, some not—that beset individuals who use gestures commonplace and innocent in their own culture but insulting or threatening in the culture in which they are working. For example, the peace sign used today in the United States (the first two fingers on one hand held up, spread apart) meant "V for Victory" during World War II. It would have been dangerous to use it in Nazi Germany, and it is an obscene gesture in some societies. In the United States, men engaged in sports (basketball, baseball, football) continually pat one another on the buttocks to indicate approval after some particularly skillful act or before a crucial play to give encouragement. This gesture is taken for granted by performers and spectators alike, provided it occurs in the proper context (sports), but it would be a highly inappropriate gesture to use walking down a public street or in a restaurant. Yet precise and meaningful as this gesture is, it is part of covert culture; people do it unconsciously, without thinking about it, unless it is called to their attention.

The use of space is also learned. People in some societies tolerate close physical contact; in others, they reject it. In large American cities such as New York, good manners require individuals to give others all the space possible in any given situation. On public transportation, in restaurants where patrons seat themselves, on beaches, "proper" behavior consists in sitting as far as possible from anyone else. If a man sits beside a woman he does not know (or vice versa) when there are alternative places available, it is usually interpreted as a sexual advance. Even if for some reason this is obviously not the case, the behavior is usually regarded as rude and disagreeable. Iroquois Indians are noted for their skill in high steel construction and for their lack of fear of heights. The reasons for this ability are far from clear, but a contributing factor may be walking habits that are part of Iroquois covert culture. Most Iroquois still place one foot directly in front of the other when walking. Unpaved paths on their Onondaga reservation may be as little as six to eight inches wide, whereas similar paths in non-Indian areas are rarely less than eighteen inches wide. If one customarily walks in an eight-inch space, one is likely to think of a steel girder as a wide, comfortable walking space.

While covert culture is hidden from us, we all remember learning the concepts of overt culture °—history dates, the proper use of "please" and "thank you," how to play basketball, and the like. We can often specify when we learned certain concepts and from whom. In the United States, hunting technology is part of overt culture. The author of the first excerpt in Chapter 4 is aware he does not know Pygmy hunting technology because he has had little opportunity to learn it. He does not regard the behavior as instinctive (although some authors still write about the "instinctive" tracking abilities of hunting and gathering peoples). Hunting knowledge is covert in some cultures, however. Ways to track and move through cover are learned in such a way and at such an age that people are not conscious of learning them. The behavior simply seems natural. In such cases, people tend to regard outsiders who lack these skills as somewhat retarded, handicapped, and possibly not quite human. The native New Yorker is apt to feel similarly about skills for coping with heavy traffic, either vehicular or pedestrian. Naturally, if an individual lacks an elementary "instinctive" skill, people will not regard him as "normal." The quotation marks are significant, because these skills are *not* instinctive; they simply seem so to people who have acquired them as part of covert culture.

From what has been said, it is obvious that covert culture differs from one society to another. This difference causes misunderstanding between peoples. Note, for example, the reaction of the author to the Pygmy treatment of animals. He admits that when they laughed and imitated the animal's struggles and suffering after they killed the *sindula*, he felt furthest from them. The Pygmies were unconcerned about inflicting pain on animals. They kicked dogs; they singed the feathers off living birds. In modern American-English tradition, the suffering of an animal is as upsetting as human suffering—possibly more so. A person who willfully causes animals to endure unnecessary pain or someone who laughs at such suffering is believed to be emotionally disturbed, cruel, inhuman, and generally untrustworthy or "bad" (and someone brought up in the American-English tradition who does such things may indeed have emotional problems). In their treatment of animals, the Ba-Mbuti behaved in a way that the author's covert culture insisted was characteristic of "bad" people. Consequently, in spite of his intellectual understanding of the Pygmies and his general sympathy with them, he could not help but feel somewhat disturbed and alienated when they exhibited this behavior. Yet in a society where kicking dogs is an expected part of the normal treatment of animals, the behavior will not indicate any character flaws.

Covert cultural differences may therefore be a source of ill-will between peoples that increased contact only aggravates, rather than reduces—a fact overlooked by proponents of "togetherness" as the solution to world tensions (Williams 1964:25). (After all, could you feel comfortable with someone who you knew frequently killed babies or regularly ate the ashes of his relatives?) The only way dislike brought about by conflicts on the covert culture level can be reduced is for members of both societies to become aware of what is causing the trouble and to develop a tolerance for something emotionally upsetting. It is possible, but far from simple.

Covert culture is extremely difficult to study in one's own culture, of course, precisely *because* it is covert. This is one reason anthropologists go into societies other than their own for extended periods of time (normally a year to a year and a half) as part of their training. Experience with the covert culture of others usually opens one's eyes to one's own, at least partially. The less experience one has with people of different cultures, the greater the proportion of one's own culture that remains covert. (This is one reason why people who are isolated often appear narrow-minded and provincial to those with more experience.)

All culture (including covert) can be studied only through its

---

FACING PAGE: A South American boy hunting with bow and arrow. In some cultures hunting knowledge is covert. *Cornell Capa/Magnum*

manifestations (manifestations of culture, remember, are act and artifacts—behavior and the consequences of behavior). An anthropologist studies these manifestations and arrives at hypotheses about the concepts motivating them. He checks these by asking questions (in the case of covert culture, the answers are never very helpful), or he tries to verify the hypotheses by predicting what behavior will occur under various circumstances. If his hypotheses are correct, his predictions will be accurate, or nearly so.

Another aspect of covert culture, and an important one, is language. It is crucial in human socialization. Both animals and man are socialized through imitation (animals may not need socialization in some areas of life because of instincts), but only man is also socialized through language. Language exerts a profound influence on our lives, an influence often greater than most of us realize. According to Edward Sapir, "The fact of the matter is that the 'real' world is to a large extent unconsciously built up on the language habits of the group" (Barnouw 1963:96). Benjamin Whorf suggested that concepts of the nature of space and time were conditioned by language structure. The Sapir-Whorf hypothesis takes the position that individual perception of reality is determined by the structure of the language the individual speaks (Barnouw 1963:97). Holders of this position agree that no true understanding of a culture is possible without complete familiarity with its language. Speakers of different languages cannot possibly perceive reality the same way. (Some philosophers conclude that because no two people ever speak exactly the same language, no individual perceives reality in exactly the same way as any other individual.)

Semanticists and psychologists have explored the effects of language on individual perception and personality. They too conclude that language strongly influences individual perceptions of situations and affects individual responses. Differences in meanings and connotations attached to certain words may have disastrous consequences for communication between individuals.

The exact nature and degree of the influence of language on socialization is by no means well understood, however. Critics of the Sapir-Whorf hypothesis point out that some societies with different cultures speak the same language, particularly so far as grammatical structure is concerned. On the other hand, other societies with different languages have cultures that are almost identical (Hoijer 1954b:102–104). The most popular position among anthropologists today would seem to be that language does indeed exert an influence on individual modes of thought, particularly by channeling them along certain lines, but does not actually control perception. Research has shown, for example, that it is easier to remember colors that have names than those that do not, although differences between the colors are perceived (Lenneberg and Roberts 1961:493–502). Still, communication and understanding across language barriers does seem to be possible and often appears as complete as communication between individuals speaking the same language.

A subtle relationship between child rearing and adult institutions has been suggested by David McClelland. His hypothesis is that "the need for achievement is responsible for economic growth and decline" (McClelland 1961:vii). The high-need achievers, McClelland says, are produced by strong independence training and achievement expectations in childhood. The excerpt would tend to support this. Etsu appears to have a strong need to achieve, and she received strong independence training at an early age. Her father seemed to feel the development of self-reliance was crucial for members of a samurai family. He illustrated the type of training a samurai child should receive by describing a lioness pushing her cub over the cliff to make it climb up from the valley because "so only can it gain strength for its life work." Japan's economy has been most impressive in its growth and vigor, especially since the end of World War II. If Etsu's training was characteristic of a significant segment of Japanese society, McClelland's hypothesis would seem to have strong support. Of course, it is poor methodology to rely on data such as this excerpt, which can give only an impressionistic idea of possibilities. To test McClelland's hypothesis, one would have to study samples of the Japanese population to determine whether they in fact *are* high-need achievers, whether their childhood training was aimed at fostering independence, whether it succeeded, and whether parents expected high achievement from their children. To show the difficulty of relying on the data contained in the excerpt, the strong emphasis on obedience and submission plus the reliance on rote memorization in studies could be used as evidence that Japanese child training was meant to and in fact did produce dependent imitators rather than self-reliant creative individuals.

PERSONALITY AND CULTURE: A COMPLEX RELATIONSHIP

The study of human beings is never simple. Most behavioral scientists have long since abandoned the search for a single cause to explain specific behavior, for they recognize that a number of factors, all of which may be important, are involved in any human interaction. In line with this awareness, modern approaches to the relationship between personality or character and culture tend to focus more on the *interaction* among genetic endowment, physical environment, idiosyncratic individual experiences, and sociocultural environment; it is the interplay of cultural demands with other factors that attracts researchers' interest. For example, recent technological advances have revealed unsuspected physical aspects of human behavior. Technology now enables man to travel more rapidly than ever before, and Western culture requires businessmen to take advantage of the new ease of travel to make their work global in scope. Because of the reported effects on the individual of rapid travel combined with the stress of engaging in prolonged and complicated business negotiations, researchers have found that man has an internal clock which is disrupted by too rapid passage from one time zone to another. Various adjustments in the expectations and behavior of businessmen and also of athletes have resulted from these findings.

Studies have been made concerning the relationship of perception to such environmental characteristics as straight lines and right angles (called a "carpentered environment" °) or curved lines and no right angles (called a "noncarpentered environment"). People raised in a noncarpentered environment are not as subject to the optical illusions that fool people socialized in a carpentered environment (Allport and Pettigrew 1957:104–113; Segall, Campbell, *et al.* 1963:769–771). The level of certain chemicals produced by the body and present in the blood (such as epinephrine, produced by the adrenal gland) has been correlated with emotional states and sensitivity (or the lack of it) to pain (Schachter and Wheeler 1962:121–128; *Science News* 1966, 90:425). Further research is necessary to learn how these chemical levels are related to child-raising practices. For example, do high (or low) levels in either parents or children correlate with harsh (or indulgent) child-raising techniques? These studies are revealing a more subtle relationship between the physical individual and his culture than had previously been suspected, and are adding to the complexity of the whole area of study. Space does not permit a more detailed discussion, but interested readers can explore the topic further through the references cited.

THE FAMILY: SEX ROLES

Look at the excerpt again. What were some characteristics other than those discussed earlier that the samurai class wanted to develop in their children? Clearly, patience, endurance, and perseverance were highly regarded. The incident when Etsu froze her fingers while practicing writing illustrates the value attached to all three. Despite being aware of the damage to her hand, neither the child nor the nurse stopped the session. Such a deliberate disregard for the personal comfort or physical well-being of a child is almost inconceivable in American culture today. Etsu was expected to finish her task slowly and carefully regardless of discomfort. In fact, the physical discomfort was assumed to contribute to her mental inspiration. It was no accident that her room was cold, since the coldest days had been chosen for the most difficult tasks, and no stove was brought into the room. Etsu's parents went out of their way to make things difficult, not easier, for their daughter.

Even though Etsu was subjected to what in the United States today might be regarded as cruel treatment, once she successfully finished her task, she was wrapped up comfortably, fed warm food her grandmother herself had prepared, surrounded with love, attention, and care. Contrast this with the cold rebuke she received from her teacher when she moved during a lesson. Assuming this difference in reaction to performance was consistent, what child would not prefer the warm, affectionate treatment, even if it meant enduring some temporary physical discomfort? When people on whom a child depends or for whom he feels affection give either cold or warm reactions according to his behavior, it is a rare child indeed who will deliberately choose to prompt the negative reaction. The source of the power of the family to socialize a child should be obvious.

The excerpt also indicates that members of the samurai class made a sharp distinction between training for boys and that for girls. Boys were permitted to sleep in a sprawled-out position, for example; girls were not. Boys studied the Chinese classics; girls normally did not. (Etsu was an exception because she was being trained as a priestess.) There were special games for boys that girls were forbidden to play (although they did do so when no one was watching—perhaps another indication that the society was shame-rather than guilt-oriented). Girls learned the necessary skills for running a household; boys did not.

All societies make some distinction between the training of girls and boys, since no society expects precisely the same behavior from both sexes. Of course there is a biological component involved—no male is likely to give birth to a child, and no female is likely to sire one. As a result of the child-bearing and nursing functions, most societies have patterns of behavior for women that can be carried out in or close to the home. As mentioned in earlier chapters, no society requires big-game hunting as a normal part of the role of women. Women are hardly ever expected to be deep sea fishermen or warriors. Women may accompany such expeditions, but it is rarely part of their normal role expectation. With these exceptions, which are based on the functional demands of the situation more than on attitudes, abilities, or inclination, role expectations for women and for men are as varied as any other aspect of culture. Thus, although the role training for men in any specific society is different from the role training for women in that society, it is also likely to be different from the training for men in other societies. The training of male children in one society may include activities restricted to the role of women in another society, and vice versa. For example, in some societies, only the men weave; in others only the women. Men make pottery in one society, women in another. Margaret Mead has pointed out that in one New Guinea society women are taught to be more aggressive and less interested in dress or adornment than the men, whereas the situation is reversed in the United States (Mead 1950: 188–189).

THE PROBLEM OF FAILURE

All societies have to cope with failures of the socialization process. A variety of factors may cause such failures. Recent studies indicate, for example, that overcrowding may be as detrimental to human socialization as it has been shown to be for laboratory rats (Ardrey 1970: 241–280). Various structural breakdowns in the family can also cause socialization problems. Harry Harlow and Margaret Harlow conducted a long series of experiments with monkeys that showed that when monkeys were deprived of all association with other young monkeys or with the mother figures, they did not develop into normal monkeys. Even sexual behavior became disturbed. The deprived monkeys could not reproduce under normal circumstances (so much for instinct!). When the experiments did finally succeed in bringing about reproduction, the deprived monkeys made poor parents. They mistreated their offspring, physically abused them, neglected them, and managed to raise a second generation of disturbed monkeys (Harlow and Harlow 1961: 48–55). The implications of these studies for humans appear clear, but researchers are being cautious. Human beings are not monkeys, however closely related the two may be. It is tempting, but perhaps unwise, to generalize from one to the other without modification. One fact does seem inescapable, however: socialization is far more important than has been suspected, even in less complex animals in whom instinctive behavior plays a more powerful role than in man.

There are other reasons for breakdowns in socialization. In a complex society, such as the United States, there are so many different groups involved in socialization (school, peer groups, various subcultures) that young people are inevitably subjected to a barrage of conflicting beliefs and values. This may be one of the factors behind the so-called identity crisis faced by many American teenagers. With strong pressure to identify with groups, and with so many groups to identify with, an individual may find himself strongly supporting diametrically opposite causes, according to the group he is associated with at any given time. A thoughtful individual must question his adopting the values of the group he is currently with, asking: What am I really like? What do I really believe? Who am I?

In addition, wherever and whenever it occurs, rapid and fundamental change in a society produces special problems of socialization. Premodern societies recently exposed to Western culture and in the process of industrializing perhaps suffer this difficulty even more deeply than does the United States, although the problem of alienation from one's own culture is also highly significant here. But any society caught in the flux of profound change will have difficulty, since many of the things adults were taught, and want to teach their children, no longer apply in the new situation, yet they carry all the emotional force of the past. Young people are often caught between attraction for the new life, realistic appraisal of the changed situation, and love or respect for parents who have not, as yet, been able to adjust to the changes. The situation should be familiar to most Americans from the stories of the conflicts between immigrant parents and their American-born children. Now, whole generations with native-born parents are suffering the same conflicts, both in the United States and in other countries. There is no immediate solution in sight, but at least books like *Future Shock* (Toffler 1970) show that people are beginning to grapple with the problem realistically instead of just bemoaning the loss of the "good old days."

The study of socialization is not limited to childhood experiences. Modern researchers are aware that events taking place later in an individual's life may also play a significant part in the development of the adult personality. Some of these later events may serve the purpose of undoing earlier childhood conditioning; others reinforce it. One experience researchers believe has the function of undoing early conditioning is the puberty rite.° This is one of the

rites de passage °(passage or crisis rites °) that marks a change in status. Crisis rites occur in all societies, but the status changes that are marked vary from one to another. The puberty rite marks the change from child or adolescent to adult. These ceremonies have attracted a great deal of attention from behavioral scientists and there is a voluminous literature on the topic. Puberty rites often involve some sort of ordeal, particularly for males, and a learning experience. The severity of the ordeal and the duration of the instruction period vary widely.

Male circumcision is a frequent feature of puberty rites. The immediate and obvious function is to make the initiate a man. Once the operation has healed, a young man is usually free to consider marriage (or sexual intercourse), speak up in the presence of the older men, command respect from the uncircumcised boys (as well as girls and women), and otherwise take on the responsibilities and privileges of adult males. This one act turns a boy into an adult. Contrast this with the ambiguous position of a young man in the United States. Laws vary from one state to another. In some states he can get a learner's permit to drive at 14 but must stay in school until he is 16. He can usually sign a legally binding document when he is 18 but in some states may not marry without parental consent until he is 20 or 21. He can be drafted at 18 but in some states cannot drink alcoholic beverages until he is 21. In most places he can be tried in criminal court as an adult when he is over 18 but the insurance rates for his car remain high until he is over 25. In American society, an individual passes through a transition state for approximately eleven years—from about age 14 to 25. During this time he is considered an adult for some purposes and a child for others—with the choice rarely left to him. There is no clear-cut ceremony or sign that he is now a full adult member of the society.

A puberty rite often dramatizes and tests some of the qualities members of the society value and expect of their adult males. In some societies, initiates are expected to be brave and show no signs of fear or pain during an extremely painful operation performed without any anesthetic (Gatheru 1965:60). In others, they are not expected to show the same fortitude. Girls usually do not have to undergo such painful ordeals, but in a few societies, they too must endure substantial pain (for example, the Kikuyu practice clitoridectomy °—excision of the clitoris [Gatheru 1965:58]).

Penalties for failure to show the desired characteristics are

FACING PAGE: Baptism, one of the first crisis rites, being performed in Ethiopia. *Victor Englebert/De Wys, Inc.*

usually well known. Group contempt, for example, may be expressed by public scorn and humiliation, including spitting on the offending initiate as an immediate reaction, and long-term rejection might even be extended to the initiate's family. The Kikuyu assume that only illegitimate boys show fear during initiation (Gatheru 1965:62).

Rewards for successful endurance are equally clear and new initiates usually delight in validating their status by demonstrating their superiority over the uninitiated. This serves to reinforce the system; the differences between circumcised and uncircumcised in terms of privileges are so obvious that the uninitiated tend to be strongly motivated to undergo the public ordeal for the sake of its rewards. Refusal to go through a puberty ceremony may mean that an individual will never be taken seriously by the rest of the society. He may be handicapped in any dealings with the people in powerful positions; he may not be able to marry (or even court a wife) and is likely to be left out of the mainstream of adult life.

Whiting and others have studied the correlations between severe puberty rites and other aspects of the society. According to Whiting, the rite serves to break any possible cross-sex identification that might occur because of a male child's close and almost exclusive association with his mother during his early infancy. Under these circumstances, the mother may appear the envied and powerful sex. The severity of the puberty rite emphasizes the boy's identity with his own sex. Whiting feels this explanation is supported by the correlation of severe, public puberty rites and either a long postpartum sex tabu or a period of a year or more when the young boy shares his mother's bed (Whiting 1961:361). Frank Young, on the other hand, feels that the rite is an expression of male solidarity and occurs particularly in those societies where male cooperation is important for both economic exploitation of the environment and defense (Young 1962:380–383). Neither of these explanations deals with the problem of female initiation. Fewer societies have female puberty rites, and in those that do the rites are rarely as painful as circumcision or subincision ° (slitting the penis from base to glans, or part way). Most female rites include only such mild ordeals as seclusion, sleeplessness, food taboos, and special, often tiring, activities. A study of female initiation shows that, as with males, severity and genital mutilation tend to be correlated with a possible conflict in sexual identity. Female initiation is also associated with matrilocal ° residence and occurs most often in societies where women make a substantial contribution to subsistence (Brown 1963: 849–850).

Many puberty rites include a period of training in the norms and beliefs of the society. This period may last from a few days to several years. The so-called bush school may be held for either sex, but it is never coeducational—each school is restricted to one sex. Most often males are the ones who receive the training and go through the public ceremony.

Even when the period of training and isolation is short, there is usually some symbolic representation of norms the society regards as important during the ceremony itself. Kikuyu initiation emphasizes the social value placed on courage and endurance. The women sing what is expected of the initiate, which of course he already knows, having witnessed similar ceremonies himself (Gatheru 1965: 59). In some societies an initiate is required to perform actually or symbolically some of the duties that will be expected of him or her as an adult. Among Navajos, for example, female initiates grind

Village girls of the Aboure tribe, dressed for a tribal rite. *Marc and Evelyne Bernheim/Rapho Guillumette*

corn; in Polynesia they weave mats or make grass skirts; in some African societies men must kill either a valuable food animal or a dangerous one, such as a lion. In the past, many societies required a young man to kill an enemy or successfully complete a difficult or dangerous task (a raid or a vision quest) before he was eligible for the puberty ceremony. All these requirements emphasize the values or behavior that an individual must have mastered to be able to perform his or her adult role successfully.

Since puberty rites generally have a public aspect when the initiate is presented to the society in his new status, the initiate has seen the ceremony many times before he himself participates as a candidate. Thus the rite has a teaching function for the uninitiated spectators. For the candidates and the initiated spectators, the rite serves to demonstrate dramatically that the candidate is capable of doing what is expected of him as an adult. It makes it easier for him to adopt the role and for others to accept him in it. This latter aspect may be more important than the literature indicates. One of the difficulties often mentioned by young adults, parents, and observers alike in the United States is getting members of the older generation (especially parents) to accept young people in their late teens and early twenties as competent adults. The United States has no public ceremony that clearly demonstrates to the older generation that the young man or woman in question has mastered the necessary adult skills, information, or values. A puberty rite cannot substitute for a college degree (which shows that its possessor has been exposed to certain aspects of his culture and society), but equally no one should demand that college graduation function as a puberty rite and insist on it before admitting a young person to adult status—as seems to happen at some social levels in the United States today.

SUMMARY

A society cannot function unless most members perform approximately as expected. Since it is impossible to force everyone in a society to behave predictably, people have to want to do what they are supposed to do. In most cases, they learn what this is while they are growing up in the family. As children, they are taught the rules, customs, and traditions of the society, they are rewarded for approved behavior and punished for incorrect performance. In this way, each child learns to value certain things and to reject or dislike others. The process is called socialization or enculturation.

Since the individual's personality is affected by the experiences he has, particularly during the first few years of life, anthropologists and some psychologists have assumed that cultures making different demands on individuals will tend to have members whose personalities are characteristic of the society and different from those in other societies. The nature of the relationship between personality and culture is complex, however. The demands of the culture do affect the personality of the individual, but the individual in turn embodies the culture and passes it along to his children. He is not simply a passive recipient. Each individual interprets and reworks the culture as he lives. The same cultural demands made on different people have different consequences. Culture and personality are dynamically interrelated, with influences going both ways.

The relationship of the physical environment and biological factors to the personality is also being investigated with a new sophistication. The interplay between the individual, his physical surroundings, his cultural surroundings, and his internal chemistry is turning out to be far more subtle and complex than was originally envisioned.

The interrelationship between various aspects of the culture, child-raising practices, and, ultimately, personality is providing new information. The function of puberty rites in undoing certain childhood conditioning; the relationship of initiation rites to structural features of the culture such as residence patterns, the contribution of women to subsistence, the organization of work groups, and so on; the relationship of basic maintenance systems to child-raising practices; the effect of the adult personality on concepts of disease causation, religious beliefs, or witchcraft; research into all these topics is producing exciting new insights into human behavior. The whole area of socialization, thought processes, education, and personality is an active and vital one in current anthropology.

Some socialization takes place throughout an individual's life, and the society as a whole plays a part in the process, but most of the early and crucial socialization takes place within the family. Chapter 6 deals with the formation and composition of families in different societies.

6 Addition of
New Members

Even with the most careful precautions and concern, individual members of the group die. If they are not replaced, the group itself will cease to exist. There are two ways in which any group replenishes its numbers: it may attract new members from other groups, or it may create new members through reproduction within the society. Attracting people from other groups is less expensive in the short run because an immigrant comes into the society as a productive adult; a child, on the other hand, must be supported for a long time until he can contribute economically to the society. But the difficulty of socializing an adult often offsets this advantage. Reproduction within the group is by far the most common method, for it is efficient and simpler in the long run. In this chapter, we focus on the more common second method for adding new members.

In reading the excerpts in this chapter, look for the ways in which people find mates, how they deal with family relationships and inheritance, how they set up households, and what happens if the households break up.

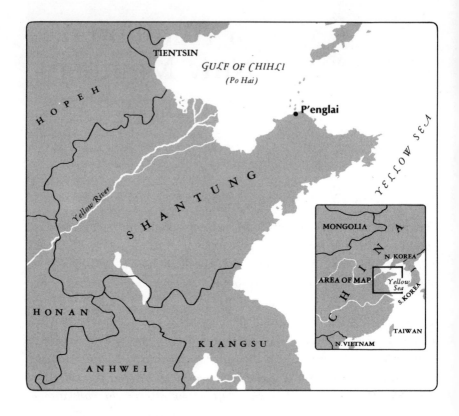

Tradition and the Chinese Bride

My father called me Little Tiger and I was my mother's youngest child.*
The name she called me is known to no one now alive. My sister and my
brother called me Meimei, Little Sister, and the neighbors called me
Hsiao Wutse, Little Five, because I was the fifth child my mother bore.
Two died before I was born.

We lived in a courtyard by ourselves when I was born. We lived near
the truck garden which had belonged to the family, to my father and my
father's uncle. . . .

The garden had once been part of the property of the Temple of the
Goddess of Mercy, the Kuan Yin T'ang. Ten generations ago, a Taoist
priest came down from the hills . . . and became the abbot of the temple.
He was our ancestor. He was a man with a square face and a strong dis-

* Abridged from *A Daughter of Han: The Autobiography of a Chinese Working Woman* by Ida Pruitt, from the story told her by Ning Lao T'ai-T'ai, pp.
11–14, 20, 29–39, 42–43, 46–47, 54–55, 66–67, 70–72. Copyright, 1945 by Yale University Press. Reprinted by permission of Yale University Press.

position. My grandfather had the same square face and I have it also. That is why my father called me Little Tiger. Also, he said, I had a strong disposition.

Our family had been well to do at one time. We had the land our ancestor left us and my grandfather and his father before him had been among those who worked as overseers on the estates of General Ch'i. When my mother married into the family we owned the garden and the house in the Chou Wang Temple section of the city and some other small houses besides. The family had servants and plenty to eat.

My father was an only son and was spoiled by his father. His parents died when he was seven or eight. He was brought up by his uncle, his father's younger brother, who made his own four sons work in the garden but sent my father to school. The uncle said that in this way he was faithful to his dead brother. My father studied the classics for about eight years, but his studies never amounted to anything. When he was grown, the uncle put him in a shop to learn business.

Money went out, the neighbors said, because my father and his cousins had too good a time, eating and playing. . . . Each year there was less than the year before. When my grandfather died, what was left was divided between my father and his uncle, the younger brother of his father.

My father tried to work in the garden but he had not the strength or the skill and he was ashamed. He sold the garden to one of his mother's aunts, to pay his debts, and went to Chefoo and peddled bread. He knew how to make bread, and carried it around the street in a basket. That was the year I was born. From the time I was conceived, the fortunes of the family went down. The destiny determined for me by Heaven was not a good one.

The neighbors said that my mother was not a good manager, that she could not make the money stretch so as to "get over the years" successfully. At New Year's time great loaves of bread were steamed in the iron cooking basin. If, when the lid of the cooking basin was raised, the loaves shrank, they were thrown into the fire. Sometimes she threw three or four cookings into the fire before the loaves came out round and full. This is what the neighbors said my mother used to do. I never saw it, for we had nothing to throw away when I was growing up.

My mother did not live the life she was brought up to live. A woman in childbed should have at least five hundred eggs to eat. When I was born she had only eight eggs. My mother's father, when he lived, sold oil in the streets, beating a small bronze gong, and supported the family comfortably. My mother had a round face and gentle ways. She was a carefully reared and sheltered person. How could such a person, living behind walls, know how to manage poverty?

. . .

Though each year our living was less than the year before, we had a good life at home. My mother was kind to us. She cooked good things for us to eat and she loved us.

My father was strict but he was good to his family. He taught us manners and what was seemly for a woman to do and what was not seemly.

. . .

When I was three or four years old we moved to the Chou Wang Temple neighborhood, to be near the garden. . . . This was the first time our family had lived in a court with others. The house had a thatched roof. Before we had always lived in houses with tile roofs.

. . .

When I was thirteen my parents stopped shaving the hair from around the patch of long hair left on my crown. I was no longer a little girl. My hair was allowed to grow and was gathered into a braid at the back of my head. It was braided in a wide loose plait which spread fan-like above and below the knot that held the hair at the nape of the neck. It was like a great butterfly. Girls do not wear their hair that way now. Part of the hair was separated and braided into a little plait down my back. When the little braid was gathered into the big braid I was a woman, and not allowed out of the gate. . . . And at the age of thirteen I was taught to cook and sew.

My father was a very strict man. We were not allowed, my sister and I, on the street after we were thirteen. People in P'englai were that way in those days. When a family wanted to know more about a girl who had been suggested for a daughter-in-law and asked what kind of a girl she was, the neighbors would answer, "We do not know. We have never seen her." And that was praise.

. . .

My sister was married when she was fifteen, and I was married when I was fifteen. I was eight when my sister was married.

My sister's match was considered a very suitable one. Her husband was only three or four years older than she and he had a trade. He was a barber. And the father-in-law was still young enough to work also. But my sister was a child, with the ways of a child and the heart of a child. She had not become used to housework. She did not know how to mix wheat bread or corn bread. She got the batter too thick or too thin, and so her mother-in-law would scold. She had no experience and could not plan meals. At one meal she would cook too much and at the next not enough. This also made her mother-in-law angry and she would scold. Though my sister had not learned to work she had learned to smoke [opium]. This also made her mother-in-law angry. She would say

A peasant home in a village outside Peking. *Marc Riboud/Magnum*

that my sister was not good for work but only for luxury. So there was bitterness.

Her mother-in-law forbade her to smoke. She took her pipe and broke it into many pieces. My sister made herself a pipe from a reed and smoked when there was no one around. One day her mother-in-law came suddenly into the room. My sister hid the pipe under her clothes as she sat on the k'ang. The lighted pipe set the wheat chaff under the bed matting afire, and her mother-in-law beat her. When her husband came home his mother told him the story and he also beat my sister. There was a great quarrel and her mother-in-law reviled her with many words that were too hard to bear.

. . . My sister went crazy. . . . she stayed with us for six months.

And she was not right for all those six months. . . . All these six months she talked to herself, and at times she was stiff and still. But she got better and the fits became less frequent.

We asked friends to talk for her to her mother-in-law and husband, and at last it was arranged that they should take her back. A separate house was rented for her and her husband so that they did not live with the old people. She got on with her husband and they liked each other, but still at times she had the spells. . . .

Seeing that my sister had so much trouble with a young husband, my father and mother said that I should be married to an older man who would cherish me. When the matchmaker told of such a one and that he had no mother—she was dead—my parents thought that they had done well for me. I was to have an older husband to cherish me, but not too old, and no mother-in-law to scold and abuse me.

Our neighbor, the man who carted away the night soil,° made the match for me. He was a professional matchmaker. He did not care how a marriage turned out. He had used the money. As the old people say, "A matchmaker does not live a lifetime with the people he brings together." The matchmaker hid four years of my husband's age from us, saying that the man was only ten years older than I. But he was fourteen years older. I was twelve when the match was made, and I became engaged—a childhood match. I still had my hair in a plait. I did not know anything. I was fifteen when I was married.

They told me that I was to be a bride. I had seen weddings going down the street. I had seen brides sitting on the k'angs on the wedding days when all went in to see them. To be married was to wear pretty clothes and ornaments in the hair.

I sat on the k'ang, bathed and dressed, in my red underclothes and red stockings. The music sounded and they took me off the k'ang. I sat on the chair and the matrons combed my hair for me into the matron's knot at the nape of my neck. They dressed me in my red embroidered bridal robes and the red embroidered bridal shoes and put the ornaments in my hair. An old man whose parents and wife were still alive carried me out and put me in the wedding chair that was to carry me to my new home. I knew only that I must not touch the sides of the chair as he put me in, and that I was dressed in beautiful clothes. I was a child, only fifteen by our count, and my birthday was small—just before the New Year. We count ourselves a year old when we are born and we all add a year at the New Year. I was counted two years old when I was a month old, for I was born near the end of the old year. I was a child. I had not yet passed my thirteenth birthday. [She continues, but in the third person.]

· · ·

The musicians in their green uniforms and red tasseled hats sat by the table in the court. There were those who played on bamboo reed flutes and those who played on wooden horns. At times the cymbals clashed. But during the ceremony of clothing the bride and while the groom, who had come to fetch the bride, drank in another room with the men of the bride's family, it was the flute that sounded. By the different motifs played those who passed by in the street or stopped to watch knew which part of the ceremony was in progress.

. . . It was time for the groom to take the bride home. The musicians stood and played. The wooden horns joined the flutes. The cymbals clashed. The drums boomed. The groom came out of the house door. He was clothed in hired bridal robes, patterned like those of a mandarin's full dress. Once or twice at least in a lifetime every man and woman is equal to the highest in the land. When they are married and when they are buried they are clothed in the garments of nobility.

The father and the brother and the uncle of the bride escorted the groom. They bowed him to his chair. Then the red sedan chair of the bride was brought to the gate . . . All cracks between the chair and the gate were covered with pieces of red felt held by the chairmen to make sure that no evil spirit should enter. A long note of the horn sounded and the bride was carried out kneeling on the arms of an old man. He was a neighbor, a carpenter who was no longer working but was spending the last years of his life in pleasant social pursuits. He was also a doctor . . . who knew what to tell the mothers when their children's bellies ached, and how to keep their faces from scarring when the children broke out with smallpox, and how to break a fever . . . He was also a manager for weddings and funerals, and he was peacemaker for the neighborhood. . . . He was what was known as a whole man. Destiny had been kind to him. His father and mother still ate and slept in his house. . . . His wife, his old partner, was the one with whom he had started forty years ago as a boy of sixteen. He had sons and grandsons. Therefore at wedding ceremonies he was much sought after to bring good luck to the new couples. . . .

Matrons whose husbands were alive patted the bride's garments into place as she folded her arms and legs. They dropped the red curtain before her. . . .

The little procession started off. There were pairs of red lanterns on poles, red banners, and red wooden boards on which were great gold ideographs. The band followed and then came the green chair of the groom. This was followed closely by the red chair of the bride. Her brother walked beside it. He carried a piece of red felt in his hands. It was his duty to hold this between her chair and all the wells and dark corners and temples they passed. He must protect her from the hungry ghosts, the souls of those who have drowned themselves in these wells and are doomed to stay there until they can persuade others to drown themselves and release them. He must protect her from the elementals that lurk in dark corners, the weasel spirits and the fox fairies, and from the little demons in the temples who might follow her home and possess her and make her leave the path of reason and do those things which people do not do. . . . Behind came the cart carrying the perfect couple, the whole couple, a middle-aged man and his wife whose parents and children lived, who were to act for the family in giving her over to her new home.

· · ·

Outside of the city the procession veered to the east . . . and went toward the sea and a village lying low and gray on the rocks of a small promontory.

It was a village of fishermen and the groom owned one of the fishing boats. He was also a farmer. . . . It was the family village of the Ning clan. All in the village were of this one clan. . . .

When I got to my new home and the wedding guests had left I found that there was a woman living in the house, a cousin's wife. She had

A Chinese fishing village on the Yangtze River. *Leblang/Monkmeyer*

lived there for many years and had borne a son to my husband. We all slept on one k'ang, the four of us. I was such a child that I told her I was glad she was there for I was frightened. Her husband had been gone many years and none knew whether he was alive or dead. . . . She lived with us for more than two years.

My husband's father was also with us. He tilled the family land and in the winter made baskets. . . .

I was but a child. We played games, the village children . . . and I. . . .

. . .

As was the custom, I went home every month to see my mother. But because my husband smoked opium and did not bring home food, I stayed longer with my mother than was the custom. Half of every month I stayed with my husband and half of every month I went home to my mother. . . .

When I left home to go back to my husband's village I would not let my mother see me cry. . . . That was because of my older sister always cried and screamed when she had to go back to her mother-in-law. And so my father would scold her.

"What can we do?" he would say. "What is done is done. What good to make such an ado?" So I was always careful not to let them see me weep. My sister's husband was good and brought them money, but her mother-in-law was cruel. I had no mother-in-law but my husband did not bring in money.

. . .

I know now that there is no need to be angry with my parents for my marriage. They did the best they could for me. They thought they were getting a good home for me. Now I know that one's destiny is one's destiny. It was so decided for me.

We slept on the same k'ang, the four of us, until just before Mantze [her first child, a girl] was born. Then the neighbors got rid of the woman for me. They were all our relatives. They said to her, "Who are you that you should live with them?"

And so she went away. . . .

. . .

Across the west wall from us lived an old uncle and aunt. He was a cousin to my husband's father. They were an old couple with no children and they were very fond of me. . . .

This old uncle was over seventy, a strong old man who loved his wine. He was good to me and hated my husband. The old aunt was a little old woman, over fifty.

I often went to their house and they fed me many meals when my husband brought home nothing for me to eat.

. . .

My husband was twenty-nine when I married him, and he had been an opium eater since he was nineteen. He took everything and sold it for opium. He could not help it. He took everything. I dared not wash a garment and put it out to dry without staying by to watch it. . . . The land had gradually gone. He had sold it.

. . .

He was a fisherman. Our village was on the seashore. There are two lives that a man with a family must not lead. One is to be a soldier and the other to be a fisherman. Fishermen go out with the tide. They may sleep all day and go out in the night watches. They learn to be idle and irregular. In the early morning, if the fishing has been successful, they take their catch, great or small, to the city . . . They sell their fish at the market and go to the counting house for their cash. The counting house is in the court of an inn. There they smoke and drink all day. What is there left to bring home? How could they escape the opium habit? And my husband was good natured and friendly. My sister's husband beat her. Mine never lifted his hand to me, but he brought me no food. Half of each month I lived at home with my mother and ate. My brother brought me grain and flour when I lived in the other half in the house of my husband.

When Mantze was born my mother came to my husband's house and took care of me. . . .

When Mantze was two and I was big with another child I left my husband and the village. This was the first time I left him and I went on foot. . . . Respectable women did not walk in the streets of P'englai. We rode on horses and squares of black cloth covered our faces. But I was angry. For three days had we quarreled. He had sold everything I possessed. I had left, of the things my mother had given me at my marriage, only a pair of silver hairpins. I liked those hairpins. He wanted to sell them. I would not let him have them. . . . These three days the four people in our house had only seven small bowls of millet gruel to eat. Then he took the hairpins and sold them for a hundred coppers and smoked his opium. We had nothing to eat. Leading my child, and heavy with the other in me, I started out. I said that we would beg.

. . . I went to my mother's house and they took me in. It was in my anger that I said I would beg, but I knew not how. I went back to my husband and when my child was born it was another girl.

. . .

Our land was gone. The old man, my husband's father, . . . could braid his baskets in town as well as in the country. What he made was barely enough to keep him alone. In town I was near my own people. We sold the house . . . We leased a room in town . . . We had a four-year lease on it. Houses were cheap in those days and easy to get.

I was twenty-one when my mother died and she was only fifty-three.

An opium house in Peking. *Brown Brothers*

Day after day I sat at home. Hunger gnawed. What could I do? My mother was dead. My brother had gone away. When my husband brought home food I ate it and my children ate with me. A woman could not go out of the court. . . . I did not know enough even to beg. So I sat at home and starved. I was so hungry one day that I took a brick, pounded it to bits, and ate it. It made me feel better.

How could I know what to do? We women knew nothing but to comb our hair and bind our feet and wait at home for our men. When my mother had been hungry she had sat at home and waited for my father to bring her food, so when I was hungry I waited at home for my husband to bring me food.

My husband sold everything we had.

. . .

[They began going to a public food kitchen which served gruel.]

One day when my husband handed the baby over to me as usual, saying, "Nurse her," one of the men in charge of the gruel station saw him do it.

"Is that your man?" said the man from the gruel station. I answered that he was.

"He is trying to sell the child. He tells people that her mother died . . ." [The husband did sell the child, but she managed to get it back.]

• • •

The old people tell us that her husband is more important to a woman than her parents. A woman is with her parents only part of her life, they say, but she is with her husband forever. He also feels that he is the most important. If a wife is not good to her husband, there is retribution in heaven.

• • •

. . . People urged me to leave him and follow another man, to become a thief or a prostitute. But my parents had left me a good name, though they left me nothing else. I could not spoil that for them.

In those years it was not as it is now. There was no freedom then for women. I stayed with him.

For another year we lived, begging and eating gruel from the public kitchen.

The father of my children was good for a while, and I thought he had learned his lesson. He promised never to sell the child again and I believed him. Then one day he sold her again and I could not get her back that time.

• • •

. . . because he sold her, I left my husband. I took Mantze and went away. I told him that he could live his life and that I would live mine. He lived in the house I had leased but I did not go home. When the lease was up I let it go. I let him live where he would. He lived from one opium den to another. I taught my daughter Mantze to run at the sight of him and to hide. What if he sold her also? I would not live with him.

⧉

The story almost has a traditionally happy ending, after some more difficulty. When Mantze was fifteen, her mother arranged her marriage (which also turned out badly). Once Mantze was married, Ning Lao began to live with her husband again. They had another child—a boy—who was his mother's great delight. Ning Lao's husband cut down on his use of opium (although he never gave it up entirely), and their life together was relatively tranquil until he died. Then she had her son to console her and to look out for her in her old age.

Most Americans would find it difficult to understand why Ning Lao remained married under the circumstances. A woman who would accept that kind of treatment today would probably be regarded as emotionally disturbed. Yet Ning Lao obviously felt she was doing the right thing and did not seriously consider any other course of action (or at least she did not mention any). Why?

WAYS OF ORGANIZING FAMILY LIFE

Family structure and the roles of immediate family members are almost always part of covert culture. Any changes in behavior or values in these areas are upsetting. People have trouble talking about the subject objectively because their emotions are too closely involved. Challenges to established patterns and beliefs are interpreted as threats to emotionally defended concepts and are therefore strongly resisted and resented. Yet there is good evidence that, like most other human behavior, family behavior and values are learned; they are not instinctive. One of the best ways to begin to appreciate this is to compare the ways other societies organize family life. Examination of the traditional Chinese family described in the preceding excerpt and the American Indian family in the excerpt that follows reveals some similarities with general American patterns and many differences.

One of the similarities is that marriage is begun with a ceremony. The details vary, but in general, friends and relatives are present, and the bride's family is involved in a great deal of expense in American and Chinese societies. The ceremony constitutes a public announcement of the marriage. This public announcement is one of the aspects that distinguishes a marriage from other types of sexual unions (Stephens 1964:5–6). Since marriage is an approved sexual union in all societies (another characteristic mentioned in the definition), there is no reason to hide it, and there may be several reasons for announcing it. In many societies, for example, an individual is not an adult until he or she assumes the responsibilities of marriage. Adult status is particularly important for men, since they are most often involved in public decision making. So long as a male is classified with the children (who are usually excluded, along with women, from public power), he is ignored, no matter what his chronological age. If he wants to have any influence, gain esteem, win prestige, be a man, he must marry. A woman also gains status by marriage, although the symbols may be less obvious in her case. In the Chinese society described in the excerpt, a woman had no chance at power (public or private) unless she had a married son who thereby gave her control over a daughter-in-law. A woman with many married sons was in an enviable position in the household, whereas an unmarried woman (or one without sons) was lowest in order of priority. Improving one's status therefore may be a powerful motivation for marriage.

The marriage ceremony is a *rite de passage* that may serve a double function. It both marks the change of status and publicly announces the marriage. In small societies, it takes very little to make a new relationship known; the "ceremony" may therefore consist of nothing more than the young couple setting up a house of their own or having a meal together (Powdermaker 1933:151–152). As societies become larger, as the change in status becomes more significant, or as the number of people immediately concerned in the marriage increases, the elaborateness of the public announcement tends to increase too. The ceremony described in the excerpt is fairly elaborate, as befits a complex culture.

Another similarity between Americans and the Chinese in the excerpt is that—ideally at least—the man provides for the family and his wife runs the home. In the American system, however, the woman was never so closely confined to her home—not even during the most restrictive period. Such limitation does occur in some other parts of the world, but it is by no means universal. American society is not unique in allowing women to play important roles outside the home. The Pygmy excerpt (Chapter 4) mentioned the active participation of women in the hunt, for example. In societies dependent on horticulture, women do much of the work in the fields (Netting 1968:125). Even societies with plow agriculture sometimes expect women to help in the fields, but such societies are generally more restrictive than those based on other methods of subsistence (Pierce 1964:27–28). Even if she contributes economically, the woman is almost never expected to be the sole provider for the home in any society, whereas in several societies the man is.

Respective obligations of spouses vary from one culture to another. It sometimes seems that the male has all the prerogatives and the female all the obligations—as in the excerpt, for example. In most cultures, privileges and obligations are more evenly divided —as in the Hopi Indian excerpt. There are almost no societies, however, that reverse the first example and give men most of the obligations and women most of the privileges. American society is perhaps one of the more extreme in this regard in some areas of family life. In attempts to allow more freedom and independence for women, legislation has sometimes given women special advantages or the court has consistently interpreted the law to the disadvantage of men in family matters. For example, from a position of virtually no control over her own children in the 1800s, the American woman has moved to an almost impregnable legal position in which the rights of the natural mother are usually held superior to those of any other individual, including the natural father. In cases of divorce or separation, women almost always receive custody of children (especially if the children are young) unless they voluntarily give up their claim.

One of the basic postulates (Hoebel 1966:23)—assumptions about the nature of things—in middle-class white American society seems to be that the male parent is relatively unimportant to the emotional well-being of the child, whereas the female is essential. Many articles in the popular press paint a gloomy picture of what happens to the home when the wife works. It is assumed that she cannot be a good mother and a working woman at the same time. With the exception of a few novelists and some psychologists, no one mentions the effect of a man's job on his family or suggests that *he* cannot be both a good father and a working man. Why not? Ignoring his family role implies that a man is not important to it except as a source of economic support and as a stud to sire children. His career is expected to come first, and if it does, no one seems to think that might be detrimental to the family. This assumption downgrades the importance of the male partner in the family and is subtly contemptuous of men as fathers.

Regardless of the arrangement, the division of labor in the family serves several functions, some of these were discussed in earlier chapters. One that is significant here is that the division forces members of opposite sexes to depend on each other. If men and women have quite different roles, both of which are important to survival, they cannot exist without each other. This can provide a powerful motivation for marriage in a system that might otherwise lack one (for example, a society such as the Trobriands in the South Pacific where premarital sex is encouraged) (Lévi-Strauss 1960:274–276).

RESIDENCE PATTERNS

Another similarity between marriage as described in the Chinese excerpt and marriage in the United States is that when Ning Lao married, she left home to live with her husband. That is the ideal in American society, although it is not always followed in practice. Ning Lao's marriage is closer to the American ideal than it should be because it does *not* correspond to the Chinese ideal. In the traditional Chinese ideal, the young couple should live with the groom's parents after marriage, as Ning Lao's sister did. This pattern is called patrilocal ° or virilocal.° The two terms are sometimes used synonymously, although there is a small distinction. Virilocal is a more precise term to use for Ning Lao's marriage, since she moved in with her husband who headed his own establishment in his family's village. His father lived with him, but it is clear that the old man was not regarded as the head of the house. If Ning Lao had followed her sister's example and moved into a household dominated by her husband's parents, patrilocal would have been the more accurate term to use.

Residence rules are useful in pointing up probable stress areas in a marriage. Who has to leave home? Who has helpful relatives nearby? (Fischer, J. 1958:508–517). Other things being equal, the individual who has to leave home and who is far from helpful relatives will be subjected to more stress in the marriage. Ning Lao's position was considerably eased by the fact that she was not far from her parents, and they were able to help for a while. If she had gone farther away, she would have been even more at the mercy of her husband and his family, as was her sister.

That the Chinese were aware of the stress on a new bride is indicated in the excerpt by the statement that the bride is supposed to visit her family frequently during the first year of marriage. If the new couple lives too far from the girl's home, however, or if her husband's family is poor, they may be unwilling or unable to afford to send her back on frequent visits. In theory, of course, the husband's relatives are supposed to look after the new bride, make her feel at home, and treat her well, so long as she behaves properly. Ning Lao was rather fortunate. Her husband's people did treat her well and looked out for her as long as they could. Her husband was amiable and did not beat her, even though he was not a good provider. The theory does not always work out that well in practice, however, as the experience of Ning Lao's sister indicates. In almost any society with patrilocal residence, there are anecdotes about treatment of new brides that was so harsh it drove them to run away or commit suicide (Pierce 1964:83; Fallers and Fallers 1960: 81). Of course, it is to the benefit of the groom's family to treat the new bride well. She is, after all, the potential mother of new heirs, essential to the continuity of the line, so it behooves any family to make her a contented wife. There are anecdotes about happy wives, too, but since happiness is rarely as dramatic or exciting as misery, these cases are apt to be overlooked by publishers and authors in favor of more sensational ones (Fernea 1969:39).

What happens in societies where the women do not leave home to live with their husband's people? What if it is the man who has to move away? Is the man subject to as much stress in a matrilocal system (the reverse of patrilocal and virilocal) as the woman is in a patrilocal one? The following excerpt describes a matrilocal system different from both the Chinese and the general American patterns.

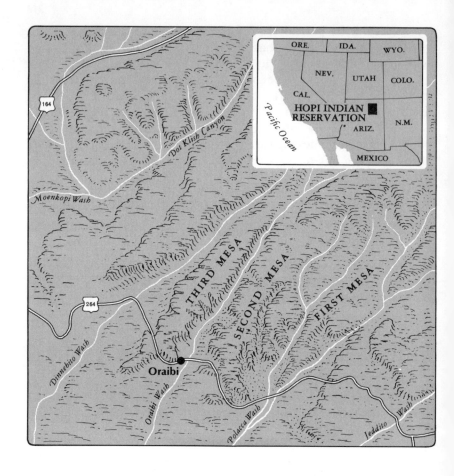

Hopi Indian Life: Courtship and Marriage

In September we returned to the Agency school.* . . .

One Friday night at a social with games I was talking to Louise of the Tobacco and Rabbit Clan. She said she was leading a hard life, that neither her father nor her stepfather seemed to care for her. . . . I told her softly that if she could like me I would help her. I said, "I love you and I will get food from the kitchen. . . ." From then on I began to look after her. . . .

* Abridged from *Sun Chief: The Autobiography of a Hopi Indian*, edited by Leo W. Simmons, pp. 111–114, 116, 131–133, 145, 155, 198, 202–203, 212–223. Copyright, 1942 by Yale University Press. Reprinted by permission of Yale University Press. Talayesva, the Sun Chief, was about sixteen at the time the excerpt starts.

214

. . .

One day Louise told me, to my surprise, that she was the daughter of my clan brother, and therefore my clan daughter. . . . This was bad news for me. . . . I had not known that Louise was the daughter of my linked-clan brother and therefore my daughter. I knew that our relatives would not like for us to be in love, and wondered what we could do. . . . we were both worried about it all.

. . .

In November, before Thanksgiving, our superior officer told forty or fifty of us that we were to go to school at Sherman, the nonreservation school in Riverside, California. . . . Louise and I planned to go together.

Before we departed I had another talk with the superintendent. I told him that Louise and I had an agreement to marry, that I was helping to support her, and that it was my right to have intercourse with her. I was not afraid to say this because I knew that for Hopi lovers who are engaged this is the proper thing. . . .

. . .

Louise and I were together on the train part of the time until we reached Riverside . . . When we had placed our baggage in the Sherman School for Indians, . . . the assistant disciplinarian told us that there would be a football game in the park at three o'clock. . . . We decided to go.

Now Susie, . . . the younger sister of Louise's mother, had gone to Sherman . . . a few weeks before. She came over with a sharp look on her face and took Louise away. I felt uneasy and feared that she might learn about our courtship and complain to our relatives that I was making love to my clan daughter.

. . .

. . . This made me think I had better drop Louise, because her mother's sister might get me into trouble. These thoughts began drawing me away from my first love. . . .

. . .

. . . At the socials I began going with a girl named Mettie from Moenkopi, which caused everybody to call her my girl.

In May, 1909, . . . we . . . packed our things to start for Oraibi.

. . .

. . . As we got off the train in Winslow we found our relatives with their wagons to meet us. . . .

I walked over to the campfire where Mettie was eating with her uncle and some other people. . . . I told her I was going out toward the railroad roundhouse to hunt for game. She whispered back that she would follow. Pretty soon I left with my rifle and hunted around until I saw her coming. We walked together toward the railroad and sat down among some bushes, where we stayed most of the afternoon. It was here that I had Mettie for the first time. I was not afraid to do it, because we were back among our own people. . . .

. . .

. . . When it was time for bed I took my blanket and lay down beside Mettie. Her uncle saw me but said nothing. I had Mettie twice more during the night. We could hear others doing the same thing, for we were sleeping close together. All the fellows were with their girls, for we were now free from the school officials and back with our uncles and fathers.

. . .

. . . I began picking fruit at the Agency in the middle of August and continued until the third week in October, living with my aunt [in Moenkopi] . . . It became public knowledge that Mettie and I were lovers. This pleased her uncles but worried her mother. At first I tried to be careful and safeguard Mettie from pregnancy because she wanted to return to school . . . Later when I found that her mother was so opposed to her marriage, I hoped that Mettie would become pregnant, because that gives a man some advantage over his sweetheart's mother. For when a girl has a baby, the mother usually wants the daughter to marry the child's father.

Other girls came into my life even while I was planning to marry Mettie. . . .

. . .

. . . Euella came over . . . to get our young clan sister, Meggie, to help her grind corn. . . . I soon went over where the girls were grinding and stood around chatting until I got a chance to ask Euella to slip out to a secret place with me. . . . After a little petting we hurried our pleasures in order to return before her family missed her. This was love-making with my little "aunt" and was the safest kind of all because I could not be expected to marry her, of course. . . .

. . .

[Mettie went back to school. Don was initiated in Oraibi and received his adult name of Talayesva. He returned to Moenkopi and continued his "safe" affair with Euella.]

On Saturday Secaletscheoma put on a dance hoping to please the gods and get help for his sore eyes. I watched the Katcinas all day and slept with Euella that night. The next morning Secaletscheoma asked me to do clown work; but I told him frankly that I was unfit for it. I did not wish to spoil the ceremony by bringing a bad wind, or to have it said that his eyes were no better on my account. My aunt was surprised until I told her the reason. Then she said, "I'm going to beat Euella for cutting me out. . . ." We often joked about love-making, but I never tried it with her. She was much older than I, the niece of my father, and the wife of my ceremonial father's brother . . . Even if she had been younger and unmarried, I would not have touched her because she was of the Sand Clan, like my father. It was all right to make love with a niece of either of my grandfathers—like Euella of the Lizard Clan, for example—but not with my father's close relatives. These aunts had teased me about love-making a great deal; but I had never tried to make a Sand Clan woman, and knew that I never would for that would not be right.

. . .

. . . I was still thinking of Mettie and received a letter from her every week; but some of the girls had written me that she had a Navaho lover, besides two Hopi boys. Mettie's mother had heard of the Navaho and told my relatives that if I waited until Mettie returned, we could marry. She did not want to lose her daughter to a Navaho. I did not want to wait.

. . .

. . . Mark, an uncle of Mettie, . . . also suggested that if I waited until Mettie returned from school I might marry her. "I hear Mettie has a Navaho friend," I replied, "and it is hard to wait. If I can find another lover, I may have to marry her."

. . .

One evening . . . my old pal Louis came from Moenkopi. [Don had gone back to Oraibi.] . . . he was as eager to go out among the girls as ever and . . . said, "I have made love with Iola of the Fire Clan before, but now she does not like me very well." I knew she was staying with her clan sister, Irene, whose parents had gone to the field house at Loloma Spring. Since we could think of no other available lovers, Louis said, "Let's take these girls by force." . . . I knew that Irene was marriageable for me but I did not know whether she wanted me or not. I argued that since Louis had had Iola before, he could get away with it, but it was too risky for me to try forcing Irene. But Louis urged until I finally agreed.

We found the girls grinding corn and decided to sneak into Irene's house and wait in the dark. Finally, as the two entered, Louis grabbed Iola and blew out the light. I caught hold of Irene and quickly assured her that she had nothing to fear. . . . We talked softly for a while and when we heard Louis and Iola at love-making, I begged Irene urgently with words of love and promises of marriage. Finally she said, "It is up to you." Then I led her, with a sheepskin, to another corner of the room where she remained passive but very sweet. After some time, she said, "Now you must ask your parents about our marrying. Let's go and leave this terrible man, Louis." I told her to be a good girl, gave her a nice bracelet, slipped out, went to the roof of my mother's house, and lay down to sleep out under the stars.

. . . When I returned from the surveyors' camp Monday evening, Irene's parents were home. After supper I went to their house. They offered me food, and the father later asked if there was anything he could do for me. Then I asked for the hand of Irene. He replied: "My daughter is not a good-looking girl. If your relatives are willing you may have her." I told him that I had my parents' consent and that they were well pleased. This was a lie, but a necessary one in order to spend the night with Irene. They agreed and arranged for us to have the next room. We had a very good time. . . . All our talk was sweet and I thought there would never be an argument between us. At cockcrow I went home for a nap on the old roof.

At breakfast I raised the subject of marriage. "I spent the night at Huminquima's," I said, "and now I want to marry his daughter, Irene." "What did they say?" asked my mother. I assured her that Irene's parents had already agreed. . . . My father spoke: "Well, I won't object, for then you would think I am against you. You are not a good-looking man, and she is not a beautiful woman, so I think you will stay together and treat each other fairly. A good-looking woman neglects her husband, because it is so easy to get another." My spirit was high when I left for work. Riding down the mesa, I waved to Irene, let out a war whoop, beat my horse into a gallop, and thought that I would always be happy.

. . .

One day the news circulated that Ira was getting married in November, and that my turn would follow four days later, making a double wedding. Both our girls belonged to the . . . Fire Clan, and their people made this plan. My brother was worried and complained, "Our father is poor and cannot afford a double wedding. What shall we do?" Then he remembered that our great-uncle . . . had approved of our marriages and said, "Perhaps he will buy a buckskin for one of us or give us some sheep for the wedding feast." I replied, "If he doesn't, we will refuse to herd for him." My father took $30 or $40 of my money to help buy the buckskins.

One evening after the crops were harvested, Ira's girl, Blanche, was brought to our house by her mother. She ground corn meal on her knees for three days, remaining in the house most of the time, but Ira was not permitted to sleep with her. I herded, and was told to keep away from Irene because she was grinding white corn meal at her house for our family.

. . .

[One morning, four days later] Iola . . . called to me, "Get up and go see what is in your house. I hear you have a pet eagle." I found Irene grinding corn with all her might. She had been brought there by her mother the night before. As I stood in the door and watched her, I

A Hopi girl, ca. 1892, wearing the coiffure that signifies her unmarried status. *The Bettmann Archive*

felt as though I were dreaming and scratched my head, seeking for words. My mother smiled and said, "Talayesva, don't be foolish." I went out sheepishly, returned to my sleeping place, yanked the cover from Dennis, who was still asleep, and said, "Get up, lazybones, it is your turn next. I am now a man with a wife. . . ."

The aunts of my father's clan, and of my ceremonial and doctor fathers' clans, ganged up and staged a big mud fight with the men of my family. They caught my grandfather, Homikniwa, and plastered him with mud from head to foot. They also poured mud and water all over my father and tried to cut his hair for letting me marry into the Fire

Clan. They made all manner of fun of Irene, calling her cross-eyed, lazy, dirty, and a poor cook, and praised me highly, asserting that they would like to have me for a husband. Dear old Masenimka, my godmother, threw mud on my father and uncles and said that she wanted me for her lover. This mud fight was to show that they were very fond of me, and that they thought Irene was making a good choice.

On the third day I began worrying about my coming bath, for I was very ticklish and did not know whether I could stand still under the hands of so many women. A little after sundown my mother told Irene to stop grinding the blue corn and sit by the fire on a soft seat. I had not seen much of her since she came to our house, and when we had spoken it was usually in a whisper. Soon her relatives came to spend the night—the same women who had stripped and bathed Ira. I thought I had never seen so many women, and even those whom I had known all my life seemed a little strange to me. I had little to say all evening, and at bedtime I took my blanket and started out. My father said, "Wait a minute, Talayesva. Where are you sleeping? I want to be able to find you in the morning." When I told him that I was sleeping with Dennis, he replied, "Be sure to leave the door unlocked so that I can wake you early. . . ."

[In the morning] My father struck a match and said, "Get up, son, and come quickly. They are preparing the yucca suds." Then he woke Dennis and asked him to see that I started. . . . When I entered the house, I saw many eyes staring at me. There were Irene's mother and her sisters, Blanche's mother and her relatives, in fact all the women of the Fire Clan, also the women of the Coyote and Water-Coyote clans, and most of my real and ceremonial aunts. They had assembled to give me a bath. My mother was assisting Irene's mother with the yucca suds. I was so timid that I took steps not more than an inch long. My mother said, "Hurry up." I laid back my shirt collar and knelt with Irene before a bowl of yucca suds. My relatives washed Irene's head and her relatives washed mine. Then they poured all the suds into one bowl, put our heads together, mixed our hair and twisted it into one strand to unite us for life. Many women rinsed our hair by pouring cold water over it. When that was completed, Irene's mother told me to take off my clothes. I felt so uncertain about my loincloth that I made an excuse to go out, ran behind the house, and checked it carefully. When I had returned and undressed, Irene's mother led me outside. My real aunts tried to bathe me first in fun, and scuffled with Irene's relatives. Then Irene's mother bathed me from tip to toe. All the women took their turn bathing me, while I stood shivering in the cold. I had to appear gentle and kind-hearted and say to each of them, "I thank you very much." They assured me that they had washed away all remaining traces of youth and had prepared my flesh for married manhood.

I hurried into the house, wrapped myself in a blanket, and stood until Irene's relatives told me to sit down near the fire. Irene's hair was arranged in the married women's style, and her mother advised her to be a good housewife. Irene and I took a pinch of sacred corn meal, went to the east edge of the mesa, held the meal to our lips, prayed silently, and sprinkled it toward the rising sun. We returned to the house in silence and my mother and sister prepared our breakfast. Before Irene's mother left, she built a fire under the piki stone. After breakfast Irene made batter and began baking piki ° [paper-thin corn bread].

. . .

My father distributed staple cotton among all our relatives and friends, asking them to pick out the seeds and return it. In a few days we butchered a couple of sheep, and it was announced from the housetop that there would be carding of cotton and spinning in the kiva for my father's new daughters-in-law. . . .

I herded sheep for my uncle . . . so that he could supervise the spinning for Irene in the Mongwi kiva, while my father had charge of the spinning for Blanche in the Howeove kiva. I returned from the sheep camp in the evening, ate supper with Irene and my family, and went to the kiva to card cotton. I had never learned to spin very well, or to weave at all. Many men were helping us. . . . Finally I was teased and reminded that it was bedtime and that I had better go. We slept together in a separate room in my mother's house. I thought I would never tire of sleeping with Irene, and she agreed that it was a good life.

The brides remained in our house for the rest of November and all the next month, for it was considered bad luck for them to go home in December. . . . The women fetched water and we hauled several wagonloads of wood in preparation for the wedding feast. . . .

In the morning, long before daylight, we arose, built fires under the pots outside, and cooked the mutton stew. Pots were boiling all around our place, and almost all the people in Oraibi were present at the breakfast feast. Then the men assembled in the different kivas to weave. Two of our uncles from Shipaulovi took back cotton string with them to weave the belts. There was work under way in all five kivas in Oraibi. . . .

One day I went to the post office . . . and received five letters . . . The fifth . . . was from my old girl Mettie . . . When I read that, I raised my head for a long breath. The Chief asked, "What is the matter, Don?" "In this letter," I replied, "Mettie says that I will always be hers." I read it to him. He smiled and said, "I think she means just that. When she comes home, I would go to see her and cheer her up." I think I would have been more excited over my wedding if she had been the the bride.

. . .

The wedding costumes were completed in January. For each bride there were two blankets whitened with kaolin, a finely woven belt, and an expensive pair of white buckskin moccasins. Soft prayer feathers were attached to the corners of the blankets. Each bride was to wear the large blanket and carry the small one rolled in a reed case when she returned to her house. The small blanket was to be carefully preserved and draped about her at death—as wings to speed her to dear ones in the House of the Dead. The beautiful belt was to serve as tail to a bird, guiding the bride in her spiritual flight.

There was a feast for our close relatives on the day that the men completed the wedding outfits. The brides made puddings, and we butchered and cooked the two sheep that Kalnimptewa had given to us. We gathered at sunset, and the brides took special pains to be good hostesses and to see that everyone was happy and well fed. After the meal they cleared the food away, and our great-uncles . . . made speeches to them: "We Sun Clan people are very thankful that you brides have come to our household and have taken such good care of us. You have proven yourselves to be good housewives by feeding us well. The wedding outfits are completed, and tomorrow you will return to your homes. We are now the same people, sisters, brothers, uncles, and aunts to each other. Look on the bright side of each day, treat your husbands right, and enjoy your lives. Visit us often so that we will be happy." The brides were expected to say: "Thanks very much for your work on the wedding outfits." . . .

Early in the morning our mother, assisted by her sister, . . . awoke the brides before daylight, washed their heads, and dressed them in the wedding outfits. They led them to the door, sprinkled a corn-meal path toward the rising sun, and placed a prayer feather upon it. The brides stepped out upon this path, followed it to the end, turned and went to their homes, carrying before them the small blanket rolled in a reed mat. There they were received by their mothers and other female relatives, who removed the wedding garments and tried them on themselves. I remained in bed for another nap and did not see my bride depart.

The brides and their relatives prepared food to bring to our house in the evening. About sunset they came with their mothers, bringing a large tub filled with food. When they returned to their houses, our own relatives were invited to come and eat. That was the occasion for giving us advice. Our great-uncle . . . spoke first: "Thank you, my nephews. You are not very good-looking, and I thought you were never going to marry. I am glad that you have chosen such fine wives. You know every woman hates a lazy man, so you must work hard and assist your new fathers in the field and with the herding. When they find that you are good helpers, they will be pleased and treat you like real sons. When

The grinding of grain in Kordofan by means of a stone slab. Similar methods are used by Indians in the American Southwest. *George Rodger/Magnum*

you kill game, or find spinach or other food plants in the fields, bring them to your wives. They will receive them gladly. Make believe that your wife is your real mother. Take good care of her, treat her fairly, and never scold her. If you love your wife, she will love you, and give you joy, and feed you well. Even when you are worried and unhappy, it will pay you to show a shining face to her. If your married life is a failure, it will be your own fault. Please prove yourselves to be men worthy of your clan."

The next day my parents killed two more sheep, made a stew, and took a large tub of food to our wives' homes. Irene and Blanche invited all their relatives to come and eat, and it was then that their uncles advised them on their family duties.

After the feast in the brides' houses, it was time for them and their relatives to prepare corn-meal gifts in exchange for the wedding costumes. The brides and their relatives ground corn for many days. . . . Many heaping plaques of fine corn meal were taken to our house—perhaps twenty bushels—to be distributed among the relatives who had assisted us. This completed the wedding obligations.

It is customary for the groom to decide when he will move into his wife's house. I remained at my house for about two weeks, visiting Irene every night. Ira stayed three weeks longer. It was necessary for me to go live with Irene early, because her father, Huminquima, was not a very good worker. Before I went, I hauled wood for them like a dutiful son-in-law. I also took part in the Soyal ceremony [one of the major Hopi religious ceremonies], observing the rules of continence. After the Soyal I borrowed Frank's team and wagon and went for an extra large load of wood without telling Irene. I returned late in the afternoon, stopped the wagon at my wife's door, and unhitched. Irene's mother shelled corn for my horses while I unloaded the wood. Irene came to the door and asked me how I liked my eggs. I thought of sneaking home, but, knowing that would never do, I timidly entered the house and ate a little of the scrambled eggs. I soon remarked that I was not very hungry, and hurried out with the shelled corn, feeling that the Fire Clan were very high-tone people. Taking the wagon to my home, I asked my mother for a square meal, which caused her to laugh. About sunset, as I returned from hobbling the horses, Irene came to our house calling, "Come and eat." She invited all my family—according to custom—but they properly declined. I meekly followed my wife to her home and sat down with the family to a dish of hot tamales wrapped in cornhusks and tied with yucca stems. But I ate so slowly that Irene's mother unwrapped tamales and placed them in a row before me. I thought, "This old lady is very kindhearted, perhaps she will do this for me always." But I was mistaken; at breakfast I had to unwrap my own tamales, and was put to work for my wife's people.

Don had some adjustments to make. He was nervous and uncomfortable with his new family. But he could always go home, as he did after his first meal with his in-laws, when he was still so timid he could not eat properly. Notice that the pattern of going back home to ease the transition occurs in the Hopi marriage as well as in the Chinese. These visits do not carry the connotation that "going home to mother" carries in the American system. That is, Don's return (and Ning Lao's) was not the result of a quarrel; it was a normal part of expected behavior. The pattern was built into the system, rather than discouraged by it.

Don's situation differed from Ning Lao's in several ways. He married within his own village and therefore was close to his relatives. Ning Lao moved into another community, one that was occupied entirely by relatives of her husband. Don's marriage was matrilocal, but he lived close by his own relatives. Uxorilocal,° which is the reverse of virilocal, is rarely used, partly because females are seldom heads of their own households before they marry. Regardless of the technical label for the residence pattern, it makes a difference when the newly married individual is separated from his family of orientation by yards instead of miles. Ning Lao and her sister would have had an easier time if they had lived next door to their parents.

Another factor that made Don's marital adjustment easier was that he was free to move about; he was not confined to the house and courtyard of his in-laws. He could get off by himself, could get his own food if necessary, and could easily leave for good, if he cared to. Ning Lao had fewer options. In her culture it was not proper for women to be seen on the street alone. She was not free to go out to work, was not trained to do anything outside the home (she said she did not even know how to beg), and was not free to travel when and where she pleased. Don was; consequently, he was under far less pressure.

Don's residence pattern corresponded to the Hopi ideal, whereas Ning Lao's varied from the Chinese. The ideal residence pattern in American society is different from either of the ideals presented in the excerpts. Here, the young couple is supposed to set up their own home in a clearly independent household. This pattern is called neolocal ° residence, and is actually not very common. Although a young couple may have a separate household in many societies, the new household is often dominated by one set of parents or the other, and this is contrary to the American ideal (Richards, A. J. 1964:210; Richards, C. 1963:25–33). In the United States, young people want to be "on their own," although in practice, during the first few years of marriage they may not be able to do so for economic or other reasons. There are an amazing number of residence patterns, and the variety of terms for them would easily fill half a page. Almost every possible combination has been tried somewhere. We have attempted here to discuss only the commoner types, not to give an exhaustive list.

Sometimes there are a series of stages in a marriage, each one correlated ° (varying or associated) with a different residence pattern. For example, Navajos during the first years of marriage tend to live several months first with one set of parents (often the wife's) and then with the other. After several years, they usually settle down on a homestead of their own (Richards, C. 1963:27; Rapoport 1954:57; Kluckhohn and Leighton 1946:57).

INHERITANCE PATTERNS

In most societies, residence rules are correlated with the inheritance pattern; they support it, or else they help solve problems posed by conflicts between the inheritance of family affiliation and inheritance of land or power. Patrilineal inheritance,° tracing descent through the male line, is usually associated with patrilocal or virilocal residence, as in the excerpt on China. The two patterns reinforce each other. Matrilineal inheritance,° tracing the line through the mother, often occurs with matrilocal residence, as illustrated by the Hopi excerpt. Again, the two patterns reinforce each other.

Societies have a variety of ways in which they classify people into groups, and birth or kinship affiliation is only one. (Other bases—sex and age—were mentioned in Chapter 4.) If a child's affiliation is determined by his mother's group, it is matrilineal; if it is determined by his father's group, the affiliation is patrilineal. Since the child is biologically the result of a combination of an equal number of genes from both parents, American society (which is aware of and concerned about this) leans heavily to bilateral inheritance,° inheritance from both sides, except in the matter of family name, which is inherited patrilineally.

Group affiliation is not the only thing that can be inherited, of course. Wealth, personal belongings, power, and a variety of intangible things also pass from one generation to the next. These may not move in the same manner as group affiliation. When a child inherits one type of thing from one parent and a different sort of thing from the other parent, the pattern is called double descent.° The Huron (Chapter 3) may have had this system, since Lahontan said they inherited their body from their mother but their soul from their father (Lahontan 1931:122). Inheritance from the father in the realm of the supernatural is supported by Jean de Brebeuf, who claimed the Huron received their supernatural charms from their fathers (Talbot 1956:71). Double descent also occurs in Africa (Ottenberg 1968:3-5). When girls always inherit only from their mothers and boys only from their fathers, the pattern is called parallel inheritance.° It is occasionally found in various parts of the world (Bock 1969:133). A society may have several patterns, one for group affiliation, another for certain types of things, and still another for different categories of things. Thus American society is bilateral for wealth and patrilineal for family name.

In certain circumstances, the residence pattern does not coincide with the inheritance of group affiliation. If marriage must take place with an outsider, the orderly succession of inherited power may cause complications in a matrilineal society, for example, since public power is almost always in the hands of the men. If land cannot pass out of the possession of the corporate matrilineal group and yet men inherit land, this may also create problems. As long as marriage takes place within the same village (endogamy,° marriage within the social unit), the transfer of power or land poses no real problem. In a matrilineal system, a man's heirs are his sister's children, not his own. The matrilineal line of succession runs from a man to his nephews instead of from father to son, the patrilineal pattern familiar in the Western world. When marriage is endogamous in the village, a man's heirs are available for training, supervision, and work on the land that will ultimately be theirs. They can take over a well-known system with a minimum of disruption, since they play accustomed roles with familiar people.

If village exogamy,° marriage outside the social unit, is the rule, however, a man and his sister would never be living in the same village under either matrilocal or patrilocal residence patterns. A man and his matrilineal heirs would be in different villages, which causes all kinds of problems. For example, if residence is matrilocal, as it normally would be in a matrilineal system, a man would leave his village while his sister stayed in it. If he inherited land in his home village, he would not be around to work it. If he inherited power through his mother, he would not be around to claim it. Patrilocal residence does not solve the problem either, because then the sister leaves the home village while he stays in it, so his heirs are not around to claim power or work land. Some societies have solved the problem with avunculocal residence,° residence with the groom's mother's brother. In this way, if a man has power or land to pass on to his sister's sons, they are living with him. His young nephews may move in as adolescents and bring wives back to his house or village when they marry. Residence in this case may appear virilocal or even patrilocal, since the couple appears to move into the groom's village or his family's home, but actually it is the village and home of the groom's maternal uncle, not the village in which the groom was born. When his children grow up, they will move away into the village of his wife's brother (to whom they are heirs), while he will receive his nephews (his sister's children), who are *his* heirs. It is a complex system from an American point of view, but apparently fairly simple in practice. It results in different areas of tension, of course. Under this system, the fact that the maternal uncle is far more of an authority figure than the father has various ramifications for father-son relationships. For example, Malinowski, who worked in such a society, found no trace of an ambivalent attitude toward the father. Father-son relations were relaxed and warm. Rather, the tension appeared between uncle and nephew. If Malinowski's observations were accurate, the genesis of the Oedipus complex described by Freud probably lies in rivalry over power, not sex (Malinowski 1953). (Psychologists have still not made sufficient use of the natural experimental situations that exist in different cultures, although some steps have been made in this direction, as mentioned in Chapter 5.)

MARRIAGE: FORMS AND DEFINITIONS

Residence patterns can vary almost infinitely because of the number of individual relationships that can be recognized and used.

The king of Akure, West Nigeria, and his wives. *Marc and Evelyne Bernheim/ Rapho Guillumette*

Marriage *form* is less variable because it has a more limited base. Since there are only two sexes, heterosexual marriage has only a few basic alternatives. It is possible to have one man marry one woman—monogamy,° which is statistically the most frequent form in the world, and the only one permitted in all societies. It is not the most popular, however. The favorite form in the majority of societies is polygyny,° one man married to several women. If this is the most popular, why is it not the most frequent on a world-wide basis? The answer lies in the birth ratio. Normally, slightly more male than female babies are born. The difference is not great, and because of the slightly higher mortality rate of male babies, the sex ratio in most societies is about even, unless something is done to disturb it—such as killing female babies (female infanticide °) or losing a large number of adult males in hazardous occupations such as warfare. If there are an approximately equal number of males and females in a society, obviously every male cannot have several wives. Usually, only wealthy older men can afford more than one wife. The majority of older men have only one, and young adult men often have none (Hart and Pilling 1964: 16–17). Of course, in a society where a few men corner all the wives, *women* will almost all be in polygynous marriages. Thus from a female point of view, polygyny is much more frequent than it is from a male point of view.

In a third possible marriage form, polyandry,° one woman is married to several men. Although polyandry does occur in a few parts of the world, it tends to be rare. Sexual jealousy does not fully explain the rarity, since wife lending, which should be as rare as polyandry if sexual jealousy were the cause, is fairly common. Polyandry seems to be correlated with female infanticide (and thus a shortage of women) combined with a low economic level (Linton 1936: 183; Stephens 1964: 45). Another reason for the rarity of polyandry and the frequency of polygyny may be the relation of the marriage form to population increase. Polygyny is highly productive in terms of numbers; polyandry is not. No matter how many husbands a woman has, she can bear only a limited number of children per year. And a woman who bears a child every year often ages rapidly and dies young. The population therefore cannot increase as quickly in the polyandrous pattern. In polygyny, however, the number of children one can can sire per year is limited only by the number of wives he has and his stamina. Societies that practice polygyny obviously have a survival advantage over polyandrous societies that might be sufficient to account for their greater frequency.

A final possible marriage form is one in which several women are married to several men. This has been called group marriage, communal marriage, or even tribal marriage (Downing 1970:119–135). It is the rarest form of all, and some anthropologists have suggested that it has never really been viable ° (able to survive) or the ideal pattern in any society (Linton 1936:182; Murdock 1949:24). To some extent, like so many other classifications in the behavioral sciences, frequency depends partly on definition. What is meant by marriage? Ethnographic accounts make it clear that a woman may be sexually shared by a number of men in many societies. Among the Siriono (Bolivian jungle Indians), for example, a man's brothers have unlimited sexual access to his wife, and he to theirs (Holmberg 1969:165). Eskimo men freely share their wives with others, even nonrelatives (Boas 1967:171). (The Siriono are reluctant to go *that* far.) But these temporary unions are not defined as marriage either by the people in the society or by outside analysts. Why not?

Any definition includes some patterns and excludes others. The broadest definition of marriage is one that can be applied to most societies but still distinguishes marriage as a particular form different from other patterns in a society. William Stephens' definition is one of the most useful:

> Marriage is a socially legitimate sexual union, begun with a public announcement and undertaken with some idea of permanence; it is assumed with a more or less explicit marriage contract, which spells out reciprocal rights and obligations between spouses and between the spouses and their future children (Stephens 1964:5).

The examples in the two excerpts clearly fit this definition, but do cases of wife lending and wife sharing? Among the Eskimo, the wife is loaned for one night or for a longer but still limited period. There is no expectation of permanence, and there are virtually no mutual obligations incurred between the man and woman. If any obligation is incurred, it is between the borrower and the woman's husband. If the relationship takes place on the woman's initiative, or without the man's asking prior permission, the husband will be righteously indignant, and violence is likely to result. Wife sharing among the Siriono is similar. It is an approved sexual union, but again there is nothing permanent about it, and there are few reciprocal obligations. A woman may sleep with a man for some food, but once the bargain has been made and the deal completed, she is not entitled to any further food from the man—unless she sleeps with him again. Her husband, on the other hand, is obligated to provide her with food even when he is not having intercourse with her for some reason or other (Holmberg 1969:166). Similarly, on Lesu (a Melanesian island in the South Pacific), a woman is expected to get

The exchange of vows in a Hindu wedding. For a complex society such as that of the Hindus, the marriage ceremony tends to be elaborate. Here the bride and groom touch hands with the bride's mother (left) and the priest. *United Press International*

shell currency from her lover to give to her husband. Her lover incurs no other obligations, nor does she (Powdermaker 1933:238). Note how different this is from American customs. On Lesu, a woman who does not collect payment for sexual services is immoral. In the United States, the term for this behavior is prostitution, and it is generally disapproved. People on Lesu would be equally shocked at a woman who engaged in sexual intercourse "for love."

What about current experiments with communal families or wife swapping in the United States? The two must be considered separately. Neither are approved sexual unions under American law, of course, but in the case of communal families, as long as "approval" is understood to apply only within the group or sub-culture itself, communal marriage might fit the definition. There have been too few studies; communal families differ too much from one another; and most communal families have been in existence far too short a time for researchers to be certain that a communal union fits the definition of marriage (Downing 1970: 119–135). Wife swapping, however, is not undertaken with any idea of permanence, and therefore it more closely resembles Eskimo and Siriono wife lending than it does any form of marriage (Bell 1971:74–83).

Marriage as defined by Stephens is virtually universal. Even the Nayar and the *kibbutz*, which may lack the family, have a form of approved sexual union that fits the definition. The Nayar are an Asiatic Indian caste in which, in the past, the wife never saw her husband after the marriage. She continued to live with her mother, sisters, and brothers, and accepted lovers on an overnight basis. Kibbutzim are communal settlements in Israel in which children are raised together in a community nursery. Notice there are several societies (including American examples) with forms fitting the definition and approved of by some subculture that are nonetheless illegal according to the formal code of the society. The study and understanding of family systems and societies in general is extraordinarily complex. Political and legal entities frequently do not coincide with cultural and social ones; legal codes do not always (and in complex societies could not possibly) embody all the values current in the society. In complex societies, there are always unwritten laws and informal codes of behavior, and there are always subgroups that hold different (and sometimes conflicting) values and that approve different kinds of behavior.

KINSHIP PATTERNS: THE FAMILY

The term *family* is, if anything, more difficult to define satisfactorily than is marriage. When it is used in American society, it is commonly held to mean parents and children—the group called a nuclear family ° in anthropological literature (Cuber 1968:432–433). Actually, this unit is more often the household than the family. When college students are asked to list the people they regard as members of their family, 95 percent list grandparents, parent's siblings ° (brothers and sisters), uncles and aunts by marriage, their own siblings' spouses (brothers- and sisters-in-law) and children (nephews and nieces); 75 percent also included their first cousins (children of their parents' siblings) (Richards, C.: unpublished research).

"Family" has had almost as many definitions as "instinct." One of the best-known anthropological statements is George Murdock's:

> The family is a social group characterized by common residence, economic cooperation, and reproduction. It includes adults of both sexes, at least two of whom maintain a socially approved sexual relationship, and one or more children, own or adopted, of the sexually cohabiting adults (Murdock 1949:1).

For years, it was assumed that the family as defined by Murdock was universal, but this assumption was challenged by both M. Spiro and E. K. Gough in separate articles on the basis of their studies among the kibbutzim and Nayar, respectively. Both groups lack common residence of parents and children, and among the Nayar, not even the husband and wife live together (Spiro 1968:68–79; Gough 1968:80–96). As with most other questions about universal human patterns, much depends on definitions. Norman Bell and Ezra Vogel dodge the question by saying that any society recognizing the statuses of father, mother, and offspring has a family system, regardless of how it is constituted (Bell and Vogel, 1968:2). If the term *father* is accepted as referring to the sociological *pater* and not necessarily including *genitor* (Goody 1962:19), then all societies have a family system because all societies recognize these statuses.

Anthropologists have been particularly interested in family structure because in many simple societies, the dynamics of family relationships are the dynamics of the social organization as a whole —that is, almost all the behavior people exhibit toward one another is determined by their family relationships. This may be difficult for a member of a complex society to appreciate. During the first twenty years of an American's life, he may very well interact with three or four times as many people (at a conservative estimate) as a member of a small society meets throughout his life. Most of the people an American knows by the time he is out of high school are nonrelatives; a member of a small society may *never* meet a nonrelative.

Societies that are simple technologically may not be at all simple in their family structure. In general, kinship complexity appears to have an almost inverse relationship with social complexity. That is, complex societies such as those found in the industrial nations of the Western world often have a simpler kinship structure than the technologically unsophisticated, small societies of sub-Saharan Africa, aboriginal Australia (which has one of the most complex kinship systems known), or the interior of Brazil. The number of people recognized and treated as kin, the varieties of specified roles that are tied to certain kinship statuses, and so on are often richly elaborated in these small, otherwise simple, societies.

People in the United States often have a great deal of difficulty with the kinship patterns of other societies. Perhaps some of the complexity is due more to the American lack of familiarity with other systems than to anything else. Complicated systems are often simple to people who grow up with them. The excerpts in this chapter shed some light on non-Western kinship systems, with the Hopi excerpt a bit more explicit than the Chinese one.

Don's society, as mentioned earlier, is matrilineal. Any society that traces descent through one line has characteristics that are unfamiliar and puzzling to members of a bilateral society. In matrilineal societies, descent is determined like last-name inheritance in the United States, but in reverse. That is, in the United States a man passes his last name along to all his children. His sons pass it along to their children, but his daughters do not. When his daughters have children, those children will bear the name of their *father*, not their mother. In a matrilineal society, a woman's children all belong to her family. Her daughters pass the affiliation on to their children; her sons do not. When her sons marry, their children belong to the family of their *mother*, not their father.

A common error in trying to understand an unfamiliar matrilineal descent pattern is to exclude *all* males from the system. Women in the United States have their father's name until they marry, and even then they keep it as their maiden name, although they do not pass it along to their children except as a given name. Similarly, in a matrilineal system men belong to the family of their mother. They continue to belong to that family even after they marry, but they cannot pass the family affiliation along to their children.

Unilineal descent carries with it other complications for American students. For one thing, it discriminates between kinds of cousins. In the American system no difference is made between cousins. There is not even a special term to distinguish males from females; all are lumped together as "cousins." The children of siblings are first cousins to each other, the children of first cousins are second cousins to each other, and so on, but this distinction is made by adding modifiers (first, second). Many contemporary Americans are not even sure just what relationship a third cousin is, anyway. In a unilineal system, however, certain cousins are members of the family and others are not. In a patrilineal system, children of the males are in the patrilineal family whereas children of their sisters are not. Similarly, in a matrilineal system, children of the females are in the matrilineal family, but children of their brothers are not. Children who are related through siblings of the opposite sex (brother and sister) are called cross-cousins,° and in a unilineal system they are normally not in the same family. This process is called bifurcation,° since it splits the matrilineal and patrilineal lines of descent. It excludes descendants of the females from the family in a patrilineal system and descendants of the males in a matrilineal system. Children who are related through siblings of the same sex, however (children of sisters or children of brothers), are called parallel cousins,° and in a unilineal system they are frequently in the same family. When parallel cousins call each other brother and sister (as they do in many societies), the pattern is called bifurcate merging,° because although the matrilineal and patrilineal descent lines split, the parallel lines are continually merged with siblings (Hoebel 1966:335–336) (see Charts 1 and 2).

Keeping track of kinship in this way gives us a number of groups not normally found in a bilineal system. First, a group of brothers in a patrilineal system (or sisters in a matrilineal one) establish families that can obviously trace their relationship to one another. This is a lineage.° As generations pass, the specific connecting links may be forgotten, but the members still assume that they are related and that they are all descended ultimately from a common ancestor even if they cannot prove it. This group is called clan,° sib,° or gens ° (Murdock 1949:67). (Sib is more popular in the United States, clan is in England.) The main difference between a clan (or sib) and a lineage is that in a lineage the connection between families can be demonstrated through genealogies, whereas in a clan it cannot. This definition creates problems in the field, because in the course of his research an anthropologist sometimes learns how families are connected when the people themselves do not know. Does he call the group a lineage then, or is it still a clan?

A larger group, called a phratry,° may be created when several clans regard themselves as somehow related or linked. In the Hopi excerpt, Don mentioned that Louise, his first love, was the daughter of a linked clan brother and therefore technically his daughter, too. This shows that the Hopi had phratries. A still larger grouping occurs when the entire society is divided into two parts, each of which is called a moiety.° Membership in a moiety may be based on kinship or on some other factor such as religion, politics, geographic location, or common interest. Membership is usually ascribed, but occasionally it may be a matter of individual choice. When it is based on kinship, the moiety may consist of many independent nuclear families, or it may be subdivided into phratries, clans, or lineages. Complexity of kinship organization increases steadily from nuclear family to extended family to lineage to clan to phratry to moiety. Additional complexity may be created by the introduction of some intermediate steps, such as a lineage segment (Sahlins

Chart 1. PATRILINEAL
Bifurcate merging

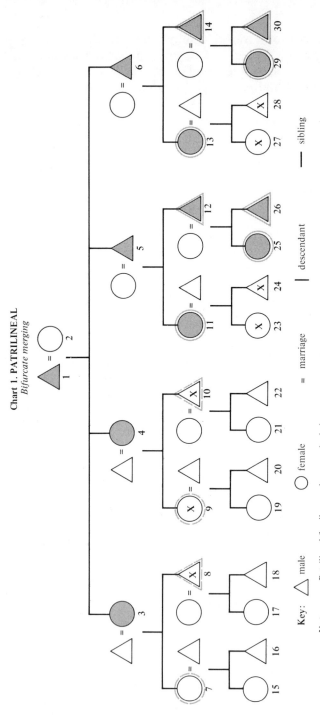

Key: △ male ○ female = marriage — descendant │ descendant — sibling

Notes: Patrilineal family members are shaded.

Individuals marked **X** are cross-cousins to shaded individuals *in the same generation*.

Individuals in the same generation outlined in gray each call each other "brother" and "sister." 11 and 12, 13 and 14, 25 and 26, 29 and 30 are brother and sister in American terminology, but 11 and 12 are parallel cousins to 13 and 14, and 29 and 30 are parallel cousins to 25 and 26. They would *not* call each other "brother" or "sister" in the United States. If they used any kinship term at all, it would be "cousin."

Individuals outlined in dotted lines are technically parallel cousins (7 and 8 parallel to 9 and 10), but usually do not call each other "brother" or "sister" in a patrilineal system because they are parallel matrilineally—through the female line.

11, 12, 13, and 14 would call both 5 and 6 "father"; 25 and 26, 29 and 30 would call both 12 and 14 "father" (since 12 and 14 call each other "brother"), and would call both 11 and 13 "father's sister" (since 12 and 14 call 11 and 13 "sister").

236

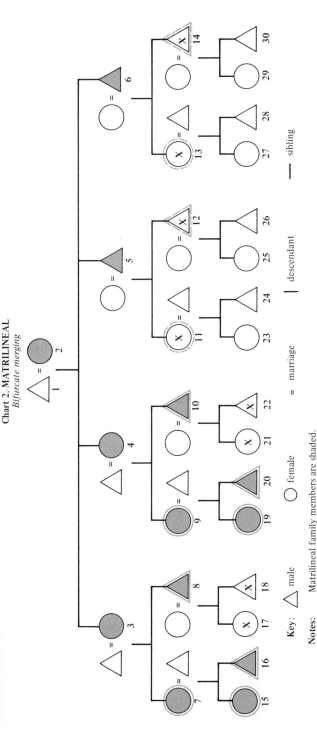

Chart 2. MATRILINEAL
Bifurcate merging

Key: △ male   ○ female   = marriage | descendant   — sibling

Notes:

Matrilineal family members are shaded.

Individuals marked **X** are cross-cousins to shaded individuals *in the same generation.*

Individuals in the same generation outlined in gray call each other "brother" and "sister." 7 and 8, 9 and 10, 15 and 16, 19 and 20 are brother and sister in American terminology, but 9 and 10 are parallel cousins to 7 and 8, and 19 and 20 are parallel cousins to 15 and 16. They would *not* call each other "brother" or "sister" in the United States. If they used any kinship term at all, it would be "cousin."

Individuals outlined in dotted lines are technically parallel cousins (11 and 12 parallel to 13 and 14), but often do not call each other "brother" or "sister" in a matrilineal system because they are parallel patrilineally—through the male line.

7, 8, 9, and 10 would call both 3 and 4 "mother"; 15 and 16, 19 and 20 would call both 7 and 9 "mother" (since 7 and 9 call each other "sister"), and would call both 8 and 10 "mother's brother" (since 8 and 10 call 7 and 9 "sister").

237

1964:181–200) or a half-clan (I Chronicles 6:61). Both Don and Ning Lao were members of clans, but the Chinese excerpt does not describe any clan function. The Hopi excerpt mentions at least one —the regulation of sex and marriage. This is frequently the province of a clan. Don also mentioned another; clans often have economic functions. His relatives helped him financially, particularly at the time of his marriage. Clans often own land. For example, Ning Lao lived in a clan village. When clans own corporate property, they frequently redistribute it periodically as needed. In the situation described by Ning Lao, however, the property apparently was owned by individual families and no mention is made of redistribution. However, since no outsiders lived in the village centuries after the clan first settled there, some agreement or rule to sell to clan members only probably existed.

INCEST RULES

Whether there are clans, lineages, or only nuclear families, societies prohibit sexual relations or marriage with certain relatives by means of an incest tabu.° Attempts to explain and understand this phenomenon have occupied researchers for decades. Part of the difficulty lies in the fact that societies vary in the specific relationships they prohibit. Only the mother-son incest prohibition approaches universality. Father-daughter sexual relations are usually forbidden, and brother-sister relations are also generally barred, but exceptions are found. In some societies, for example, brother-sister marriage has been required. The ancient Egyptian, Hawaiian, and Inca cultures are the best-known examples, but even in those, brother-sister marriage was expected only of royalty and was barred to commoners.

Unilineal societies may carry the incest prohibition much further than bilateral cultures in certain relationships, yet allow marriage between other categories of kin that would be forbidden in a bilateral society like that of the United States. For example, all parallel cousins in the line of descent call one another brother and sister in many unilineal societies. (In a patrilineal society, children of sisters are also technically parallel cousins, but since they belong to their fathers', not their mothers', families, they will not be in the same family unless their fathers are also brothers or the society has exogamous moieties; the same is true in reverse in a matrilineal system, where the children of brothers are also technically parallel cousins.) See Chart 3. Kinship patterns fall into only a few major

Chart 3. EXOGAMOUS MATRILINEAL MOIETY

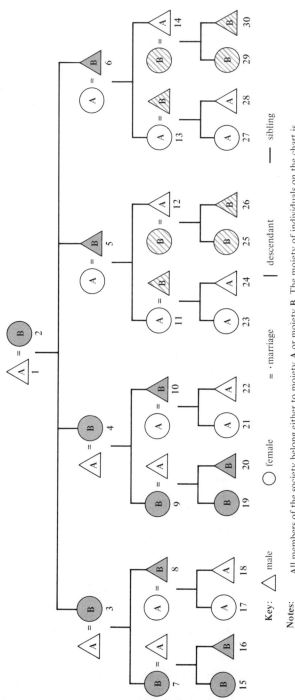

Key: △ male   ○ female   = · marriage | descendant   — sibling

Notes: All members of the society belong either to moiety **A** or moiety **B**. The moiety of individuals on the chart is indicated by the letter **A** or **B** in every case.

Members of the matrilineal *family* are shaded gray.

Members of moiety **B** (the moiety of the matrilineal *family* charted) who are *not* also members of the matrilineal family have cross hatching instead of gray shading.

In this type of moiety system, *all* parallel cousins (traced through either matrilineal or patrilineal lines) are in the same moiety, while all cross-cousins are in the opposite moiety.

categories (see Table 1). Once these are memorized, the student usually finds the maze of new terms and patterns in monographs a little easier to understand. (It is always clearer to demonstrate kinship patterns than to describe them verbally.)

When a society follows a unilineal bifurcate-merging pattern for generations, people may call each other brother and sister and be restricted by incest regulations although they have only the most tenuous biological relationships. On the other hand, the same society that regards as incestuous a relationship Americans would accept with no qualms might very well encourage the marriage of first

Table 1. Kinship Terms

Descent Type	Same Term for	Distinct Term for
*Parental generation**		
Bilateral–generational	mo, mo si, fa si fa, fa bro, mo bro	no one no one
Bilateral–lineal	mo si, fa si mo bro, fa bro	mo fa
Unilateral–bifurcate merging	mo, mo si fa, fa bro	fa si mo bro
Unilateral–bifurcate collateral	no one no one	mo, mo si, fa si fa, fa bro, mo bro
Ego's own generation †		
Bilateral–Hawaiian	sibling, cross-cousin, parallel cousin	no one
Bilateral–Eskimo	cross-cousin, parallel cousin	sibling
Unilineal–Crow, Omaha, Iroquois	sibling, parallel cousin	cross-cousin
Unilineal–Sudanese	no one	sibling, cross-cousin, parallel cousin

* In the bilateral–generational type, all related females in the parental generation are called by the same term, and all related males in that generation are called by the same term. At the opposite extreme is the unilateral-bifurcate collateral where mother, father, mother's siblings, and father's siblings are each distinguished by a separate term.

† In the Hawaiian system, all relatives of the same generation call each other by the same term, equivalent to brother or sister in American terminology. At the opposite extreme, in the Sudanese system, siblings, cross-cousins, and parallel cousins are all distinguished by separate terms. Therefore, Sudanese follow the same principle of terminology for one's own generation that bifurcate collateral does in the terminology for the parental generation.

cross-cousins, which many Americans *would* regard as incestuous, or the marriage of a man and his sister's daughter which is definitely an incestuous match in the United States (Evans-Pritchard 1965: 215).

Why do incest regulations exist? Are they necessary? One assumption has been that inbreeding would have harmful genetic effects. Yet how could this have been a conscious reason in societies with no understanding of genetics? Moreover, biologically a cross-cousin is as close as a parallel cousin, yet many societies require marriage with a cross-cousin but regard parallel-cousin marriage as incest. One of the earliest explanations was that people brought up together are not sexually attractive to each other. This explanation was more or less discredited by Freud, who held that, on the contrary, people brought up together would naturally be attractive to one another, and to avoid the disruptive effect of sexual competition within the family, stringent prohibitions had to be set up. The clinching argument seemed to be that one does not have to prohibit something if it is literally unthinkable. Some recent cross-cultural evidence seems to indicate that the first explanation is sounder than the Freudian argument would make it seem. Among the Chinese, a child bride is sometimes brought into the groom's house to be raised with her future husband. Although there is no cultural brother-sister tabu in this situation, of course—in fact, the pair are constantly encouraged to act as husband and wife—the pair almost always find each other sexually unattractive when it is time to consummate the match. This form of marriage produces fewer children and has a higher divorce rate than does the usual marriage pattern (Wolf 1966:883–898; Westermarck 1921; Freud 1920:294).

Claude Lévi-Strauss, a modern theorist, relies heavily on a structural-formalist ° explanation. He regards incest prohibitions as essentially arbitrary and cultural (since they are so variable), rather than anything demanded by biological imperatives. He says that incest regulations force families to depend on one another, just as the division of labor forces individuals to depend on one another. This creates a larger number of interdependent people and gives the group a survival advantage. Groups with incest regulations therefore prospered, while those who were inbred died out not so much for biological reasons as for social ones (Lévi-Strauss 1960:261–285).

THE REGULATION OF MARRIAGE: STABILITY

The specific attitude of a society toward sexual behavior in general is probably a factor in the explanation of the incest tabu in any particular society. Wolf's data on the Chinese, for example, might not be replicable ° (repeatable) in societies with different attitudes toward sex. Females can engage in sexual activities even when they are not aroused, but men cannot. If the culture teaches men that they can be aroused only by certain combinations of circumstances, they will not be easily aroused by others. If, on the other hand, the culture teaches men that they have a steady and constant recurring need—like hunger—which can be satisfied by almost any means, specific characteristics such as age, close proximity since childhood, physical appearance, or even common humanity may be irrelevant. (Intercourse with nonhuman animals is by no means unknown, of course.)

For a man of China, the tie with the family of orientation, the consanguine ° tie (a bond of blood relationship), was held to be the most important. For women, however, this bond was supposed to be severed at marriage. A woman was expected to separate herself emotionally and physically from her parents and turn her attention to her new family. Children served to cement this new bond. They, particularly the males, were important to a woman's husband's people and were her main source of status in that family. Through them she could develop the emotional attachment to her family of procreation,° the one formed by marriage, that she had lost when she left her family of orientation.

For many societies like the Chinese, marriage is regarded as far too serious a matter to be left entirely up to the young. Ning Lao was given no choice at all—neither whom she was to marry nor when. She treated her daughter the same way. When both marriages turned out badly, Ning Lao blamed destiny, not her parents or herself. In China, marriage was arranged by the parents, and children—particularly the females—had little to say about it. Don, however, chose his own partner, but he had to get parental approval or he could not have married properly; marriage among the Hopi was expensive and required a great deal of cooperation from the extended family in terms of wealth and labor. His potential bride's family had to cooperate too, so their approval was equally necessary. The failure of Mettie's mother to approve his earlier affair had prevented that marriage. Societies seem to fall along a continuum. At one extreme, the parents make all the decisions, and the young have no say in the matter, not even veto power. At the other extreme, the young make the decisions of when and whom to marry, and parents may not even meet the prospective spouse until after the wedding. Patterns in most societies fall somewhere in between the two.

Marriage frequently entails a great deal of labor or expense on the part of either or both families. Societies vary as to which family bears the brunt of the cost. In the United States, most of the expense lies in feeding and entertaining large numbers of people, and it is supposed to be borne by the bride's family. A girl must have the approval and cooperation of her family if she is to have a "big" wedding (unless she has money of her own). In some societies, there is a transfer of wealth from one family to the other. When the wealth comes from the bride's family, it is called a dowry.° The dowry may be distributed in different ways: (1) It may be given to the bride herself for the purpose of setting up her new home or for the rearing of her prospective children; (2) it may be given into the control of the husband for similar purposes; or (3) it may be given to the family of the groom. If the wealth comes from the groom's family, it is called bride ° or progeny price,° or bride wealth ° (Hoebel 1966:344–346). This is never given to either the groom or the bride, but always goes to the bride's family. Generally, the explanation is that the bride or progeny price is given to compensate the bride's family for the loss of her services or for the loss of the offspring their daughter will bear. It validates the right of the husband to the services of his wife, the right of his family to their children, or both. Progeny price would not be expected in societies where descent is matrilineal, of course, since children are not lost to the family. Bride price may appear, however, if the family loses the services of an economically important member in cases of patrilocal or avunculocal residence.

When wealth or labor is involved in a marriage—as in the Hopi ceremony, for example—the families have a vested interest in the stability of the marriage. They do not want to have to go through the whole process again for the same people, for one thing. For another, when wealth is given up, it may be forfeited by the family whose child is at fault in a divorce. That is, if the offspring of the recipient family is to blame, they may have to return the wealth. If the offspring of the donor family is at fault, they may get their child back, but lose their wealth (and then have to spend more to get their offspring married again!). Such families, therefore, are directly involved in the success of the marriage. (This may be one reason why they do not like to leave it up to the children.) Even when a marriage is dissolved by the death of one of the partners and no one is held to blame, families often try to maintain a tie that has been established with considerable effort. To this end, they substitute another person for the deceased. This pattern is called sororate ° if a female substitutes for her sister and levirate ° when a male substitutes for his brother. The Hebrews practiced levirate (Genesis

38:6–26). The most common question an American asks at this point is, "What if the man is already married?" or "What if there is no brother (or sister)?" Most societies that practice levirate or sororate also permit polygamy ° (plural spouses), so taking on an extra spouse is no problem. Such societies are also often unilineal, and there are always a number of people called "brother" or "sister" who will serve perfectly well as substitutes for a real brother or sister.

American society tends to regard biological relationships as crucial (Schneider 1968:23–25). Because in Western society generally, determination of biological paternity is vital in inheritance, there is also heavy emphasis on female chastity. The only way biological paternity can be determined with certainty is to ensure that only one male has access to the female. The more emphasis placed on biological paternity (the *genitor* aspect of fatherhood), the more people in the society try to ensure that the female has no sexual access to any male other than her husband. She must be a virgin when married (to be sure she is not carrying another man's child), and she must restrict her activity after marriage to her husband (or again he might be confronted with a child he did not sire).

Other societies are far more flexible in this regard. In a matrilineal society, the biological father is of little significance. So long as a man's rights to his wife's sexual services are not compromised, he should not be concerned about the men she gets involved with. In much of Melanesia, men generally are not particularly bothered by a wife's affairs, although since individuals vary in all societies, some men are more reluctant to share their wives than others (Powdermaker 1933:247–248; Malinowski 1929:321–324). Even a patrilineal society may regard the sociological father as more important than the biological sire. In some groups, for example, the true father is regarded as the man who feeds the mother during her pregnancy and the child during its infancy. The contribution of the man who sired the child (unless he is the same man) is held to be less important in determining fatherhood. After all, the life of the child depended on the man who brought in food. He "grew" the child in a very real sense (Schapera 1941:244–245).

In societies where marriage is arranged and managed by the family rather than by the partners themselves, attitudes toward romantic love are not very favorable, if the concept exists at all. Ning Lao gives no indication of a romantic attachment to her husband. This may not be surprising to Americans, considering his behavior, but it is surprising that she gives no indication of being disappointed about the lack of romance in her marriage, or even of being aware that it was missing. Her expressions of disappointment are confined to her husband's performance as a provider. It might be possible to get a similar statement from some subgroups within contemporary American culture, but the prevailing stereotype is that marriage is (or should be) based on love. When love is missing, the lack is legitimate grounds for complaint or even divorce. The American stereotype of romantic love as a basis for marriage is almost unique to the English-speaking world. In the Hopi excerpt, Don talks of love, but his behavior belies his words from a non-Indian point of view. If he "loved" Mettie, how could he decide to marry Irene so easily? And why was he unable to wait the short time till Mettie came home, particularly after he knew that her mother no longer opposed the match? Don himself admitted he probably would have been more excited about his marriage if Mettie had been involved; yet he also said he "loved" Irene. This does not quite fit the prevailing American concept of love.

When cases of romantic love do occur in parts of the world where marriage is normally arranged, it is often regarded as a misfortune. Such cultures may view romantic love as a dangerous mental aberration that causes people to forget their obligations, fail to perform various duties, neglect important people, and generally behave badly. Legends and folktales in such countries are full of the disasters caused by romantic love (Goodman 1949: 89–132, 480–483). Even English-speaking societies had such stories before the concept of romantic love took firm hold. All the great love stories of the past—Tristan and Isolde, Romeo and Juliet, Hero and Leander, for example—are tragedies. Tristan and Isolde were enchanted by a love potion, and their madness led them to betray their obligations to King Mark, Isolde's husband. Romeo and Juliet both ignored and betrayed obligations to their families, and died. Leander's love for Hero led him to lose his life attempting to see her (Leach 1949: 11, 25, 26; Hamilton, E. 1945: 135–138).

If husbands and wives do not love each other, why do they stay together? Societies vary widely in the relationship they expect between husband and wife. In some, the pair are held together only by their mutual concern for their children or by pressure from their respective families. In many societies, the birth of a child is crucial to the perpetuation of the marriage, and childless couples do not stay together long. The birth of a child is consequently an important event, and crisis rites occur in as many societies as puberty rites. Although they may involve only the mother and child, in some societies, the father also has an important part to play in the ceremonies. The couvade,° a practice widespread in the Amazon area and among the Island Carib requires that the father, as well as the mother, be confined at the birth (sometimes for a longer period). He may complain of labor pains, observe food tabus, and endure various ordeals as well. The purpose of the couvade is usually said to be to ensure the well-being of the child (Steward and Faron 1959:303, 324, 370).

The relationship with affinal relatives ° (in-laws) has preserved or destroyed marriages in many societies (including our own). Chapter 4 discusses two of the techniques (joking and avoidance) commonly used to prevent or ease tension between affinal and blood relatives. In societies where consanguine (blood) ties to the family of orientation are paramount for both men and women, the conjugal ° (marriage) ties may be brittle and relations between the two almost hostile (see below).

Stability in marriage obviously depends neither on romantic attachment nor on happiness. Ning Lao's marriage was stable, in the sense that she married only once and was never divorced, but it certainly was neither romantic nor happy. Don's marriage, based on romantic love of a sort and his own choice, was also stable in the same sense as Ning Lao's, but it too falls short of the American ideal of a happy marriage. (The American divorce rate, however, shows quite clearly that a substantial number of marriages based on this ideal founder.) Stability in marriage does not seem to have much to do with Judaeo-Christian morality, either. Ning Lao's husband was hardly a shining example of "goodness." He had one premarital and extramarital affair; he had one illegitimate child we know about (he may have had more). He smoked opium, did not provide for his family, and sold one of his children. Yet he never sought a divorce and lived with Ning Lao again as soon as she let him. He fathered another child by her. His marriage was certainly stable in the sense of enduring. Don also fails to provide a model for Judaeo-Christian morality, at least so far as his sexual behavior is concerned. He engaged in a variety of premarital and extramarital affairs, but this behavior did not affect the stability of his marriage.

One obvious factor involved in the stability of marriage is the ease or difficulty of obtaining a divorce. If it is difficult or if there is strong social disapproval, there will be fewer divorces. The divorce rate has gone up steadily in the United States as divorce has become easier and more acceptable. In one sense, therefore, a divorce rate represents only the ease with which a divorce can be obtained. It cannot serve as an index of either morality or marital happiness in the society. Another factor in the high American divorce rate is the fact that most people get married. That sounds facetious, but it is not. Many societies have a high rate of consensual unions,° people living together without marriage. The frequency with which people in these societies change mates is never reflected in divorce statistics. Marriage and divorce statistics indicate the official bureaucratic definitions in the society. In many countries these definitions do not reflect closely the realities of the situation.

There have been various studies of the causes of stability in marriage in different societies. Most of them tend to show that divorce rates are closely tied to factors in the social structure of the society. Divorce is generally most frequent in societies where descent is reckoned through the mother and where the social system also tends to emphasize consanguine ties at the expense of conjugal ties, for example (Gluckman 1968:464–468; Ackerman 1968:469–478). Although in no society is divorce fully approved, societies vary in the stringency of the disapproval and in the disruptiveness of divorce. In the United States, divorce and separation are highly detrimental to the children, partly because they are so emotionally dependent on a limited number of people. Since the household is small, a home broken by either divorce or death of a spouse generally lacks an adult representative of one of the sexes. It therefore cannot provide all the necessary models for the proper socialization of the child unless substitutes can be found. In societies with extended family households, the problem is not so acute. The child is almost always socialized by several adults of both sexes, and the loss of one is not quite so traumatic.

SUMMARY

All societies regulate the sexual behavior of their members. At a minimum, the society classifies individuals into permissible and nonpermissible sexual partners through incest rules. The specific relationships prohibited or permitted vary widely from one society to another. In order to have any incest prohibitions at all, of course, it is necessary to recognize kinship affiliations. Membership in or exclusion from a kinship-based group is determined in various limited ways. A child can be affiliated through his mother, his father, or both parents. Societies organized around affiliation through one parent rather than through both have a variety of characteristics in common, such as the occurrence of lineages and clans, discrimination of cross and parallel cousins, frequently including preferred cross-cousin marriage, and levirate and sororate. The latter is made easier by another practice frequent in unilineal societies—classificatory kinship,° in which relationship terms are extended to include relatives who would be excluded in American kinship terminology.

Marriage exists in all societies, although the family (as defined by Murdock) does not. Marriage may be arranged entirely by the parents and be a matter for general extended family concern, or it may result from the independent choice of the young couple and be regarded as entirely their own business. Wealth frequently changes hands at a marriage. Sometimes the bride's family must distribute wealth, sometimes the groom's family gives up wealth, and sometimes both families exchange items. In any of these cases, the young couple usually must depend on assistance from their families to marry.

Residence after marriage varies widely from one society to another, and is occasionally variable even within the same society. A change in residence places some stress on the individual who has to leave home, particularly if he or she is cut off from supportive relatives. Residence rules may reinforce the group affiliation pattern or serve to correct problems when group affiliation and some important element in the society are not passed along in the same way from one generation to the next.

The family is a major source of socialization for the young. It is frequently the group within which the individual first learns the values and traditions of his culture and internalizes the beliefs and rules that make it possible for him to function in his society and enjoy doing it. Socialization is not the only answer to the question of why man supports his society, however. Without a feeling of esprit de corps and morale, man—apparently alone of all the animals—does not have the motivation to continue living. Where does man find answers to the questions of why he lives and why he should want to go on? In the next chapter, we discuss the problem of maintaining morale and motivation, another prerequisite for the survival of society.

7 Maintaining
Morale and Motivation

Man has always asked, Why am I here? What is it all for? Why do we do what we do? He is often anxious about the future, death, and many other things beyond his control. Man seems to be the only animal who broods about the future. For a society to survive, for the individual members to survive, they need not only material things such as food, clothing, and shelter, but also a reason for living and for behaving responsibly. People must have a feeling of loyalty to the group, a feeling of satisfaction and a sense of rightness in what they do and what is expected from them. Otherwise they give up as individuals or as members of society, and either they or the society fails to survive. For a society to function well, its members must have reasonably high morale, motivation to live and to live according to its norms. What is the source of this morale, this motivation? Much of it comes from an individual's socialization, but this is not the only source. Art, folklore, literature, and religion also provide man with answers, with motivation, and with morale.

In this chapter we focus mainly on religion, which seems to have some priority over the fine arts. Archeological evidence indicates that the arts had their origin and first flourished in the service of religion. Once established in man's general culture, however, many of the arts developed along other lines, and today they serve independently to bolster morale and motivation.

In the following excerpt, note what seem to be the major worries of people in the society, the questions they ask, and the source or the type of answers they receive. What kind of specialists do they have? How is life made exciting, interesting, and more secure for them?

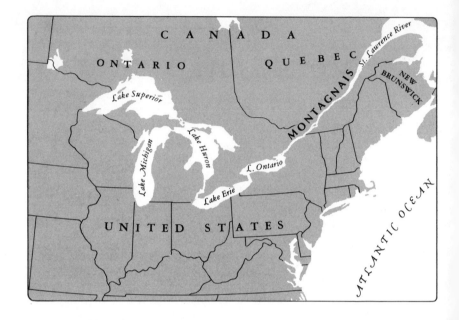

Sorcery and the Montagnais

Towards nightfall, two or three young men erected a tent in the middle of our Cabin; they stuck six poles deep into the ground in the form of a circle, and to hold them in place they fastened to the tops of these poles a large ring, which completely encircled them; this done, they enclosed this Edifice with Castelognes [woolen blankets], leaving the top of the tent open; it is all that a tall man can do to reach to the top of this round tower, capable of holding 5 or 6 men standing upright.* This house made, the fires of the cabin are entirely extinguished, and the brands thrown outside, lest the flame frighten away the Genii or *Khichikouai*, who are to enter this tent; a young juggler slipped in from below, turning back, for this purpose, the covering which enveloped it, then replaced it when he had entered, for they must be very careful that there be no opening in this fine palace except from above. The juggler, having entered, began to moan softly, as if complaining; he shook the tent at first without violence; then becoming animated little by little, he commenced

---

* Abridged from "Le Jeune's Relations, 1634," in Ruben G. Thwaites (ed.), *The Jesuit Relations & Allied Documents* (Cleveland: Burrows Bros., 1897), Vol. 6, pp. 163–171, 193–201. Odd-numbered pages are in English; even-numbered, in French. The report by the French Jesuit Paul Le Jeune was made after he had spent a winter with the Montagnais Indians in eastern Canada. The complete report is published in Vols. 6 and 7.

250

to whistle, in a hollow tone, and as if it came from afar; then to talk as if in a bottle; to cry like the owls of these countries, which it seems to me have stronger voices than those of France; then to howl and sing, constantly varying the tones; . . . disguising his voice so that it seemed to me I heard those puppets which showmen exhibit in France. Sometimes he spoke Montagnais, sometimes Algonquain, retaining always the Algonquain intonation, which, like the Provençal, is vivacious. At first, as I have said, he shook this edifice gently; but, as he continued to become more animated, he fell into so violent an ecstasy, that I thought he would break everything to pieces, shaking his house with so much force and violence, that I was astonished at a man having so much strength; for, after he had once begun to shake it, he did not stop until the consultation was over, which lasted about three hours. Whenever he would change his voice, the Savages would at first cry out, . . . "listen, listen"; then, as an invitation to these Genii, they said to them, . . . "enter, enter." At other times, as if they were replying to the howls of the juggler, they drew this aspiration from the depths of their chests, *ho, ho.* I was seated like the others, looking on at this wonderful mystery, forbidden to speak; but as I had not vowed obedience to them, I did not fail to intrude a little word into the proceedings. Sometimes I begged them to have pity on this poor juggler, who was killing himself in this tent; at other times I told them they should cry louder, for the Genii had gone to sleep.

Some of these Barbarians imagined that this juggler was not inside, that he had been carried away, without knowing where or how. Others said that his body was lying on the ground, and that his soul was up above the tent, where it spoke at first, calling these Genii, and throwing from time to time sparks of fire. Now to return to our consultation. The Savages having heard a certain voice that the juggler counterfeited, uttered a cry of joy, saying that one of these Genii had entered; then addressing themselves to him, they cried out, . . . "call, call"; that is, "call thy companions." Thereupon the juggler, pretending to be one of the Genii and changing his tone and his voice, called them. In the meantime our sorcerer, who was present, took his drum, and began to sing with the juggler who was in the tent, and the others answered. Some of the young men were made to dance, among others the Apostate [Pierre Antoine Pastedechouan, the Montagnais interpreter who had been baptized and then had turned back to his native religion], who did not wish to hear of it, but the sorcerer made him obey.

At last, after a thousand cries and howls, after a thousand songs, after having danced and thoroughly shaken this fine edifice, the Savages believing that the Genii . . . had entered, the sorcerer consulted them. He asked them about his health (for he is sick), and about that of his wife, who was also sick. These Genii, or rather the juggler who counter-

feited them, answered that, as to his wife, she was already dead, that it
was all over with her. I could have said as much myself, for one needed
not to be a prophet or a sorcerer to guess that, inasmuch as the poor creature was already struck with death; in regard to the sorcerer, they said
that he would see the Spring. Now, knowing his disease,—which was a
pain in the loins, or rather an infirmity resulting from his licentiousness
and excesses, for he is vile to the last degree,—I said to him, seeing that
he was otherwise healthy, and that he drank and ate very heartily, that
he would not only see the Spring but also the Summer, if some other
accident did not overtake him, and I was not mistaken.

After these interrogations, these fine oracles were asked if there
would soon be snow, if there would be much of it, if there would be Elks
or Moose, and where they could be found. They answered, or rather the
juggler, always disguising his voice, that they saw a little snow and some
moose far away, without indicating the place, having the prudence not to
commit themselves.

So this is what took place in this consultation, after which I wished
to get hold of the juggler; but, as it was night, he made his exit from
the tent and from our little cabin so swiftly, that he was outside almost
before I was aware of it. He and all the other Savages, who had come
from the other Cabins to these beautiful mysteries, having departed, I
asked the Apostate if he was so simple as to believe that the Genii entered
and spoke in this tent. He began to swear his belief, which he had lost
and denied, that it was not the juggler who spoke, but these *Khichikouai*
or Genii of the air, and my host said to me, "Enter thou thyself into the
tent, and thou wilt see that thy body will remain below, and thy soul
will mount on high." I did want to go in; but, as I was the only one of my
party, I foresaw that they might commit some outrage upon me, and, as
there were no witnesses there, they would boast that I had recognized
and admired the truth of their mysteries.

· · ·

I must set down here what I saw them do on the twelfth of February.
As I was reciting my hours [prayers] toward evening, the sorcerer began
to talk about me: *aiamtheou*, "He is making his prayers"; then, pronounc-
ing some words which I did not understand, he added: *Niganipahau*,
"I will kill him at once." . . . Just as I was thinking that he wanted to
take my life, my host said to me, "Hast thou not some powder that kills
men?" "Why?" I asked. "I want to kill some one," he answered me. I
leave you to imagine whether I finished my prayers without any distrac-
tion; for I knew very well that they were disinclined to kill any of their
own people, and that the sorcerer had threatened me with death some
days before,—although only in jest, as he told me afterward; but I did
not have much confidence in him. . . . I wished to learn if they had me

in mind, and so I asked them where the man was that they wished to kill; they answered me that he was in the neighborhood of Gaspé, more than a hundred leagues away from us. I began to laugh, for in truth I had never dreamed that they would undertake to kill a man a hundred leagues away. I inquired why they wished to take his life. They answered that this man was a Canadian sorcerer, who, having had some trouble with ours, had threatened him with death and had given him the disease from which he had suffered so long, and which was going to consume him in two days, if he did not prevent the stroke by his art. I told them that God had forbidden murder, and that we never killed people; that did not prevent them from pursuing their purpose. My host, foreseeing the great commotion which was about to take place, said to me, "Thou wilt have the headache; go off into one of the other cabins near by." "No," said the sorcerer, "there will be no harm in his seeing what we do." They had all the children and women go out, except one who sat near the sorcerer; I remained as a spectator of their mysteries, with all the Savages of the other cabins, who were summoned. All being seated, a young man comes bearing two pickets, or very sharply-pointed sticks; my host prepares the charm, composed of little pieces of wood shaped at both ends like a serpent's tongue, iron arrow-points, pieces of broken knives, bits of iron bent like a big fishhook, and other similar things; all these are wrapped in a piece of leather. When this is done, the sorcerer takes his drum, all begin to chant and howl, and to make the uproar of which I spoke above; after a few songs, the woman who had remained arises, and goes all around the inside of the cabin, passing behind the backs of the people who are there. When she is reseated, the magician takes these two stakes; then, pointing out a certain place, begins by saying, "Here is his head" (I believe he meant the head of the man whom he wished to kill); then with all his might he drives these stakes into the ground, inclining them toward the place where he believed this Canadian was. Thereupon my host comes to assist his brother; he makes a tolerably deep ditch in the ground with these stakes; meanwhile the songs and other noises continue incessantly. The ditch made and the stakes planted, the servant of the sorcerer, I mean the Apostate, goes in search of a sword, and the sorcerer strikes with it one of these pickets; then he descends into the ditch, assuming the posture of an excited man who is striking heavy blows with the sword and poniard; for he has both, in this act of a furious and enraged man. The sorcerer takes the charm wrapped in skin, puts it in the ditch, and redoubles his sword-cuts at the same time that they increase the uproar.

Finally, this mystery ends, and he draws out the sword and the poniard all covered with blood, and throws them down before the other Savages; the ditch is hurriedly covered up, and the magician boastfully asserts that his man is struck, that he will soon die, and asks if they have not heard his cries; they all say "no," except two young men, relatives of his, who say they have heard some very dull sounds, and as if far away. Oh, how glad they make him! Turning toward me, he begins to laugh, saying, "See this black robe, who comes here to tell us that we must not kill any one." As I am looking attentively at the sword and the poniard, he has them presented to me. "Look," he says, "what is that?" "It is blood," I answer. "of what? Of some Moose or other animal." They laugh at me, saying that it is the blood of that Sorcerer of Gaspé. "How?" I answer them, "he is more than a hundred leagues away from here." "It is true," they reply, "but it is the Manitou; that is, the Devil, who carries his blood under the earth." Now if this man is really a Magician, I leave you to decide; for my part, I consider that he is neither Sorcerer nor Magician, but that he would like very much to be one. All that he does, according to my opinion, is nothing but nonsense to amuse the Savages. He would like to have communication with the Devil or Manitou, but I do not think that he has. Yet I am persuaded that there has been some Sorcerer or Magician here, if what they tell me is true about diseases and cures which they describe to me; it is a strange thing,

A magician undergoes convulsions in order to prophesy the outcome of his tribe's forthcoming war expedition. From an eighteenth-century engraving. *The Bettman Archive*

in my opinion, that the Devil, who is visible to the South Americans, and who so beats and torments them that they would like to get rid of such a guest, does not communicate himself visibly and sensibly to our Savages. . . .

Unfortunately, Le Jeune never revealed whether the Gaspé sorcerer died. Apparently he was so sure of his evaluation of the situation that he never bothered to check after he returned to Jesuit headquarters in Québec. Our curiosity must remain unsatisfied.

Le Jeune lived with the Montagnais to learn their language and to convert as many of them as possible. He was terribly sincere, and he firmly believed in the existence of a supernatural that intervened in the lives of men. In this he and the Montagnais agreed. Le Jeune, however, was convinced that the Manitou (the Montagnais word for supernatural) was the Christian devil. In 1634, the suggestion that a supernatural being worshiped by other peoples might be equated with the Christian God would have been regarded as scandalous or blasphemous.

BELIEF SYSTEMS

Le Jeune did not realize how many beliefs he and the Montagnais held in common. Their differences in behavior were so apparent and Le Jeune's bias was so strong that he was unable to examine the Montagnais belief system with any objectivity. A careful study of his report, however, reveals many of the Montagnais religious beliefs, and incidentally sheds light on Le Jeune's concepts too. A list of concepts and practices is given below.

Concepts about the Supernatural

Montagnais

A. Based on the first ceremony described by Le Jeune:
1. There are a variety of *Khichikouai,* or spirits of the air.
2. Flame (or light?) frightens them.
3. The spirits speak aloud under certain circumstances and may answer questions asked by humans.
4. The spirits manifest their presence physically by shaking walls,

whistling, hooting like owls, speaking, shooting sparks, and making a variety of other noises.

5. The spirits can predict the future and know what is happening in distant parts of the world.
6. Men have souls that can separate from their bodies.
7. Supernatural beings can interact with each other and with human souls.
8. Human singing and dancing are important for dealing with the supernatural.
9. Irrelevant conversation may interfere with the success of a ceremony. (The evidence for this statement is indirect. Le Jeune was asked to keep quiet, but since he and others did not, yet the ceremony was a success, it would appear that silence was not absolutely necessary, although it was perhaps desirable.)

B. Based on the second ceremony described by Le Jeune:
1. Men can cause disease or can kill other men by supernatural means.
2. The supernatural can transmit material things over a considerable distance.
3. Acts performed in one location can have an effect in another regardless of how far apart they are, because of (2) above.
4. One can protect oneself from supernatural harm by supernatural methods (in the case described, by supernaturally attacking the individual believed to be responsible for the difficulty).
5. Weak individuals may be harmed by witnessing certain ceremonies. (The evidence for this statement is indirect. Le Jeune was first warned that he would get a headache if he stayed for the ceremony, but when the sorcerer said "there will be no harm in his seeing what we do," he was allowed to remain. The women and children, however, except for the single female participant, were sent out of the cabin. The belief is widespread that it is dangerous—to the individual or to the group—to have unauthorized observers at certain ceremonies.)

Le Jeune

A. Based on the first ceremony he described:
1. Demons and a variety of evil spirits exist.
2. There is a specific evil force called the devil.
3. Humans can interact with these evil supernatural beings.

B. Based on the second ceremony he described:

1. There is a good supernatural being called God. (From other data we know Le Jeune believed there is only one God, but there is no direct evidence for this in the excerpt itself.)
2. This God forbids murder.
3. It is possible for humans to cause and cure disease supernaturally. (Le Jeune thought "real" magicians among the Montagnais might have done so at one time, "if what they tell me is true about the diseases and cures which they describe to me.") We know from other sources by and about Le Jeune that he believed in the existence of angels who were allied with the forces of good.

It is easy to see from the list that Le Jeune and the Montagnais shared more beliefs that either of them realized. First, both believed in supernatural beings with will and consciousness. In addition, both believed that men and the supernatural could interact; that one individual could harm another by means of the supernatural; and that there was a variety of supernatural beings capable of a variety of actions. From other sources of data about past Christian religious beliefs, it is possible to add more shared concepts. Both Le Jeune and the Montagnais believed that man had a soul that could separate from the body; that supernatural beings knew what the future held and what was happening in other parts of the world; that the supernatural could be used as protection against supernatural attack.

There is no major area of the globe entirely free from such beliefs, even today, although they may appear in different combinations in specific individuals or groups. The belief in supernatural beings with will and consciousness is called *animism* ° and is one of the most widespread concepts about the supernatural. The belief was first defined by E. B. Tylor (Tylor 1965:10–21), who noted its almost universal occurrence and suggested it had developed from speculation about dreams, which are consciously experienced by almost everyone. Tylor also described a special kind of belief in supernatural beings—the worship of animals and of natural features of the environment—that he called "nature worship" (Tylor 1965: 10). R. R. Marrett, another student of religion in the same period, coined the term *animatism* ° for a belief in the life force of usually inanimate natural objects (LaBarre 1964:26–29). This term is so close in sound to the word *animism* that it has plagued generations of students. Moreover, the distinction between animism and animatism is not always easy to determine in actual religious systems; it is sometimes impossible to learn whether an individual worships a spirit housed in a rock (animism), or believes that the rock itself has an awareness, consciousness, and supernatural powers (animatism). The people of a society themselves may not be sure, or they may disagree on the correct interpretation. Tylor's terminology is the more useful here, since people who venerate a rock can be classified as nature worshipers in any case. We shall therefore use his term, and not that of Marrett.

Another widespread belief is that the supernatural is a mindless force, analogous to electricity, with *no* will, awareness, or consciousness. This concept is called *mana* ° and is similar to the Western idea of "luck." It is not so pervasive as the concept of animism, although it appears in many parts of the world. Mana can be used for either good or evil purposes, since the force itself has no awareness and is no more intrinsically "good" or "evil" than electricity. Objects, locations, people, and animals can have mana. If a person knows how to deal with the mana in something, he can use it to bring himself good fortune, but if he is untrained or supernaturally weak (a child, for example), contact with the mana may bring him disaster, just as contact with a high-tension wire may harm an unprotected person. The attitude toward mana is therefore ambivalent. Everyone wants to increase his own store of mana, and thereby his good fortune, but everyone also wants to avoid contact with more mana than he is equipped to control. Individuals with a great deal of mana (which is usually indicated by their fine health, wealth, and general good fortune) are dangerous to others and are therefore feared, respected, envied, and admired. Objects that belong to them or things they handle may become infested with an unusual amount of mana, making them dangerous to people who have a lesser amount. Contact with such people and their belongings is often hedged about with precautions and restrictions, called *tabus.*° The terms *mana* and *tabu* come from the South Pacific, where these concepts have been elaborately developed. The important difference between the concepts of mana and animism is that animistic beings have awareness and will, whereas mana does not. One cannot plead or bargain with mana, but it can be thoroughly controlled by anyone with the proper knowledge. Supernatural beings are less predictable or controllable, but they can be reasoned with, propitiated, and even outwitted. There is no clear evidence in the excerpt that the Montagnais had a mana-like concept of the supernatural, but data in Le Jeune's full report indicate that they might have had.

Le Jeune and the Montagnais both believed that men could harm each other by supernatural means, and both believed the cause and the cure of most diseases were supernatural. Le Jeune attributed some diseases to "natural" causes, but all could be cured by God, and some—particularly epidemic diseases—might be sent by God to punish individuals or whole societies. Diseases caused by men using the supernatural were manifestations of the devil's power and were not the work of good supernatural beings. The Montagnais did not make such fine distinctions: they apparently felt that all diseases, at least all serious ones, were supernaturally caused, either by the supernatural acting independently or at the command of some sorcerer. Because the belief that the supernatural is the ultimate cause of all disease is widespread, in most societies religion is intimately involved in the treatment of illness. In the United States large segments of the population believe that prayer is an important supplement to medicine, and some groups depend almost entirely on supernatural treatment (Eddy n.d.: 1–17).

From the list of beliefs given above, it is more difficult to determine the differences between Le Jeune and the Montagnais than it is to discover similarities. Some apparent differences are actually only modifications of shared concepts. For example, both shared the general belief that men and the supernatural interact. The Montagnais, however, believed that the spirits spoke aloud to men and answered their questions. Le Jeune did not agree. As a Christian, he held that such communication could occur only under special circumstances with special individuals (Joan of Arc, for example). As the report indicates, he obviously did not accept the idea that the spirits engaged in casual chitchat about the weather with a cabinful of Indians. Both Le Jeune and the Montagnais believed man had a soul that could separate from his body, but Le Jeune held that this normally occurred only after death. As in the case of visions, there might be exceptions, but he thought they were rare, and certainly not the almost routine occurrences that the Montagnais thought them to be.

Other beliefs held by the Montagnais were unacceptable to Le Jeune even in modified form; some he felt applied only to evil spirits. He did not believe that supernatural beings were frightened by flame (although Christian folk belief would accept the idea that light, especially daylight, was frightening to evil spirits). The Montagnais thought the spirits whistled, hooted like owls, and shook tent walls. Le Jeune did not believe that good spirits engaged in such antics, and although he might have agreed that evil spirits could behave that way, it is clear from the report that he tended to blame all the noise and activity on the Montagnais sorcerer himself.

In Le Jeune's religious system, man had no certain control over the forces of good. Man could supplicate or by performance win the good will or pity of the supernatural, but the suggestion that man could in any way control God was abhorrent. The concepts of the Montagnais were very different. To them, the supernatural was subject to the control of man; one only had to know the proper method. This difference between control and persuasion is often accepted as one of the distinctions between magic and religion, magic being defined as a system for control over the supernatural (Hoebel 1966:467). In general, anthropologists have accepted this definition, and regard magic and religion as two different approaches to the supernatural distinguished by the presence or absence of the power to control. Not all agree, however. A. Van Gennep, an early theorist, regarded religion as a body of theory and concepts about the supernatural, and magic as the techniques for dealing with the supernatural based on those beliefs (Van Gennep 1960:13). He placed religion and science on the same analytical level as two different conceptual approaches to understanding the universe. Magic, the practice based on religion, was therefore on the same analytical level as what we call technology—the practice based on scientific theory. Van Gennep's definition is easier to apply than the other, because all religious systems attempt to influence the supernatural in some way. Using his definition, all techniques for doing so are designated magic, regardless of whether they are thought to coerce the supernatural, and all beliefs about the supernatural are classified as religious concepts, whether they depict the supernatural as subject to human control or as an omnipotent being whose good will depends upon man's submission. Van Gennep's definition helps one avoid the ethnocentric trap of regarding practices of familiar systems as "religious" and those of unfamiliar systems as "magical."

The question of the universality of magic and religion is often raised. The answer is largely a matter of definition. To Le Jeune and other Jesuits, whose definition of religion included specific beliefs (in one God, in the divinity of Jesus, in the virgin birth, and in a host of other dogmas), the Montagnais either had no religion or worshiped the devil. Definitions used by anthropologists today vary, but can be roughly summed up: Religion consists of attitudes and beliefs about the supernatural. Based on this definition, most anthropologists state that all societies have some form of religion. But some anthropologists regard this definition as unsatisfactory. For one thing, it leaves the word "supernatural" undefined; for another, many students of religion have pointed out that the distinction between "natural" and "supernatural" is by no means universal, nor is it consistent even in societies that make such a distinction. Most of the Western world would classify as supernatural all phenomena beyond the power of man or man-made devices to cause, sense, control, or comprehend. Instances of such phenomena will vary according to the technology of each society, so that a precise definition of the word that will hold across cultural boundaries has not yet been made. What can be said so far is that all societies appear to have concepts and beliefs dealing with what the Western world would classify as the supernatural. Perhaps an anthropological definition should read as follows: Religion consists of attitudes and beliefs about what Western civilization classifies as supernatural. While this definition is ethnocentric, it makes it possible to categorize practices and beliefs for analysis, and perhaps even more important, makes explicit something that has long been implicit in the definition.

The anthropologist Murray Wax suggested in a recent essay that the whole concept "religion" is a "folk category of the Western Judaeo-Christian tradition," and that the category may not exist in other parts of the world (Wax 1968:228). He prefers a classification based on "magical" and "rational" thinking. Magical thinkers, according to Wax, regard the universe as "a 'society,' not a 'mechanism'; that is, it is composed of beings' rather than 'objects'" (Wax 1968:235). He regards this classification as less ethnocentric than the other.

Whichever definition of magic or of religion is accepted, there are certain similarities in practices that can be identified. Much of the behavior for manipulating the supernatural uses materials that have been in contact with the person or thing to be affected, mimics the desired result, or both. James Frazer has classified such behavior under the general term *sympathetic magic,* based on what he calls the Law of Sympathy, which assumes that things act on each other even at a distance because of a "secret sympathy" between them (Frazer 1955:52). Frazer also divided this general principle into two subordinate laws: the Law of Similarity or Imitation, and the Law of Contagion or Contact. The first states that things that resemble each other influence each other, like produces like, and effect resembles its cause; the second states that things once in contact continue to affect each other after contact is broken (Frazer 1955:52ff.). Le Jeune's report describes one Montagnais ritual based at least partly on imitative magic. The charm used in the assassination sorcery contained things that could cut and wound. The sorcerer made dagger thrusts and sword slashes in the air to harm his opponent. The presence of blood on the weapons was confirmation that the thrusts had actually penetrated the body of his enemy. Had the Montagnais sorcerer also used something formerly in contact with his opponent's body (such as clothing, fingernail or hair clippings, or excrement), he would have been using the Law of Contagion.

Sorcery and witchcraft are practiced in many parts of the world today, with a recent resurgence of so-called Satanic cults in Europe, England, and the United States. Many practices reminiscent of the Middle Ages have been adopted by elements of modern society once thought immune to such beliefs (Holzer 1971:4–6, 71–85). Sorcery is the term usually reserved for magic practiced with evil intent, but magic for socially acceptable goals also uses the same principles. Thus the Nootka put a model of a swimming fish into the river when salmon runs are delayed, and peoples in many parts of the world engage in ritual sexual intercourse to encourage fertility in the plant and animal worlds (Leach 1949:867).

Read Le Jeune's excerpt again and you will find evidence of a profound and yet subtle difference between European and American Indian religious concepts that Le Jeune probably never realized existed. Le Jeune's God prohibited murder, yet Le Jeune accepted the idea that evil supernatural beings might assist humans to kill other humans. He divided the supernatural world (and the natural world as well) into categories of good and evil beings. His God, the saints, angels, and other assorted supernatural beings were "good" and would never under any circumstances do anything that Le Jeune would regard as "evil." Misfortunes that befell men where held to be the work of the devil or were merited punishment for man's sins and therefore "good" for him. The Montagnais had no such dichotomy of good and evil beings. Some supernaturals were more powerful than others, or had special competence in certain areas, but none was regarded as invariably good or bad. The Montagnais beliefs were characteristic of those of American Indians in general; the Old World good-evil dichotomy hardly seemed to exist in the New. The Indian approach was incomprehensible and reprehensible to European clerics (as it is to many people today), although it was certainly attractive to less pious Frenchmen.

All of what Robert Redfield has called the Great Traditions have attached moral values to the supernatural, whereas most of the Little Traditions (like that of the Montagnais) have not (Redfield 1960: 40–59). From parts of Le Jeune's report it is clear that to the Montagnais, violation of a supernatural regulation, such as the requirement that certain animal bones be burned instead of given to dogs, was a dangerous and even a stupid thing to do, since it might result in hunting failure, but it was not "wrong" in the European sense.

A man could do it if he could get away with it, but he was taking a risk. Behavior that harmed another person was "bad," but there was little concern over supernatural punishment; instead, the wronged individual was likely to retaliate immediately (and violently) with the full support of public opinion. Sins—offenses against the supernatural—were of consequence only if the supernatural reacted and then were of general concern only if the reaction appeared to threaten the society as a whole. At that point, the individual's actions were judged "crimes"—offenses against society —and social pressure was directed against him (see Chapter 4).

This classification led to the evaluation of actions in context. Stealing from another Montagnais was a crime, but since Europeans were not Montagnais, stealing from them was not. It was also proper to take another person's belongings in retaliation for certain offenses. Stealing, therefore, was not intrinsically bad; it was classified as wrong according to who took from whom and under what circumstances. Apparently, if a Montagnais got away with something normally regarded as a "crime" or a "sin," he felt no guilt about it and was unconcerned unless he became ill. In that case, his act might be used by a religious specialist as an explanation for his sickness, which was attributed to retaliation by a sorcerer or a supernatural. The Montagnais (like many other peoples) had a concept of an afterlife, but one's fate was not determined so much by one's conduct during life as by the circumstances of death and the subsequent treatment of the body. (Compare Norse beliefs that men who died in battle went to Valhalla, whereas those who died naturally did not—saint or sinner in life, it made no difference.)

Still another contrast between Le Jeune and the Montagnais lies in the degree of exclusiveness of the belief system. Christianity is classified as an "exclusive" religion. It rejects inclusion of gods from other systems (although a surprising number turn up as "saints" with new names but old ceremonies). Since the Christian God is believed to be omnipotent and in control of the entire universe, belief in other gods is assumed to be either mistaken or the worship of evil supernatural beings. The Christian, Islamic, and Judaic religions will not permit believers to hold other religious beliefs simultaneously. An inclusive religion, on the other hand, permits believers to accept a variety of different beliefs simultaneously. A member of an inclusive religion sees no difficulty in participating in his own religion and in Christian services as well.

Exclusive religions are apt to proselytize more often than are inclusive ones. Le Jeune himself was a missionary. In his system, it was possible for people born into one religion to become members of another—the Christian faith—simply by accepting certain beliefs and undergoing certain rituals. The rituals are examples of the class of ceremony called *rites de passage* (passage rites) by Van Gennep (Van Gennep 1960:3), other examples of which have been mentioned in Chapters 5 and 6. Such ceremonies mark the transition of an individual from one status to another, and all societies have them in some form. The ceremonies may involve the supernatural and so be religious in nature, or they may be secular. Because they so often deal with dramatic events in the life cycle, they are sometimes called "crisis rites."

All the Great Tradition religions accept converts (although Judaism still does so reluctantly). Tribal religions, on the other hand, are limited to members born or adopted into the group (Dobyns 1960:114–117, 444–458). Christianity began as a tribal religion; it took explicit doctrinal change to open the belief to non-Jews (Walker 1959:23). The change was vital to the spread of Christianity, which otherwise would have remained a Jewish sect. Two tribal religions cannot compete for recruits, since neither has a mechanism for accepting any. Members of tribal religions often resist conversion to one of the Great Tradition religions because they do not believe such a thing is possible. Le Jeune was often frustrated by this lack of comprehension. When he pointed out that the French regularly violated Montagnais tabus without any of the expected unpleasant consequences, the Montagnais were unshaken in their faith because they did not think the two situations were comparable. The French were not Montagnais, so what they did in regard to tabus was irrelevant. When Le Jeune tried to insist that the Montagnais abide by certain restrictions, they could not understand why they should have to abide by French rules. They persisted in thinking in terms of a French heaven and a Montagnais afterworld. Relatives had themselves baptized so they could all be in the same afterworld, or refused baptism because they did not want to be separated after death. Some individuals who claimed to have visited heaven and returned insisted that the Montagnais were badly treated there by the French. The idea of a single heaven and hell was a difficult concept to communicate.

PRACTICES

The Montagnais and Le Jeune differed far more in their practices than they did in their beliefs. A list of practices taken from the excerpt is given here. If we compare the two lists and add what is generally known about Christian practices of the time, some obvious differences are revealed. Christians usually have permanent religious buildings separate from their homes and do not normally erect a special structure inside the house for each ceremony. Most of the major Christian groups do not expect their religious leaders to go into a trance, nor do they want them hidden from sight during ceremonies. Christians tend to be suspicious of trances and of hidden activities.

Religious Practices

Montagnais

A. Based on the first ceremony described by Le Jeune:

1. For certain ceremonies, the Montagnais build a separate structure inside their dwellings.
2. All lights and fires are extinguished for ceremonies.
3. One religious specialist, isolated and out of sight, makes various noises and is responsible for shaking the walls of the religious structure. (In other societies such behavior usually indicates that the specialist has gone into a trance, but since Le Jeune was not observing the "juggler" directly, he reported nothing that enables us to be certain about this.)
4. All the spectators are expected to participate by calling out encouragement to the spirits, by singing, by dancing, and in general by obeying the directions of another specialist.
5. Another specialist, who is not isolated and who is not in a trance state, carries out the interrogation of the spirits.

B. Based on the second ceremony:

1. Women and children are deliberately excluded from some ceremonies. (They were probably not present at the first ceremony either, but Le Jeune gives no information about this.)
2. Certain females may actually play a part in some ceremonies.
3. The specialist does other things besides direct the singing and dancing. He mimics the activities he is trying to cause, digs in the ground, sings and dances himself, and so on.
4. Spectators take an active role in some ceremonies and may assist the specialist directly in addition to singing and dancing at his command.

Le Jeune

A. Based on the first ceremony:

The only direct evidence of Le Jeune's behavior is his statement that he talked to the Montagnais during the ceremony. He was also, clearly, an observer of what was happening, and not in any way a participant. His reactions provide some indirect evidence as to what his behavior as a religious specialist probably was, and of course other information is available from a general study of Jesuit practices.

1. Whatever behavior Le Jeune might have engaged in as a religious specialist, it clearly was *not* the sort of behavior he was witnessing among the Montagnais.
2. Christian religious specialists would not take an active part in non-Christian ceremonies, although they might observe them.

B. Based on the second ceremony:

1. Christian religious specialists recited prayers even when there was no specific ceremony in progress.
2. There were a certain number of prayers that were to be recited, and this task was to be completed regularly (daily) in spite of distractions.
3. Christian specialists did not engage in activity designed to kill people.

The role of women in Christian ceremonies is almost unique among the world's religions. On the one hand, women are supposed to be devout spectators, present at almost all ceremonies. On the other hand, until recently women were not supposed to participate in the ceremonies *except* as spectators or in very minor roles. In many of the other religions of the world, women are either excluded entirely from participation or even observation of many ceremonies or else are permitted to become religious specialists themselves. Le Jeune reports that women (except for one with a special role to play) were excluded from the ceremonies. This complete exclusion of women must have seemed strange to the Jesuit, and the active participation of the only female exception, even stranger. Moreover, in Le Jeune's religion, nonspecialists were not allowed the sort of active role the Montagnais seemed to expect from their average male citizen (and the exceptional female).

The Montagnais differed from Le Jeune's society in the kinds of specialists they had. All except the simplest of societies have specialists who deal with the supernatural. (In the simplest societies, each individual acts as his own "specialist," but even there, some may be recognized as better at it than others.) The Montagnais, with a relatively simple society based on hunting, had at least two types of part-time religious specialists. Neither of these behaved the way Le Jeune expected such persons to behave in *his* system. In other words, the French and Montagnais roles of the religious specialist had quite different contents. Le Jeune distinguished the two Montagnais types by using the term *juggler* for one and the terms *sorcerer* or *magician* for the other. From Le Jeune's point of view, the term *juggler* was more derogatory; it meant a trickster, a ventriloquist, a sleight-of-hand artist. He compared the juggler at one point to the puppeteers of France. A magician or sorcerer, on the other hand, was one who could interact with evil supernatural beings. Although Le Jeune called one of the Montagnais a magician or a sorcerer, he wrote that he would leave it to the reader to decide "if this man is really a Magician," or not. Le Jeune obviously thought he was not. A more subtle indication of Le Jeune's skepticism is that when he wrote about a "real" magician or sorcerer in this excerpt, he used a capital "M" or "S," but when he wrote about the Montagnais specialist, he always used a lower case "m" or "s."

Several characteristics of the religious specialists anthropologists call *shamans* ° are mentioned by Le Jeune in the excerpt. A shaman is supposed to have personal supernatural power, whereas a priest does not. Le Jeune indicates that the Montagnais believed the juggler could separate his soul from his body and could continue to control it. His detached soul could shake the tent and could attract supernatural beings to the tent. The disembodied spirit could also make a variety of noises. In other reports of similar ceremonies, the religious specialist might be bound before being placed in the tent (Leach 1949:56–57). The activity that then takes place is regarded as proof that the spirit, and not the physical body of the specialist, is making its presence felt and heard. On some occasions, the bound specialist disappears from the tent and appears outside after the ceremony. (Perhaps this is what Le Jeune observed when he mentioned that the juggler "made his exit from the tent and from our little cabin so swiftly, that he was outside almost before I was aware of it.")

A shaman often intervenes with the supernatural world for the benefit of man. A priest generally explains the will of the supernatural to man, but his intervention, if any, is usually limited to suggesting a course of action to the petitioner and occasionally performing a ritual or prayer for him. Le Jeune describes the effort made by one specialist to attract the spirits and by another to interrogate them. In the second ceremony, he reports the attempt of one sorcerer to use the supernatural against another. In some societies, a shaman may invade the supernatural world and even do battle with supernatural beings to compel them to grant human wishes (Howells 1962:127).

Another characteristic of shamans is that they are highly indi-

A Zulu medicine man warding off a coming hailstorm. *Courtesy of the Ameri-can Museum of Natural History*

vidualistic and neither learn nor teach a highly organized body of doctrine. A shaman may learn a few specialized techniques from other shamans, but such knowledge is individually held and individually passed from one to another. Most of the shaman's power and knowledge comes from direct personal revelation obtained through visions and dreams. A priest ° is a member of an organized group of religious specialists and learns an organized body of doctrine, often in a special school. The Montagnais had no such school or organized doctrine. Other parts of Le Jeune's report indicate that the Montagnais specialists were highly individualistic. Their specialists are accordingly classified as closer to shamans than to priests. The distinction between a shaman and a priest is useful for purposes of analysis, but as is true of so many human patterns, the behavioral reality is often closer to a continuum than to a dichotomy. Many religious specialists seem to behave in ways that are intermediate between the analytical extremes. In dealing with specific societies, anthropologists have therefore tended to use a term in the local dialect, or to translate it, if possible, into such terms as "star gazer" or "fortune teller."

Le Jeune mentions some other characteristics of religious behavior. Absolute darkness was required for the ceremony, the spirits being reluctant to approach in the light. This fondness for darkness and dislike of light as characteristic of spirits is a belief held the world over. Many religions believe that night is a time for heightened supernatural activity. Folk Christianity, particularly in the past, generally assumed that nocturnal spirits were evil. A form of light is involved in almost all Christian ceremonies, and expressions such as "ye are the light of the world" form a part of Christian religious writings. Other Middle Eastern religions (for example, Zoroastrianism) also correlate darkness with evil and light with good, but such a correlation is by no means universal.

Participants in the Montagnais ceremonies were expected to sing and dance. In American Indian rituals, dance is often a form of prayer as important to the proper conduct of a ceremony as verbal prayers and songs. The removal of dancing from religious ceremonies is almost unique to Christianity and may have been a reaction to its importance in other religions that were regarded as devil worship.

When the spirit or soul was separated from the shaman's body, it manifested its presence by sparks and noises. Thus, the hooting of owls and the strange voices mentioned in the excerpt are still regarded by some American Indians as evidence of supernatural activity. The owl particularly is frequently associated with the supernatural, perhaps because of its nocturnal activities. Le Jeune reported that the Montagnais disagreed as to exactly what happened inside the tent during the ceremony. Some felt the shaman had actually disappeared; others thought only his soul moved. Le Jeune regarded this disagreement as evidence that the Montagnais beliefs were false, since *his* system had no tolerance for disagreement. The

Montagnais, without a formally organized doctrine, were less concerned with individually variant beliefs.

Spirit possession of religious specialists is another characteristic found the world over. It is known in Christianity, although it has usually been regarded as characteristic of fringe sects, or as possession by the devil. Saints or individuals capable of performing miracles have not usually been regarded so much as possessed by supernaturals as being able to influence or attract their favor in some way.

THE ORIGINS OF RELIGION: SOME HYPOTHESES

What is the origin of religion? Why does man engage in this kind of behavior at all? A believer would answer by pointing out the need to take some account of the supernatural world, but that answer does not satisfy everyone. Is it possible to find another basis for the origin of religion? As far as we know, man is the only animal who wonders where he came from, or what his purpose in life may be. Wolves, sparrows, ants—all go through life untroubled by the search for identity or meaning that bedevils man. Modern theology and much of modern philosophical thinking are still devoted to man's search for understanding, for purpose, for some higher or more certain reality than what appears immediately obvious. Man also is apparently the only animal who can lose motivation and, as a result, die. Other animals may give up the struggle because of exhaustion or privation, but apparently only man can worry or brood himself into suicide. A detailed discussion of all the hypotheses that have been advanced to account for this behavior or for the origin of man's religious beliefs is too complex and extensive for us to take up here. We can, however, make a beginning.

How old is religion? How long has man engaged in religious behavior? What is the earliest evidence for its existence? These are questions we can answer. The earliest documents recovered so far are from the cradle of civilization in Mesopotamia, and they reveal an already well-established system. Religion began long before writing. Evidence from earlier periods is necessarily indirect, but inferences have been made from the available data, and analogies from modern or historical religious systems have been used to support those inferences.

Art, dating from the Upper Paleolithic period (in Europe some 25,000 to 15,000 years ago), is helpful. Cave paintings of creatures that are part human, part animal can hardly be representations of

A cave painting by bushmen in Bechuanaland. *De Wys, Inc.*

reality; they are more likely symbolic of supernatural beings. Small figurines with exaggerated female sexual characteristics and no facial features, hands, or feet are also more likely representations of a fertility principle than portraits. Some of the famous cave paintings of the type found at Altamira in Spain or Lascaux in France show wounded animals. One suggestion is that these paintings were made to ensure success in the hunt by imitating the desired result (Howell 1965:148). If this suggestion is correct, the paintings would indicate that one of the major principles of magic had already been developed. Some of the paintings were done in virtually inaccessible parts of the caves. Their location is difficult to explain on the basis of an esthetic motivation for art. In other cases, several paintings were superimposed, although other parts of the cave walls were left empty. Again, this is difficult to explain if the paintings were being done for esthetic reasons. If, however, one speculates that a particular spot was believed to be supernaturally powerful, then the choice is a logical one. The cave paintings therefore suggest that some of the major concepts of religion had developed by this time.

Art itself early served to maintain man's motivation and morale. With surprising suddenness, artistic evidence appears on the archeological scene. Necklaces, beads, and other ornaments were made, tools were decorated or carved far beyond utilitarian needs. We do not know the reasons for this florescence of art. It may have had something to do with the biological evolution of man's brain, or there may have been some other cause. Additional archeological research may shed some light on the issue (Chard 1969:154).

Were there any other art forms besides carving and painting at this time? From some of the paintings we can infer that dancing was present, but the verbal arts left no direct traces until the beginning of writing, thousands of years later. If there was dancing, there may have been music, but again, there is no direct evidence as yet. Folklorists have traced the spread of certain tales, or themes in tales, usually attributing greater antiquity to tales or themes that have spread farthest. Because of the varying capacity of different peoples for travel, however, this is a risky generalization. Further elucidation of the age and origin of the verbal arts probably awaits the development of a functional time machine.

During recorded history at least, all the arts have served to entertain, instruct, and inspire men. There is no reason to assume that their function when they first appeared was substantially different. They almost surely enhanced the effectiveness of religion and have shown throughout history a strong capacity to assist in the maintenance of morale and motivation in their own right, even when they were not directly tied into the service of religion.

The cave paintings and statuettes, however, are not the first evidence we have of religious beliefs. Neanderthal man, who lived 70,000 to 150,000 years ago during the last glacial period, and whose skeletal remains are associated with the cultural assemblage known as Mousterian,° buried his dead, sometimes with grave offerings, and often sprinkled or painted them with red ocher ° (a natural iron-oxide pigment) (Chard 1969:222). We do not know anything else about the religious beliefs of this early kind of man, but we assume from the burial evidence that he believed in some sort of afterlife.

For an earlier time, we cannot rely heavily on present evidence. It has been suggested that Pekin man, a type of *Homo erectus* ° who

FACING PAGE: One of the Colossi of Memnon, built to guard a funerary temple in Egypt. From ancient times men have buried their dead with elaborate grave offerings and monuments. *Elliot Erwitt/Magnum*

lived from 250,000 to 500,000 years ago, may have extracted brains from the skulls of his dead for religious purposes (Roper 1969: 427ff.). So many alternative explanations have been advanced for the available evidence, however, that we cannot make even that tentative suggestion with any certainty. As more and more information is accumulated on the early forms of man, it is possible that we will be able to answer questions about the antiquity of religion more positively. At present, it appears that Neanderthal man may have been the first to have had some form of religion, but future discoveries may reveal that religion is even older.

THE FUNCTIONS OF RELIGION

What accounts for the wide distribution and persistence of religion? Why do people react with so much emotion to a threatened change in religion? (Witness the furor over the American Supreme Court decision to keep prayers and Bible readings out of the school; the protests over changes in the Roman Catholic mass; the turmoil over the Pope's encyclical *Humanae Vitae.*) One approach to these questions has been to concentrate on the functions religion seems to serve in society. The various hypotheses by anthropologists and sociologists seem to fall into three major categories:
1. Religion relieves anxieties in areas of life over which man has little or no control.
2. Religion integrates and binds together members of the society.
3. Religion justifies and explains customs and traditions.

In Le Jeune's report of the first ceremony, questions were asked by the sorcerer about weather conditions, the location of game, and the outcome of specific cases of disease. An examination of ceremonies in other parts of the world frequently reveals a similar preoccupation with weather, food sources, and individual well-being. These are all matters that bear on individual and consequently on societal survival. They are all areas in which man, particularly non-Western man, has little or no control. Humans everywhere are concerned with health (particularly when it is bad) and with food (particularly when the supply is not adequate or reliable). The relationship of the weather to food is obvious for agricultural peoples, but weather is also significant to hunters, although not in quite the same way. The Montagnais depended on snow in winter to track game more easily. With snowshoes, they could travel over deep snow that exhausted or confined heavier mammals such as moose, elk, and deer. The pronouncement of the spirits that they saw "a little" snow must have been disheartening to the Montagnais, but at least they would not sit in camp waiting for snow. The moose were far away, which was also bad news, but at least a man could hunt other game and would not waste his time trying to find moose.

Le Jeune scorned the spirit response in regard to the health of the sorcerer and his wife because the prophecies seemed obvious to him, but were they so obvious to the sorcerer? The sorcerer's own disease may have been uncomfortable enough to make him uneasy about the possible outcome. In the case of his wife, he might have hoped that the spirits could suggest a course of action to save her. In any event, even though the prediction about his wife was

A religious procession on Good Friday in San Fertello, Italy. *David Seymour/ Magnum*

bad, he was no longer anxious because he *knew* what would happen. Psychologists tell us that uncertainty may be harder to bear than an unpleasant certainty. The second ceremony Le Jeune described indicates how an individual may relieve anxiety by positive action. It would therefore seem that the Montagnais evidence supports the hypothesis that religion relieves anxieties. Other anthropologists have pointed out that religion may also create anxiety. The Christian sinner, the Navajo who touches a corpse, the Polynesian who breaks a tabu—all suffer varying degrees of anxiety directly caused by religion. The religion itself usually provides a way to cope with such anxieties, however.

Another function suggested for religion is that it serves to integrate the community. There are many activities that bind people together, of course, and not all of them can be classed as religious. Suggesting that one function of religion is to integrate a community is *not* the same as saying that *only* religious rites integrate a community or that integration of a community is the *only* function of religion. Examine the excerpt by Le Jeune once again. Adult males of the community were called in to cooperate in the ceremonies. In the ritual aimed at killing an enemy sorcerer, the situation clearly defined group members as defending one of their own against external hostility. Both ceremonies emphasized the bonds between group members and reinforced their sense of community. But women and children were excluded from these ceremonies. Would this not work against the integration of the society? The very fact of exclusion could add to the solidarity of the men and could even increase a sense of solidarity among the women, since they were all in the category of excluded people. Historical documentation reveals integrative elements other than religious ones that bound women and children into the larger society. The Montagnais example as presented in the excerpt supports the hypothesis that religion may serve an integrative function in society.

The description of other rituals also tends to support the hypothesis. Any of the crisis rites, religious or otherwise, serves to integrate a society by uniting people in a cooperative endeavor, by clearly making public a change in the status of members, and by reaffirming group concepts. (Reciting values or behaviors appropriate to the new status is often a part of crisis rites.) When crisis rites involve the supernatural, religion is again playing an integrative role in the society. Individuals or groups within a society may feel a special relationship to things in the environment, which are called *totems*.° Ceremonies involving these serve to integrate the society. The strength of the bond that some peoples feel exists be-

A meeting of Black Muslims in the United States. Greater numbers of followers seem to be attracted to religious movements in a society under stress. *Roger Malloch/Magnum*

tween them and an animal or object in the environment has intrigued researchers for years, yet the similarity of totemism to modern Western practices of selecting a group mascot or symbol went unnoticed for some time (Linton 1936:424–426). The use of a group symbol is clearly integrative regardless of whether the supernatural is involved. When it is involved, then once again religion is helping to integrate the society.

Another type of religious behavior, called revitalization,° nativistic revival,° or messianic movement,° is also of interest. Under certain circumstances, a society may experience a religious upheaval. A charismatic leader appears, a "new" doctrine is promulgated (which actually may be only a modification of an old doctrine), followers are attracted, converts with strong and even fanatical convictions increase, and the whole society may be swept up in a mass movement that often radically and permanently changes the nature of the system. Studies of such cases seem to indicate that they occur when a society is suffering severe stress or has just passed through a period of disaster and demoralization (Mooney 1965:2ff.). The new religious formulation appears to strengthen and reunify the society. Not enough is known about these movements yet to be able to explain precisely why they have this effect. One suggestion is that the new doctrine relieves anxieties caused by the stress and provides an acceptable rationale for changes (or persistences) in behavior. By doing this, the movement reestablishes the morale and motivation of individuals in the society. Since this is a prerequisite for survival, a revitalization movement once again makes a system viable.

The integrative hypothesis has been criticized on the basis that religion has caused innumerable conflicts and friction both within and between societies. Violent conflicts based on religion still occur today (the current Protestant-Catholic trouble in Northern Ireland is an example, and the Middle Eastern situation is aggravated by the religious differences of the participants). However, cases where religion divides rather than integrates all appear to be instances of competition between two or more belief systems. Apparently, so long as there is only one religious system within a society, it serves to integrate the members of that society. Competition between two or more systems, however, creates intense factionalism and may completely rupture the society. The most severe competition between religious systems occurs if both are exclusive and missionary religions. Two tribal religions either cannot compete for members, or—if the belief system is inclusive—may assimilate.

Religion is also said to support the values of the society by providing an explanation and justification for customs and traditions. The short excerpt by Le Jeune does not illustrate this characteristic, but his longer report does. For example, bones of certain game animals were burned rather than being thrown to the dogs, because the Montagnais believed the generalized spirit of these animals would be offended if dogs ate the bones and would then not permit any more of the animals to be caught. Le Jeune and other Europeans were continually being frustrated in their attempts to change Indian behavior (as distinct from their beliefs) because the Indians protested that the new behavior was offensive to the supernatural or that continuation of the old behavior was essential to maintain good relationships with the supernatural.

These functions (which are not necessarily the only possible functions a religion may perform in a specific society) help to explain the emotion an attack on religion arouses. To a believer, an attack on his religion cannot be regarded simply as a matter of criticism of some abstract philosophical hypothesis. It is a threat to his personal survival, to the society in which he lives, and to the values in which he believes. It should not surprise anyone that missionaries so often become martyrs.

SUMMARY

One of the prerequisites for the survival of a society, then, is the maintenance of morale and motivation among its members. People in the society must get satisfaction and justification from doing what needs to be done. Man seems particularly prone to questions about the value of life and of what he is doing as a member of society. In modern society, particularly recently, individuals have been torn by doubts as to the worth of many of the basic assumptions, values, and practices of the system. It is extremely difficult, perhaps impossible, to arrive at an objective conclusion that this way of life is better than that way. In most societies of the past and in a few of the present, such questions have been settled by an appeal to tradition (this is the way our fathers did it, so it is good enough for us), to ethnic group pride (I am a Hopi and this is the Hopi way), or to the supernatural (this way is best because it is the way God commanded). All these reasons provided most members of a given society with a reason for what they did and with a deep satisfaction and security when they performed properly in the expected manner. The rewards for meeting expectations, however demanding, were consequently greater than the difficulties and frustrations encountered in trying to meet them. Perhaps a perception of this satisfaction is the source of the idyllic picture of "savage life" so often presented by the uneasy and critical members of an industrialized society.

Today, none of these ancient supports seem acceptable to members of mass industrial societies. There have been attempts to shore up customs by appeals to logic, to utility, to humanitarianism, or to some other rational foundation, but so far nothing has gained the general emotional commitment of earlier methods. Until something is found that can permit or create the kind of satisfaction and security people previously obtained from the proper performance of their societal roles, modern societies will continue to be disrupted by the dissatisfied, the alienated, and the discontented.

8 Concepts
and Trends in
Anthropology

Man has been interesting to man for centuries. C. Leonard Woolley reports that there was a kind of museum in Ur, one of the earliest sites of civilization (Woolley 1965:204). Herodotus is famous for his descriptions of "foreign" cultures. Since the beginning of writing (and possibly long before), there has been speculation about foreign or "different" cultures and about the possible reasons for the variations. Anthropology—the study of man—is only the most recent label attached to this interest.

A SHORT DESCRIPTION OF THE FIELD

Modern anthropology, as the word is used in the United States, is divided into two major areas. One, physical anthropology,° deals with man as a biological organism; this is the only part of the discipline most Europeans call "anthropology." It includes the study of physical variation in man, human diseases, human physical development, geographic distribution of biological characteristics, processes of evolutionary change, and any other physical or biological matters involving man. Because of the interest in evolution, some physical anthropologists have also engaged in extensive study of primates other than man and in paleontology ° (the study of fossils). Very little information from physical anthropology was used in this book, and that mostly in the first chapter. The other major division of anthropology deals with man as a social and cultural being. Here man's learned concepts are studied through the behavior stemming from them. This division has three distinct branches: linguistics,° archeology,° and cultural anthropology.

Linguistics is the study of the structure of language. People interested in this field have occasionally pursued their studies without paying any but incidental attention to the speakers or the meaning of the sounds made. They have concentrated on sound patterns and the organized structure of the speech itself. Many, of course, have studied other culturally motivated human behavior besides speech or have concentrated on ascertaining the meaning of words. Still, linguists often differ from other anthropologists in being less involved with the people they study. We have used some of the research in linguistics in the chapter on socialization.

Archeology at times can be as divorced from human behavior as linguistics. Some archeologists have concentrated on the physical characteristics of artifacts such as pottery, metal objects, or stone tools to such an extent that these have completely overshadowed their makers. Other archeologists have paid more attention to the human behavior that resulted in or made use of the artifacts found. Classical archeologists traditionally were interested in reconstructing the past. In their almost exclusive concentration on the art objects and inscriptions of early civilizations in the Mediterranean area, however, they discovered much about kings, rulers, and the upper classes, but very little about the daily life of ordinary people, and they ignored the rest of the world almost entirely. Traditionally, archeologists working in this area have been allied with classics departments rather than with anthropology. In recent decades, anthropologists using a wide variety of new techniques for analysis and recovery have been concentrating on a fuller reconstruction of past cultures not only in the Mediterranean area, but all over the world. The trend in this direction has led to articles calling archeology the new social science. Archeological data are used in this book especially for material included in the first and second chapters.

Throughout this text, however, we have been primarily concerned with the third branch, cultural anthropology. In the United States, the term *cultural anthropology* is more or less restricted to this branch, although both archeology and linguistics deal with culture at least occasionally, and their data (artifacts or verbal behavior) are all culturally motivated. In most of the rest of the world, what Americans call cultural anthropology is referred to as "ethnology" and is regarded as distinct from "anthropology." The British compromise and refer to "social anthropology." Unless all these terms are kept in mind, books on "anthropology" written by Europeans can be confusing to Americans.

Only a brief introduction to the field of cultural anthropology (or ethnology or social anthropology) is contained in this volume. For example, each of the separate topics discussed in Chapters 1 through 7 could serve as the basis for one or more college courses. The data of anthropology are incredibly rich, and any introductory text can present only a bare minimum or run the risk of overwhelming the student. Two major interesting areas of anthropology have not even been mentioned as such, since they are broad enough to encompass all the topics we have discussed. Applied anthropology (also called culture change) and theory were left for this chapter, although some theoretical concepts have been integrated into previous chapters when appropriate.

It should be clear by now that anthropology is a field that offers something for almost everyone. If a student is interested in chemistry or biology, he could easily specialize in some phase of physical anthropology; if he is interested in law, the subdiscipline of primitive law and government beckons; if his interest lies in the area of economics, the subfield of economic anthropology is open; if his interest is in the humanities, particularly art, folklore, music, or dance, these fields, too, are recognized subdisciplines in anthropology. The field of culture and personality is closely allied with psychology, while that of social organization is closer to sociology. There is virtually no field of interest that does not relate to anthropology in some way. Even nuclear physics has become involved in the development of more accurate ways to date archeological and paleontological material.

DIRECTED SOCIAL CHANGE

Applied anthropology is one of the most exciting and controversial areas of anthropology today because it is immediately involved in problems of directed social change. This involvement raises a host of ethical questions. Who has the right to judge other people? Who says that one way of life is better than another? What justification has anyone for changing the lives of other people? None of these questions is easy to answer, although some people seem to think they are. Many individuals would immediately insist that no one has any right to judge other societies, that one way of life is just as good as another, and that no one has the right to direct other people's lives. Unfortunately, it becomes difficult to maintain this distant perspective when, for example, people plead for help to stop an epidemic that is wiping out their children. It is difficult to tell them that since one system is just as good as another, their own medical concepts and techniques should be able to cope with the epidemic. If their system were effective, they would not be asking for help. The fact that their system cannot cope with the epidemic while Western medical technology *can* suggests that it may be possible to show that one system really is better than another, at least for some purposes. At that point the ideal of cultural relativity ° is threatened and must be either abandoned or radically modified.

Perhaps Western medicine is more effective for treating certain kinds of sickness, but medicine is only one aspect of culture. Even if we can evaluate medical concepts comparatively, can we judge others? And if we can, should we? Can we not just help people with their medical problem and leave the rest of their culture alone? This is the position many people, including doctors who actually deliver medical help, have taken. They are there to heal the sick, and they have no intention of meddling with the rest of the culture. Unfortunately, that is impossible. Culture is an organized whole, not a random collection of bits and pieces. It is not possible to change one part without having any effect on the rest. If we put ourselves in the position of simply delivering treatment, is that not a new imperialism? The poor have-not countries must depend on outsiders to save their very lives. What people would not resent this, and resent the society that kept a monopoly on its vital medical knowledge? Most human beings want some control, particularly in this vital area of life and death. They not only want treatment, they want to understand the process and be able to practice it themselves. Are we being fair if we deny the information to them? Most people would answer "No" on humanitarian grounds alone, regardless of the political implications denial would have. So we find ourselves committed to helping countries that ask for aid not only by giving them treatment, but also by training their own people in modern medical technology and concepts.

Western medicine does not consist simply of injections, pills, and surgery. It is based on a coherent body of theory that must be imported along with techniques if the whole system is to work. We must at least teach the germ theory of disease, since it is the cornerstone of our medical technology. The germ theory, however, is almost certain to be in disagreement with medical concepts in premodern societies, and these concepts are apt to be imbedded in religion. Remember that weather and disease control are the two main topics with which religion is involved around the world. The germ theory may run counter to the recipient society's religious concepts; if people accept the basic concepts of Western medicine, their belief in their own religious system may weaken. If one area of religious faith is undermined, other areas of religion are usually weakened too. Since only medical concepts are being introduced, nothing is available to replace lost religious faith. This can be disastrous for the culture if no one has anticipated the problem.

Besides endangering the religion of the society and thereby running the risk of undermining the morale and motivation that keeps it vital, other areas of life will be affected by the introduction of modern medicine even if the germ theory is never accepted by the majority of the people. Western medicine teaches that health depends on certain sanitary practices. Regular baths and the careful disposal of excrement instead of keeping it around in an outhouse are not whimsical notions on the part of the older generation. They have the practical functions of keeping down vermin, skin problems such as impetigo,° and dangerous disease organisms. The almost immediate outbreak of disease when water systems are disrupted and the incidence of head lice among the unwashed generation in the United States indicates that the American population is not protected by any special Providence. It is subject to the same laws of disease propagation as the rest of the world, however distasteful that thought may be to some Americans.

In trying to introduce modern Western medicine to societies that have asked for it, changes have to be promoted in such areas of life as where people urinate and defecate; what they eat and how they prepare it; how often they wash themselves and their clothing, and so on. In addition, by changing the death rate in these countries without also changing the birth rate, modern medicine is making a major contribution to the population explosion that is rapidly making the earth too small for us all. If urination, defecation, diet, and cleanliness are thought to be sensitive topics, wait till birth control is attempted! Changing the sexual habits of a people is usually incredibly difficult, yet can the attempt be avoided? Moreover, there the change agent is doing just what we said should not be done at the start of this section, and it does not seem to matter whether the change agent is a member (or employee) of the elite governing group in the country being changed or an imported specialist. If local elites attempt to bring about the changes described, they are almost sure to be accused of being puppets of Yankee imperialists, communist dupes, Uncle Toms (or an equivalent term), or the sad results of brain washing. The change agent, native or foreign, will inevitably have been trained outside his own country and the tragedy of the foreign-trained specialist is that he usually finds himself as alienated from his own people as is any outsider. The *change* itself is the problem, more than the agent. We got into the mess by (1) agreeing to help people who asked for it and (2) trying to avoid a new imperialism by spreading our knowledge instead of keeping it a monopoly—surely both laudable goals from humanitarian as well as political points of view.

Very well, let us avoid the impasse by refusing to aid people in the first place, or by refusing to share knowledge with them. Imagine the screams from the rest of the world. Besides, have we any right to play God and doom people to die when we could save them? Especially if they ask for our help? This moral dilemma is one most of the younger generation (and many of the older) have so far either not realized or have refused to face. It is much easier just to parrot the simple answers mentioned at the beginning of this section. One reason why more people have not confronted the dilemma earlier is that they do not realize it is impossible to solve a major problem in a society without changing that society in some way. Doctors prompted by the most humane motives think only of the lives they are saving. They either do not think about how these additional people are to be fed, housed, clothed, and protected by the society, or if they do, they accept no responsibility for helping to accomplish it—after all, their field is medicine, not social planning. In a society unable to take care of its present population adequately, future increases pose a dreadful threat.

Since culture is not a random assortment of discrete items, it is not possible to change just one thing. All the parts are interrelated. When people have tried to make only one change—even with the best intentions and at the urgent request of the society involved—other changes have occurred anyway. Because they have been unanticipated for the most part, the results have generally been disastrous. The annals of culture change are full of the dismal results of sincere but misguided assistance.

How can the unhappy consequences of change be avoided? While it may not be possible to escape them entirely, their effects can certainly be reduced. If people working in other cultures—in any capacity whatsoever—accept the facts that (1) culture is an organized whole and (2) changing one part is bound to cause changes in other parts, they will realize that to do their job well they must understand the specific culture of the society they are working in and some of the dynamics of how cultures in general function and change.

THEORY: A BRIEF SURVEY

In this context, the importance and relevance of theory should be obvious. Theory attempts to explain interrelationships and systems so that they can be better understood, predicted, and controlled. Without some theoretical understanding, anyone trying to work in a cross-cultural situation is in the position of a man looking for a gas leak with a lighted candle. He may accomplish his task, but he will destroy everything around him in the process.

Unfortunately, theory is still weak in cultural anthropology. The field is relatively new, data are still pouring in, and all the information has not yet been integrated into a single coherent body. We have learned a few things, however, and there have been various attempts to establish a theoretical base for anthropology. A rash of data production has usually been followed by a spell of attempting to digest the mass of facts. Theories and generalizations spawned during such a phase have prompted more field research to test them. Because most of the theories have not survived without major modification, the process is still one of cycles, each of which adds a bit of real understanding.

Even though the task is far from complete, some progress has been made in understanding and organization of data over the years. As recently as 1940, there were still some people (such as Alfred Kroeber) who were masters of the entire field of anthropology, including the physical, archeological, linguistic, and ethnological branches. This is not possible today. Although all well-trained anthropologists have some familiarity with every branch, no one can now claim expertise in all. The data explosion has hit the social sciences too.

One of the earliest "schools" in anthropology grew out of the excitement surrounding Charles Darwin's formulation of evolution and natural selection. In this approach, whose most famous exponents were Edward Tylor and Lewis H. Morgan, it was held that all societies had passed through various stages of development from primitive to civilized. But the pattern of *unilinear* evolutionary development did not stand up under the impact of additional data. It has been almost entirely abandoned in American anthropology, although it *still* crops up occasionally in newspapers and in popular articles. Since World War II, however, a modified version has been revived. Today most anthropologists would accept certain evolutionary generalizations *applied to mankind's culture as a whole:*

1. It is possible to demonstrate a continuum from simple to complex in several areas of human behavior such as law, government, technology, and economy. It is not necessary, however, to postulate that every society experiences each level, or even that change has always occurred in the direction of simple to complex. (We know of societies that have abandoned agriculture to take up

hunting and gathering, for example, although the latter is usually regarded as a simpler subsistence form.)

2. In certain aspects of culture such as economy, law, and technology, complex developments are *dependent* on preexisting simpler forms, although these need not have been developed in the society with the complex form. (Thus the development of the equipment for riding a horse—saddle, bridle, bit, stirrup—could not have occurred until after animal domestication; yet the society that first rode horses was apparently *not* the society that first domesticated animals.)

No single society can be shown to have passed through all the stages of simple to complex in all aspects of life where such a progression has been found. Societies change, appear, disappear, combine, and separate. There is not one that has an unbroken continuity back to the beginning of man, and yet all are equally old in the sense that the members of any one have as long an evolutionary history as the members of any other. Mischa Titiev (a well-known anthropologist currently associated with the University of Michigan) presented four generalizations (he called them "laws") that apply to the development of man as a whole:

1. The law of increasing reliance on culture
2. The law of expanding use of natural resources
3. The law of the declining percentage of individual knowledge, with its corollaries (*a*) increasing specialization and (*b*) necessary cooperation
4. The laws of the conservation of time and human muscular energy (Titiev 1963:369–382).

Modification of some of these generalizations has been necessary. For example, the rules of the conservation of time and human muscular energy do not hold completely in certain aspects of life, such as religion, recreation, and art. Games are not usually promoted on the basis that one is quicker or easier to play than another. A new religious belief is not adopted because it is faster and less physically demanding to practice. Innovations are not accepted in art solely because they are easier and quicker. Although a few developments follow the pattern of the conservation of time and human muscular energy, many do not. Other factors determine acceptance or rejection of innovation in these aspects of life. The law of increasing utilization of natural resources also needs some modification, since there is good evidence that industrialization has actually decreased utilization of the food resources exploited by

hunters and gatherers.   There may have been an overall increase in
the variety and quantity of exploited resources *in general* and certain resources—such as minerals—may be exploited much more
intensively, but this increase has not occurred in *all* resources.   Despite these minor modifications, Titiev's laws or tendencies are useful to know and can easily be applied to situations of culture change.
The importance of the law of the declining percentage of individual
knowledge and its corollaries has already been stressed several
times.   Innovations that run counter to trends are less likely to be
adopted than those which promote them.

When the first negative reaction to the evolutionist approach
developed, anthropologists began to focus on the description of cultures and the distribution of specific characteristics as traits.°   A
few exponents went to the extreme and tried to trace *all* cultures to
a single origin.   This approach is still popular in the nonscientific
literature.   People who attribute all civilization to Atlantis or Le-
muria, or who attribute Polynesian culture to the South American
Andes, are intellectual descendants of the extreme diffusionist
school.°   One of the most exaggerated positions was promoted by
G. Elliot Smith, who attributed all civilization to Egyptian missionaries fanning out over the world to spread Egyptian culture and the
worship of the Sun God.

People interested in folklore have traced stories or single story
elements ° all over the world.   Frazer, in his extensive collection of
religious beliefs and practices (published in *The Golden Bough*),
organized a great deal of data which were used by diffusionists who
were not as extreme as Smith (Frazer 1955).   A more complex formulation postulated several centers of culture that spread a variety
of patterns.   The complex interaction of all these was held to be
responsible for the astonishing variations in culture found in different parts of the globe.   Wilhelm Schmidt and Fritz Graebner were
primarily responsible for this hypothesis, and they formed what was
known as the culture-historical ° school (Herskovits 1951:510–514),
but which is better known by its German name of *Kulturkreiselehre*, translated as the culture sphere or circle school.   Its modern
descendants no longer look for single centers, but they still trace historical connections between cultures on the basis of the distribution
of culture elements ° (Fischer, J. 1971:personal communication).

The extreme diffusionists and even the culture-historical school
were eventually discredited by the continuing influx of new data.
Critics pointed out that many of the traits diffusionists labeled as
identical bore only a superficial resemblance to one another and
were actually no more alike than the words *nein* in German and *nine*

in English. Alexander Goldenweiser pointed out that for some things there is a "limitation of possibilities." That is, there are a finite number of ways to make an effective canoe paddle or a container to hold water. A round piece of cloth (or even wood) will not work for either purpose. As mentioned in Chapter 6, there are only four basic forms of heterosexual marriage. Consequently, if similarly shaped water jars or similar marriage forms appear in different parts of the world, there is no need to postulate diffusion to explain the similarity; the limitation of possibilities and independent invention will do.

On the other hand, the possible decorations for water jars are almost infinite. Therefore, if two water jars found in widely separated parts of the world are not only of identical shape but also have the same coloring and decoration (particularly if the decoration depicts some fabulous creature that never really existed), the jar becomes good evidence of diffusion between the two places; it indicates that there was some type of contact, either direct or indirect. The more complex the items being compared and the more arbitrary the associations between the component parts, the more likely they are to be related when they closely resemble each other. Conversely, the more simple the two items and the more closely they copy something found in nature, or the more functional the associations between component parts, the more likely they are to have been independently invented, unless there is good evidence to prove otherwise.

Even though the extreme diffusionist position has been largely abandoned, the significance of diffusion to cultural development is widely recognized today. Man is not highly original, but he is quite imitative. Throughout man's history, a good idea has spread with amazing rapidity, even when transportation was dependent on manpower alone. The spread of ideas without any accompanying physical objects is called stimulus diffusion ° and is much more difficult to trace, of course, than the diffusion of material objects. Enough cases of stimulus diffusion have been documented, however, for us to know it occurs, probably more often than we think. Linton illustrates the point in his classic description of a "100 percent American." He points out that almost everything an American believes and does has its origins outside the United States (Linton 1937:427–429). The importance of understanding the process of diffusion should be obvious.

There is a well-known truism that it is difficult to make people change, but this particular truism is false unless it is modified. It is ironic that some of the same people who talk about the difficulty and slowness of change may complain about the rapid spread of Coca-Cola. Government agents who cannot induce people to cut down their herds to help erosion control or cannot persuade them to kill animals to stop the spread of hoof and mouth disease find themselves equally unable to *stop* the spread of marijuana smoking, the manufacture of illegal liquor, or some other "undesirable" change. People are not necessarily resistant to change, per se; they just will not change in the direction the change agent wants them to. Knowledge of the principles of diffusion can help a person do his job more effectively with less chance of harming the people he is working with.

Distribution studies have led to the development of other concepts as well. The concept of "culture area," ° for example, is still used today (Wissler 1922). This idea was originally developed by Clark Wissler to assist museum curators in organizing their material for display purposes (Herskovits 1951:183). Put simply, it states that people in one geographic area resemble each other culturally more than they resemble people elsewhere; the boundaries of a culture area are drawn both geographically and culturally. The concept saves a great deal of work. For example, all the tribes in the American Plains culture area resemble the Piegan in basic outline. Everyone who has read this book and can remember details from the first excerpt already knows something about the Cheyenne, Arapaho, Sioux, Comanche, Pawnee, and so on, as well as about the Piegan. They all depended on the buffalo, which they hunted much the same way. They all lived in movable skin-covered lodges (the *tipi*), usually made in more or less the same manner. They all had roughly the same division of labor and depended on the horse for transport. They all essentially lacked pottery, agriculture, and canoe travel. Even their religious beliefs were similar. Details of each culture varied to the extent that tribes could be distinguished by the arrows they left in their victims or by the tracks their moccasins made in the dirt, but the basic resemblances were striking.

Knowing in detail about one group in a culture area makes it possible to concentrate on the specific ways in which a new culture differs from the one already known. This can be an obvious help to a doctor, anthropologist, or some other change agent going to work in a large geographic area such as the upper Amazon drainage. He does not have to learn a completely new set of data for each of the tiny tribes he may encounter. Once he understands the basic patterns of the culture area, he can concentrate on details, and feel, correctly, that he already knows something about each new group he meets.

George P. Murdock has made the most significant contribution to organizing the massive amount of data accumulated during the first half of the twentieth century by establishing the Human Relations Area Files (HRAF). He set up a classification system that could be used to arrange ethnographic data (Murdock 1950). Into the HRAF were then coded vast bodies of material, both published and unpublished, on different peoples in the various culture areas of the world. This classification has been quite useful for certain kinds of research, although some people may have tried to get more out of the material than is there. There has been criticism that data are not always reliable and that cross-cultural comparisons have sometimes compared things that were not actually comparable. Still, for many researchers, HRAF makes easily available material that would take a lifetime of work to accumulate on one's own. (Students can also make good use of the files to write papers on carefully defined problems within one society. Hardly any library in the world would have available *all* the sources classified in the files.)

As anthropologists became familiar with more and more cultures, they noticed that each one seemed to have a distinct "style." The personality or character of the members of each culture seemed distinguishable. Frenchmen, for example, were obviously different in behavior and temperament from Englishmen, Russians, Japanese, or Americans. The relationship between culture and personality became a major focus of interest. Ralph Linton and Cora Du Bois, working with the psychoanalyst Abram Kardiner, developed the concept of the modal personality—a cluster of personality traits that appear most frequently in a culture (Barnouw 1963:110) (see Chapter 5). Ruth Benedict, one of the early pioneers in American anthropology, thought that each culture was organized around a central pattern she called a configuration.° This pattern encouraged certain personality developments and inhibited others. She also said that the main configuration could be correlated with psychological types, such as Dionysian and Apollonian (Benedict 1934:79). Her hypothesis had no sooner been expressed than other anthropologists began to modify it on the basis of additional data. Morris Opler pointed out that most cultures were not organized around one focus but had several, which he called themes ° (Opler 1945:198–206). Hoebel followed much the same track, only he used the term *basic postulates* ° to refer to the major concepts that gave a culture its unique character (Hoebel 1964:13). Other anthropologists became interested in what people of different cultures regard as "good" or "bad." Of the several anthropologists who became absorbed in the study of values, Clyde Kluckhohn is probably one of the best known.

CURRENT VITAL ISSUES

Values, themes, configurations, or basic postulates are crucial concepts in applied anthropology. New elements may be accepted or rejected on the basis of how well they fit with the fundamental concepts of the culture. Elements that are accepted are often reworked to conform more closely to the underlying organization of the culture. A change agent who tries to introduce something that is incompatible with this basic structure is bound to have difficulty. To succeed, he has to change either the basic structure of the culture (which is almost impossible to do) or his innovation. If the basic themes and values are known, the innovation can be preadapted to fit better, and the inevitable reworking may be anticipated. It may even be possible to guide the reworking to ensure that it does not invalidate the entire change. (Some American Indian groups, taught to screen doors and windows, but never really understanding why, reworked the innovation by leaving doors propped open and failing to repair holes in the screen. Consequently, although they *have* screens, these are not accomplishing the purpose the change agent intended when he introduced them.)

Margaret Mead, the anthropologist who is best known to the American public, pointed out that it might be easier to introduce almost an entire new culture at once rather than to try to change an old one bit by bit (Mead 1956:411). Partial changes always create so many problems of adjustment and the new clusters of traits are so unpredictable at the present state of knowledge that a massive rapid change is sometimes both simpler and safer.

The whole area of the relationship between culture and the individual personality (called either psychological anthropology or culture and personality) is a vital one today. The focus of attention has changed somewhat from national character and modal personality studies to searches for specific cross-cultural uniformities and generalizations (such as the studies by Whiting and Child mentioned in Chapter 5). A great deal of research is currently going on, and information on the topic is steadily increasing.

At about the same time as the interest in values and personality and culture was occupying the attention of some American anthropologists, others were trying to understand specific patterns in a society by looking at how they functioned. Malinowski and Alfred Radcliffe-Brown were the principal leaders in this approach (Keesing 1964:150–155). The basic concept—that a specific pattern in a culture can be explained by its present function rather than by its history—has, like so many other formulations, been modified with time and new data. The same function can usually be served by a variety of different patterns. Why, therefore, should a society have one rather than another? Simply to point out that a particular pattern serves a particular function does not answer the question. Functionalism ° is by no means dead in modern anthropology, however; it is important to programs of directed culture change, for example, since it is essential to know precisely how something functions in a society before it is safe (or in some cases even possible) to change it.

One of the most popular theoretical approaches in cultural anthropology today is structural formalism, whose chief exponent is the French anthropologist Claude Lévi-Strauss. Some of his hypotheses have already been mentioned (in Chapter 6). This theoretical position appears to run almost directly counter to the interest in values, at least superficially. Structural formalism accounts for the presence of certain behavior by the demands of the system itself —the formal underlying structure—and not by the values (conscious or unconscious) held by members of the culture. Values would be a consequence of the formal structure, rather than a causal factor. Thus Lévi-Strauss attributes incest prohibitions to the fact that families must be interdependent for the efficient survival of society rather than to frustrated human desires or the fear of biological damage. The division of labor has little to do with innate male-female differences; it exists instead because it forces people to depend on each other, again serving the basic structure of the system (Lévi-Strauss 1960: 261–285).

The work of Leigh Minturn and William Lambert on family structure and child-training patterns tends to support the hypotheses of Lévi-Strauss. They point out that many training patterns are followed not because the women (or men) involved consciously choose to follow them or even because they unconsciously imitate the patterns their parents followed, but because the demands of the family structure make it almost impossible to do anything else. An American mother coping alone with three preschool children cannot (even if she *wants* to) employ the techniques of a South Pacific mother who never has to spend more time on child care than she wants to because she can turn the child over to other people once it is weaned, and sometimes even before (Minturn and Lambert 1968: 551–557.

Structural formalism is not an entirely new approach. Émile Durkheim used it to account for patterns of suicide, and Kroeber suggested it in his work on culture as superorganic (Durkheim 1951;

Kroeber 1917:163–213). According to the Redfield definition given at the beginning of this book, culture is an underlying formal structure of learned and shared concepts that motivates observable behavior. Lévi-Strauss has given new impetus to the concept that culture is a shared mental phenomenon that changes according to its own rules.

THE FUTURE

What is the most likely future direction for anthropology? At the present time, it is a growing discipline in the social sciences—which themselves are still growing while many other fields have stopped or begun to decline. The growth of anthropology has slowed in the past few years, but in the light of continuing and ever increasing undergraduate interest, growth is likely to continue on that level at least. What anthropology "school" is likely to dominate the field in the next decade or so?

It is difficult to try to predict the future of anything as vital and changeable as the study of man. In the first place, anthropology is not likely to head in any *single* direction. Modern anthropologists do not follow "schools" in the same way their predecessors did; they tend instead to be more eclectic and pragmatic. They will use any theory or methodology that seems appropriate, valid, and useful to their research problem, regardless of its origin. It is possible to indicate some trends and some vital areas of interest in anthropology, but a theoretical or factual breakthrough could occur tomorrow and set the whole field off in directions that are totally unpredictable on the basis of current knowledge.

Three major areas of current interest have just been discussed —applied anthropology, psychological anthropology, and structural-formalist theory. Other areas in which interest and research attention have been increasing in the last decade are urban anthropology, ethnosemantics or cognitive anthropology, industrial anthropology, medical anthropology, educational anthropology, and the use of computers in model or system building as well as in analysis.

Industrial anthropology is still mainly the province of physical anthropologists, who have been involved in it for some time in matters of design and industrial safety. Cultural anthropologists have started moving into the field and will probably continue to do so as management employs more minority-group members and begins to run into the inevitable cross-cultural misunderstandings.

Urban anthropology is an obvious development. As anthropologists began studying more complex societies such as that of India, it was inevitable that they would become involved in studying cities. The subcultural differences between rural and urban populations in a single society or between different classes within one city are often of the same magnitude as cultural differences between separate societies. To a middle class *WASP* (White Anglo-Saxon Protestant), Chinatown in New York, Spanish Harlem, or the black ghetto is as culturally alien as a foreign country. Anthropology has much to contribute to the understanding of urban problems, since so many of these problems are generated by cross-cultural contacts. At present, most urban studies are made by sociologists, but anthropological interest in the area may increase more rapidly in the future.

Medical anthropology includes both the study of non-Western medical concepts and the problems of introducing Western medicine to various parts of the world (including parts of the United States). The cultures of medical practitioners and medical institutions are also subjects for study. More and more medical schools and hospitals are employing anthropologists to find answers to persistent and perplexing problems or are including anthropology as part of their training programs.

The interest in educational anthropology (the cross-cultural study of educational methods, goals, and content) is one of the more recent, but it is growing rapidly. Several publications dealing with educational systems and educational technology in various parts of the world have recently appeared. In this subfield as well as in the others mentioned, interest will probably increase in the future.

Ethnosemantics is an area that combines linguistics and social anthropology more closely. Using the rigorous methodology of linguistics, attempts are made to map out the boundaries of the meanings of words used in a particular culture—thus the term *cognitive anthropology*, which is also used for this new field (Berlin 1970: 3–18). Some of the developments showing broadly based universally applicable generalizations are proving highly exciting and controversial.

The increasing use of computers is a fairly new development for anthropologists, who have traditionally shied away from mathematical approaches. For years, one of the main differences between anthropologists and sociologists was that sociologists used the survey for collecting data which were then analyzed by statistical methods, whereas anthropologists used participation-observation and made a qualitative analysis of their data. Recently, however, archeologists have turned to computers to analyze the thousands of pottery shards found in rich sites, and cultural anthropologists have begun to use surveys and computer analysis. Even more recently, cultural anthropologists have begun to experiment with computers for building model cultural systems. It is still too early to tell how productive this trend will be, but it is likely to draw increasing attention in the future.

One serious problem must be confronted in the coming decade, since it is currently causing a bitter controversy in anthropological circles, and that is the problem of the most appropriate apportionment of involvement and objectivity—the question of where, when, and how the personal values of the anthropologist should be engaged. Although the issue is not precisely either theoretical or methodological, it affects both areas. There is no simple answer to the question, but many people are trying to provide one. There are extremists on both sides: those who feel objectivity cannot be attained and should not be sought and those who feel that values have no place in any field that claims to be a science.

Most anthropologists probably prefer some position between the two extremes, but a hot controversy is raging about just where along the continuum the field and its practitioners should be. Anthropologists are human beings, citizens of particular political entities, and bearers of particular cultures. In studying other peoples, they have traditionally made use of their personal characteristics by reporting their own reactions as fully as possible when they have participated in the study culture. In other words, they tried to use their own cultural biases to increase understanding rather than to obscure it. Since Malinowski's time, anthropologists have always undergone a considerable amount of field training to make them alert to their own biases and to teach methods of research that would help them avoid the biases that remain covert. Although they participated as much as possible in the daily life of the peoples they studied, anthropologists traditionally were supposed to remain analytical, aloof from any long-range real consequences of the research. The first anthropologists to engage in applied research were looked upon somewhat skeptically, for in the eyes of many, this was no longer "pure" research. But now anthropologists, in common with other scientists, have become increasingly concerned about the use to which their research is being put. They have begun to criticize one another because some do work for financial sponsors of which others disapprove, because some fail to protect informants adequately from detrimental consequences of the research, or because some allow their research results to be censored and withheld from the profession. In addition, some anthropologists have felt that their professional associations should take a strong stand on political questions, while others think they should not.

All these topics are sources of heated controversy. Since the subject of anthropological research is man himself, questions of this sort are perhaps even more pressing and sensitive than they are in other scientific fields. In the physical sciences, for example, researchers do not normally have to worry about the element of awareness or choice in their study objects. As far as we know, an atom does not care if someone splits it. A chemical does not decide to react differently because it knows it is part of an experiment or because it does not like the experimenter. Metals do not become apathetic and turn to alcoholism or suicide because their organization is disrupted by accident or design. People do, and this infinitely complicates the situation for anthropologists.

Both involvement and objectivity are probably essential in anthropology. Part of the controversy seems to come from confusion over when objectivity is (or is not) appropriate, and who should be allowed to make significant decisions. Involvement of values is probably inevitable in decisions over what research should be done and who should pay for it. Anthropologists are human, and each will probably do a better job if he is studying a topic he prefers. Money for research comes from public and private sources. The values of the anthropologist and those of the people who control the funds enter into decisions over what research will be supported and actually done.

Research that is evaluated by those who control the money as urgent, significant, or most promising for some purpose or other will probably get funds. Of course, it is difficult to determine in advance what research will be productive. It is probably impossible to make an objective decision, so the real question is whose values should determine the choice—those of the scientists, the elected officials, the people providing the money, or the chosen money managers. Naturally, the researcher wants to be able to decide what to study; he may even feel that he knows best what *should* be studied. Similarly, the people footing the bill want some say in the matter. In addition, if the person controlling the funds is using public money, he is normally accountable in some way and therefore must be able to justify his decisions either to other elected officials (Congress, for example) or to the public at large. If the funds are provided by private individuals it may be possible to ignore public values, but then the individual who provides the funds must be satisfied. Because his values may be quite different from the general public ones, he provides some source of diversity in what research eventually is supported. Those managing public funds are not noted for their support of unusual projects.

Adding fuel to an already heated controversy, some anthropologists have taken it upon themselves to act as the conscience for the whole profession. Other anthropologists, who feel perfectly capable of making moral decisions themselves, resent this. Just as medical doctors may be prepared to accept a code of ethics regarding their treatment of patients, but not any regulation of what branch of medicine they should specialize in, anthropologists may be ready to accept an ethical code dealing with their relationships to the people they study, but not any dictates as to what they should study or for whom they should work.

Another thorny issue is what happens to the results of the research. There is a strong objection to anthropologists being subjected to censorship, but there is an equally strong objection to disseminating information that might be used in some way against the study group. It is, however, difficult to both conceal and reveal the same information. It is also difficult to determine just what information might be used "against" a people at some future date. Furthermore, the decision as to what is harmful is in itself a value judgment. What would be interpreted as damaging by one group in the controversy might be regarded as beneficial by another.

An entirely different dimension is the problem of how much values should or do enter into the research itself. It is, of course, difficult to be objective about behavior that violates one's own covert culture, but it can be attempted. People in other professions have been trained to be objective. A good medical doctor will not overlook a potentially fatal disease just because he dislikes the patient, nor will he refuse to recognize an embarrassing problem because he likes the patient. Surely anthropologists can be equally objective studying other cultures. Doctors recognize their own lack of objectivity regarding medical problems in their own families and customarily send intimate friends and family members to other doctors for diagnosis and treatment. Similarly, anthropologists recognize that there are special problems involved in studying their own culture and usually are not permitted to do so for their first field experience. A peculiar exception to this is that both American and English institutions, when training foreign-born anthropologists such as Asiatic Indians, Pakistanis, or Africans, often encourage them to study their own cultures. They thereby lose a fine opportunity to have an anthropologically trained outsider make a study of American or English culture. In addition, it forces the foreign anthropologist to miss a valuable part of his training. Why allow foreign anthropologists to do something most American or English anthropologists are forbidden to do? The answer seems to be that anthropologists normally study "foreign" cultures, and an African or Indian culture is "foreign" (to the American or Englishman of course), so it is therefore acceptable—ethnocentrism in its worst form!

Deliberately falsifying or distorting data in any way contravenes the whole purpose of science; it is incompatible with any serious study of human behavior. A behavioral scientist who does more than slightly disguise his study population to protect them from curiosity seekers is doing incalculable harm to the understanding of people. Honest mistakes cause trouble enough without deliberate distortions. Understanding of genetics was hampered for almost twenty years by one researcher's insistence that he had proof of the inheritance of acquired characteristics. When independent observers finally could examine the evidence, they found it was fraudulent. Scientists had been hoaxed and theories based on the "proof" were useless. The concept was dropped from genetics until a Soviet scientist named Lysenko resurrected it. Because of political intervention by Stalin, scientists who opposed Lysenko were silenced. Politics could not control growing plants, however, and experiments based on the inheritance of acquired characteristics which were designed to improve Soviet agriculture uniformly failed (*Encyclopaedia Britannica* 1970, 13:614–617).

Because most people writing about human behavior have a particular position to support, their statements are often self-seeking and therefore suspect. Where can the city planner, or anybody who wants to improve the human condition, turn for the accurate information he needs? If even the behavioral sciences are distorting their data to serve their own interests, however sincere those interests may be, who can be relied on? No one can make any sensible plans in the absence of reliable data. If a population is increasing by 4 percent per year and food production is increasing only 2 percent in the same period, it will not help anyone to be told the opposite. People will starve, because they need real food, not false statistics.

In summary then, values in anthropology are probably inevitable in choices over what is to be investigated, whose support will be accepted, and what is to be done with the results of the research. Arguments can and will continue over who should decide these questions—the anthropologists themselves, the financial supporters, public officials, a professional association, or some combination of all of these. Values must not be allowed to influence the data themselves, however. Regardless of what choices are made in other aspects of research, the data must be gathered and reported as accurately and objectively as possible, or there is no hope for any increased scientific understanding of man.

Anthropology, as a field, is faced with serious choices in this area which may determine its future usefulness as a science of man. If it is to continue as a science, there are a variety of areas that will probably receive increased attention: education, medicine, industry, urban centers, cognition, psychology, the use of computers for model building, and the application of anthropology. Other areas not apparent at present may prove to be exciting and fruitful. The field is a fast-growing one that offers promise for future generations who are particularly interested in "the proper study of mankind"— man (Pope 1958:107).

Glossary

achieved status a status that one attains through his own efforts.

affinal relatives in-laws.

animatism the belief that inanimate or nonsentient things, such as rocks, trees, the wind, and other aspects of nature, have a will and consciousness.

animism the belief in a supernatural being or beings with consciousness and will.

archeology the study and reconstruction of past cultures through their artifacts and the physical traces of their activities.

ascribed status a status assigned to a person whether he likes it or not by virtue of certain characteristics that he possesses.

atlatl a spear thrower, usually wood. It may also be bone, ivory, or a similar solid material.

Australopithecus africanus (Telanthropus or Homo habilis) an early hominid believed by some to be directly ancestral to man; first found at Taung, South Africa, by Dart in 1924.

Australopithecus robustus (Paranthropus) an early hominid believed by some to be another species of Australopithecus, but held by others to be a different genus. It is not believed to be ancestral to man.

avunculocal residence the residence of a married couple with the groom's mother's brother.

barter an exchange wherein goods or services are given directly for other goods or services. No medium of exchange such as money is used.

basic maintenance system a system that satisfies the biological survival needs of a group, for example, a means of subsistence.

basic postulates assumptions about the nature of things; may be true or false.

bifurcate merging a system of kinship terminology that excludes one line of descent from the family (bifurcation) but combines cousins of the other line with siblings (merging).

bifurcation the excluding of descendants of one line from the family— for example, descendants of males in a matrilineal system and descendants of females in a patrilineal system.

bilateral inheritance equal inheritance from both parents.

bolas a weapon composed of two or more stone balls tied together on long strings, thrown to entangle birds or game animals.

bride price wealth transferred from the groom's family to the bride's family as part of the marriage process.

bride wealth another term for "bride price."

bung the plug that stops the hole in a barrel.

buckskin tanned deer hide.

capital wealth in any form that is used or could be used to produce more wealth.

capstan an upright windlass. A large cylinder with a cable or hawser (thick tow rope) wound around it. It usually has several spokes at the top so more than one person can help turn it and a ratchet to keep it from slipping back as force is released.

carpentered environment an environment characterized by straight lines and right angles.

caste an endogamous social group whose members are ascribed to it at birth for life.

chilblains painful swellings or sores caused by exposure to the cold.

chinook the warm wind on the west central and north central plains of the United States in winter.

civilization a technical term referring to a society that possesses a set of attributes such as monumental public works, writing, science, and so on. It is not to be confused with "civilized" in the sense of "urbane" or "sophisticated."

clan a unilineal descent group whose members assume they have a common ancestor but cannot trace their precise relationship to each other.

class a social group whose members have approximately the same socioeconomic status. Membership in a class, unlike that of a caste, may be changed.

classificatory kinship a variety of relationships combined under one term. For example, "uncle" is a classificatory term since it applies to mother's brother, father's brother, mother's sister's husband, and father's sister's husband.

clitoridectomy excision of the clitoris.

Cold Maker the Piegan personification for the cold winter weather.

competitive cooperation group cooperation to accomplish a group goal, combined with individual competition to see who can do the most to help attain that goal.

configuration the overall orientation or characteristic around which a culture is organized; it provides a focus or a style that permeates the entire culture.

conjugal pertaining to marriage.

consanguine related by blood.

consensual union the relationship of a couple willingly living together without being married.

cooperative competition individuals cooperating in a team that is competing against other teams.

copyright property rights to a particular organization of words or sounds (as in music).

correlated related to or varying with something.

correlation the degree of mutual correspondence between two variables (two sets of data, two kinds of social phenomena, and so on).

coulée a deep gulch or ravine, usually dry much of the year.

counterculture group a group whose culture is opposed to the culture of the mainstream of society.

couvade the custom in which the father ritualistically imitates the pregnancy and delivery of the mother.

covert culture those concepts which people take for granted, do not remember learning, and often are not aware that they know.

crime an offense against people or society.

crisis rite a ceremony marking a major change of status. It is also called *rite de passage* or passage rite.

cross-cousins children of opposite-sexed siblings, for example, the child of a father's sister or a mother's brother.

cultural relativity the idea that one culture is just as valid as any other, and that the characteristics of a culture can be evaluated only in the context of that culture.

culture those organized concepts, mainfest in act and artifact, learned and shared by man as a member of society.

culture area a geographic area within which separate societies have cultures that share more characteristics with each other than they do with cultures outside the area.

culture-bound accustomed to thinking solely in terms of the values and beliefs of one's own society and culture.

culture elements separate characteristics that go to make up a whole culture; sometimes called culture traits.

culture historical Herskovits' term for the German *Kulturkreiselehre* or culture circle (sphere) school. A school of thought with heavy emphasis on tracing the distribution and origin of culture traits.

diffusion the process by which cultural concepts move from one society to another.

diffusionist school the school of thought that attempts to explain all culture as the product of diffusion from a single center or at most a few sources.

divination the attempt to foretell the future or reveal the unknown by the use of techniques usually involving communication with the supernatural.

dominance control or influence over others. Any social group, human or animal, has a dominance structure. A dominant individual has preferential access to space, sex, food, or other "good things."

dominance structure the pattern of dominance in any social group.

double descent descent in which one sort of things (land, physical appearance, and so on) is traced through one parental line and other things (money, intellectual qualities, and so on) are traced through the other line. A child inherits from both parents, but inherits different kinds of things from each.

dowry wealth transferred from the bride's family to the groom's family, the groom, or the bride as part of the marriage process.

dumb barter *see* silent barter.

egalitarian pertaining to equality.

emic classification of characteristics of a society according to the way in which members of that society classify them.

eminent domain the right of a government to take private property for public use, giving just compensation to the owner.

emulative competition competition in which one attempts to outdo his competitor.

enculturation the teaching of beliefs and traditions of a society to the young or the uninitiated.

endogamy marriage within the social unit.

ethnocentric judging all other groups by reference to the standards, values, and characteristics of one's own group.

etic classification of characteristics of a society according to some external system of analysis.

exchange system a situation that exists only if there is both a demand for something and a differentiation in suppliers.

exogamy marriage outside the social unit.

extended family a group that includes relatives other than the parents and offspring.

extended households those in which a variety of relatives other than the members of the nuclear family live.

family of orientation the family one is born into.

family of procreation the family that one begins after marriage.

female infanticide the killing of female babies.

fish weirs traps built in shallow water to catch fish, usually stretching across a stream, river, or estuary.

flintlock the firing mechanism of a gun in which gunpowder is exploded by a spark produced by sticking a piece of flint in the hammer against a piece of metal; it is obsolete.

folkways customs and traditions observed by people in a society; positive beliefs about how to act and what should be done.

foragers individuals who harvest the wild produce (animal or vegetable) of their environment but consume it on the spot instead of collecting it to share with others.

formal sanction a punishment or reward that is explicit, known in advance, and impersonally applied to all. As punishment it frequently involves force and is usually applied by specialists.

functionalism the concept that a specific pattern in a culture can be explained by the purpose it currently serves rather than by its history.

functional status a status based on what one does in a society, such as that of a carpenter or a plumber.

genitor the biological sire.

gens a patrilineal group whose members assume they have a common ancestor but cannot trace their precise relationship to each other; a synonym for "clan."

government a network of statuses whose primary roles are political.

grave goods artifacts placed in a grave with the body.

harrow *see* spring-tooth harrow.

Homo erectus the name given to one of the early forms of man; also called pithecanthropines. Sinanthropus pekinensis (Peking or China man) and Pithecanthropus erectus (Java man) are included in this group.

Homo habilis *see* Australopithecus africanus.

horticulture a form of food production depending on hand tools, with mixed crops rather than single crop fields; also called gardening.

hospice an inn, or a refuge for the sick or poor.

impetigo a contagious skin disease caused by staphylococci. The skin appears to blister, the blisters break, and a heavy scab-like crust forms. Removing the scab and washing the area with green soap (a disinfectant soap) is the usual treatment.

incest tabu the prohibition of sexual intercourse, marriage, or both with relatives regarded as especially close.

informal sanction a punishment or reward that is spontaneous, varying according to the circumstances and individuals involved. As punishment it usually involves shame or ridicule and is most often applied by nonspecialists in the area of law enforcement.

institution a set of norms or rules focusing around a particular aspect or problem in society. Examples of institutions are the religious system, the economic system, and so on.

internalize to incorporate in oneself the values, concepts, and so on of another or of a group.

kumamolimo the central meeting place of the BaMbuti Pygmy religious ceremony called the molimo.

latent function a real but unintended function (sometimes unrecognized by the society).

law a rule or command in a society backed up by severe sanctions applied with the approval of society; also called a legal norm.

levirate marriage of a man to his brother's widow or of a woman to her deceased husband's brother.

lineage a unilineal descent group whose members can trace their relationship to each other.

linguistics the study of the structure of language.

lodge a type of American Indian dwelling; may refer to skin, brush, or log structure, either earth-covered or not.

mana a supernatural force with no will, awareness, or consciousness.

manifest function a function explicitly intended by members of the society.

market an exchange involving a number of buyers and sellers with the price varying according to what is asked and paid by the people involved.

matrilineal inheritance descent traced through the female line.

matrilocal pertaining to a marriage arrangement in which the bride and groom live with or near the bride's parents; sometimes used synonymously with "uxorilocal."

messianic movement a religious revival usually occurring when a society is under severe stress. It is generally headed by a charismatic leader who serves as a prophet, messiah, or martyr.

molimo a ceremony of the BaMbuti Pygmies and the instrument used in it.

modal personality the cluster of personality traits that appears most frequently in a culture.

moiety one of two parts of a society.

money a medium of exchange that is durable, portable, standardized, divisible, and relatively stable in value.

monogamy the practice of having one spouse at a time.

mores folkways that are particularly involved with social welfare; they usually consist of stringent tabus or prohibitions rather than prescriptions of positive action.

Mousterian a particular assemblage of artifacts, dating from 40,000 to 150,000 b.p. (before present) and most often associated with Neanderthal man.

mulcted fined.

nativistic revival a mass movement, frequently religious, usually occurring when a society is under severe stress, and attempting to reestablish a legendary or remembered glorious past.

Neanderthal an early form of man with wide distribution dating from between 40,000 and 150,000 years ago. There is some controversy among experts as to whether this form is ancestral to modern man or is a side branch that became extinct.

neolocal pertaining to a marriage arrangement in which the bride and groom move to a new residence where they are relatively independent of both sets of parents.

night soil human excrement.

nuclear family parents and offspring.

obligatio rights and duties.

ocher a natural iron-oxide pigment, usually red or yellow.

overt culture those concepts of which people are aware and consciously teach or learn.

Paleolithic old stone age.

paleontology the study of fossils; a branch of geology.

parallel cousins children of same-sexed siblings.

parallel inheritance girls inherit only from their mothers and boys only from their fathers.

Paranthropus *see* Australopithecus robustus.

parfleche a rawhide container, usually shaped like a box or a suitcase and used for storage or transport, especially of food.

particularistic exchange an exchange in which the emphasis is on the social relationship between participants rather than on the economic aspect.

pater the sociological male parent.

patrilineal inheritance descent traced through the male line.

patrilocal pertaining to a marriage arrangement in which the bride and groom live with or near the groom's parents; sometimes used synonymously with "virilocal."

pemmican meat pounded together with fat and berries and dried; a nourishing food, easy to store.

percussion cap a small metal cap containing gunpowder that explodes when struck.

personalistic exchange economic decisions made on the basis of social (or personal factors).

phratry a group of linked clans.

physical anthropology the branch of anthropology that deals with man as a biological organism.

piki paper-thin corn bread.

pithecanthropines *see* Homo erectus.

polyandry the practice of having more than one husband at a time.

polygamy the practice of having several spouses at one time.

polygyny the practice of having more than one wife at a time.

porcelain ceramic artifacts. In the *Jesuit Relations* it usually refers to trade beads which quickly replaced shell. (It was sometimes used to refer to strung shell too, however.)

power the ability to make binding key decisions.

prestation the giving of a gift to create a social obligation.

priest a member of an organized group of religious specialists who learns an organized body of doctrine, often in a special school.

private law the injured party has the right to revenge himself on the offender if he can.

procreation the producing of young.

progeny price wealth transferred from groom's family to bride's family; a synonym for "bride price." It gives the groom's family rights over the offspring (real or potential) of the match.

projective system a belief system of a society which deals with an aspect not easily subject to scientific experimental proof (religion, mythology, explanations of disease causation in premodern non-Western societies, and so on).

property right a right to control, exploit, use, enjoy, or dispose of a valuable thing.

puberty rite a ceremony to mark passage from adolescence or childhood to adulthood.

public law a system wherein society takes the part of the injured person and specialized members apprehend, judge, and punish the offending individual.

quirt a short-handled whip, usually with a braided rawhide lash.

reciprocal gift-giving the exchange of gifts thought to have an equivalent value.

redistribution the turning over of goods to a central location or organization which then distributes them to other members of the society.

red ocher a natural iron-oxide pigment used in Mousterian graves.

rennet the membrane lining of the stomach of a calf, or an extract of this, used to curdle milk.

reparations payments in the nature of fines made by the loser in a war to the winner; or by a society causing damage, to the victims.

replicable able to be duplicated.

revitalization a renewal or revival that breathes new life into a culture that has been under stress and growing disorganized.

rite de passage a ceremony that marks a major change in status; also called "rite of passage," "passage rite," or "crisis rite."

role the behavior expected of an individual in a particular status.

role conflict when two or more of an individual's roles (with conflicting expectations) are activated simultaneously.

sanction reward or punishment.

scalar status a status determined by rank or access to wealth and power.

shaman a religious leader who is highly individualistic, does not have an organized doctrine, and usually intercedes on the side of man. His knowledge usually comes from direct revelation.

sib a unilineal descent group whose members assume they have a common ancestor but cannot trace their precise relationship to each other; a synonym for "clan."

siblings brothers and sisters.

silent barter an exchange that takes place without face-to-face contact.

sin an offense against the supernatural.

sindula the water chevrotain, an animal hunted by the BaMbuti Pygmies in Africa.

smooth-bore musket a gun without rifling (grooves) in the barrel; it is not very accurate.

socialization teaching the young how to get along in a group.

social norm something that members of a society agree should or should not be done.

sondu an antelope, hunted by the BaMbuti Pygmies in Africa.

sororate marriage of a woman to the widower of her sister, or of a man to his deceased wife's sister.

spring-tooth harrow a farm implement with teeth that spring back and forth used to break up clods of earth left after plowing. When used as a verb, it is the process of breaking up clods and smoothing the fields.

status a position in a society.

stimulus diffusion the spread of ideas rather than physical artifacts.

story elements the discrete themes or pieces from which a story is composed.

structural formalism Lévi-Strauss' approach that attempts to explain culture by discovering the underlying basic formal structure.

subincision slitting the penis from the base to the glans, or part way.

suppressive competition competition in which one attempts to destroy or pull down his rival.

sutler a person who follows an army to sell supplies—especially food and liquor—to soldiers.

tabu (taboo) a prohibition or caution usually but not always involving the supernatural.

Telanthropus *see* Australopithecus africanus.

themes major basic concepts of a culture that underlie most of its observable behavior and articulated beliefs.

totem something in nature that is believed to have a special and significant relationship with a particular group.

toque a round close-fitting cap.

train a wooden sled with runners, usually drawn by one horse; used on the frontier.

traits discrete observable characteristics of a culture; the smallest meaningful and observable parts of a culture.

transhumance seasonal shifting of people from one area to another.

transvestite a person who dresses like a member of the opposite sex.

travois two long poles, two ends on one side of which were crossed over the back of a horse, with the other ends dragging on the ground. Goods and people were transported on nets of rawhide or rope strung between the poles.

universalistic system one in which economic decisions are made on the basis of technical factors such as cost, quality, efficiency, rather than on the basis of social factors.

universalistic exchange exchange with emphasis on economic rather than social factors.

uxorilocal the reverse of virilocal; a marriage arrangement in which the bride and groom live in the bride's parents' home. It is sometimes used synonymously with "matrilocal."

vermilion bright red mercuric sulfide (or any other similar red earth) used as a pigment; also refers to a bright yellowish-red color.

viable able to survive.

virilocal pertaining to a marriage arrangement in which the bride and groom live in the groom's home. It is sometimes used synonymously with "patrilocal."

Bibliography

ACKERMAN, CHARLES
  1968 "Conjunctive Affiliation and Divorce," in Norman W. Bell and
    Ezra F. Vogel (eds.), *A Modern Introduction to the Family.* New
    York: Free Press, pp. 469–477.
ALLPORT, G. W., and T. F. PETTIGREW
  1957 "Cultural Influence on the Perception of Movement: The
    Trapezoidal Illusion among Zulus," *Journal of Abnormal and So-
    cial Psychology* 55:104–113.
ARDREY, ROBERT
  1961 *African Genesis.* New York: Dell.
  1970 *The Social Contract.* New York: Atheneum.
ARMILLAS, PEDRO
  1964 "Northern Mesoamerica," in Jesse Jennings and Edward Nor-
    beck (eds.), *Prehistoric Man in the New World.* Chicago: Uni-
    versity of Chicago Press, pp. 291–329.
BARNOUW, VICTOR
  1963 *Culture and Personality.* Homewood, Ill.: Dorsey Press.
  1971 *An Introduction to Anthropology.* Homewood, Ill.: Dorsey
    Press.
BEALS, ALAN R.
  1964 *Gopalpur.* New York: Holt, Rinehart and Winston.
BELL, NORMAN W., AND EZRA F. VOGEL
  1968 *A Modern Introduction to the Family.* New York: Free Press.
BELL, ROBERT R.
  1971 *Social Deviance.* Homewood, Ill.: Dorsey Press.
BELSHAW, CYRIL S.
  1965 *Traditional Exchange and Modern Markets.* Englewood Cliffs,
    N.J.: Prentice-Hall.
BENEDICT, RUTH
  1934 *Patterns of Culture.* New York: New American Library.
BENNETT, JOHN W., AND MELVIN M. TUMIN
  1964 "Some Cultural Imperatives," in Peter B. Hammond (ed.),
    Cultural and Social Anthropology. New York: Macmillan.
BERLIN, BRENT
  1970 "A Universalist-Evolutionary Approach in Ethnographic Se-
    mantics," in Ann Fischer (ed.), *Current Directions in Anthropol-*

ogy. Vol. 3, No. 3, Part 2. Washington, D.C.: American Anthropological Association, pp. 3–18.

BIRDWHISTELL, RAY
  1970 "Ways We Speak Body Language," *New York Times Magazine,* May 31, pp. 8–9.

BOAS, FRANZ
  1967 *The Central Eskimo.* Lincoln: University of Nebraska Press.

BOCK, PHILIP K.
  1969 *Modern Cultural Anthropology.* New York: Knopf.

BOHANNAN, PAUL (ED.)
  1960 *African Homicide and Suicide.* Princeton, N.J.: Princeton University Press.
  1967 *Law and Warfare.* Garden City, N.Y.: Natural History Press.

BRACE, C. LORING
  1964 "A Consideration of Hominid Catastrophism," *Current Anthropology* 5(1):3–19, 32–38.

BRÉBEUF, JEAN DE, S. J.
  1897 "Huron Relation of 1636," in R. G. Thwaites (ed.), *Jesuit Relations & Allied Documents.* Vol. 10. Cleveland: Burrows Bros.

BROWN, JUDITH K.
  1963 "A Cross-Cultural Study of Female Initiation Rites," *American Anthropologist* 65(4):837–853.

BULFINCH, THOMAS
  n.d. *Bulfinch's Mythology.* New York: Modern Library.

CAMPBELL, BERNARD G.
  1966 *Human Evolution.* Chicago: Aldine.

CHAGNON, NAPOLEAN A.
  1968 *Yanomamo: The Fierce People.* New York: Holt, Rinehart and Winston.

CHARD, CHESTER S.
  1969 *Man in Prehistory.* New York: McGraw-Hill.

CHILDS, EBENEZER
  1906 *Recollections of Wisconsin since 1820.* Vol. 4. State Historical Society of Wisconsin, pp. 153–195.

CLARK, ELMER T.
  1937 *Small Sects in America.* Nashville, Tenn.: Cokesbury Press.

CLIFTON, JAMES (ED.)
  1968 *Introduction to Cultural Anthropology.* Boston: Houghton Mifflin.

CLINTON, DEWITT
  1817 A Memoir on the Antiquities of the Western Parts of the State of New York Addressed to the Honorable Samuel L. Mitchill a Vice-President of the Literary and Philosophical Society of New York. Read before the society, 13 November 1817.

COHEN, YEHUDI A.
  1968 *Man in Adaptation: The Cultural Present.* Chicago: Aldine.

CUBER, JOHN F.
  1968 *Sociology: A Synopsis of Principles.* New York: Appleton-Century-Crofts.

DEUSCHLE, KURT, AND HUGH S. FULMER (EDS.)
  n.d. "Progress Report Concerning the Period April 1957–March 1, 1959." Navajo-Cornell Field Health Research Project.

DOBYNS, HENRY F.
  1960 "The Religious Festival." Ph.D. thesis, Cornell University, Ithaca, N.Y.
  1966 "Estimating Aboriginal American Population," *Current Anthropology* 7(4):395–416, 440–444.
DOBYNS, HENRY F., AND ROBERT C. EULER
  1970 *Wauba Yuma's People.* Prescott, Ariz.: Prescott College.
DOWNING, JOSEPH
  1970 "The Tribal Family and the Society of Awakening," in Herbert A. Otto (ed.), *The Family in Search of a Future.* New York: Appleton-Century-Crofts, pp. 119–135.
DRUCKER, PHILIP
  1963 *Indians of the Northwest Coast.* Garden City, N.Y.: Natural History Press.
DURKHEIM, ÉMILE
  1951 *Suicide.* New York: Free Press.
EDDY, MARY BAKER
  n.d. *Science and Health.* Boston: published by trustees under the will of Mary Baker G. Eddy.
EKHOLM, GORDON F.
  1964 "Transpacific Contacts," in Jesse Jennings and Edward Norbeck (eds.), *Prehistoric Man in the New World.* Chicago: University of Chicago Press, pp. 489–510.
EKVALL, ROBERT B.
  1968 *Fields on the Hoof.* New York: Holt, Rinehart and Winston.
Encyclopaedia Britannica
  1966, 1970 Warren E. Preece (ed.). 24 vols. Chicago: William Benton.
EVANS-PRITCHARD, E. E.
  1965 *The Position of Women in Primitive Societies and Other Essays in Social Anthropology.* London: Faber and Faber.
FALLERS, L. A., AND M. C. FALLERS
  1960 "Homicide and Suicide in Busoga," in Paul Bohannan (ed.), *African Homicide and Suicide.* Princeton, N.J.: Princeton University Press, pp. 65–93.
FERNEA, ELIZABETH WARNOCK
  1969 *Guests of the Sheik.* Garden City, N.Y.: Doubleday.
FISCHER, ANN (ED.)
  1970 *Current Directions in Anthropology.* Vol. 3, No. 3, Part 2. Washington, D.C.: American Anthropological Association.
FISCHER, JOHN L.
  1958 "The Classification of Residence in Censuses," *American Anthropologist* 60(3):508–517.
FISCHER, JOHN L., AND ANN FISCHER
  1966 *The New Englanders of Orchard Town, U.S.A.* New York: Wiley.
FORDE, C. DARYLL
  1968 "The Kazak: Horse and Sheep Herders of Central Asia," in Yehudi A. Cohen (ed.), *Man in Adaptation: The Cultural Present.* Chicago: Aldine, pp. 299–309.
FORTES, MEYER
  1962 *Marriage in Tribal Societies.* Cambridge, Eng.: Cambridge University Press.

FRANKFORT, HENRI
1964 "The Cities of Mesopotamia," in Peter B. Hammond (ed.), *Physical Anthropology and Archaeology*. New York: Macmillan, pp. 344–361.

FRAZER, SIR JAMES GEORGE
1955 *The Golden Bough.* London: Macmillan.

FREUCHEN, PETER
1961 *Book of the Eskimos.* Greenwich, Conn.: Fawcett.

FREUD, SIGMUND
1920 *A General Introduction to Psychoanalysis.* Translated by Joan Riviere. New York: Liveright.

GATHERU, R. MUGO
1965 *Child of Two Worlds.* Garden City, N.Y.: Doubleday.

GILBERT, GEORGE B.
1939 *Forty Years a Country Preacher.* New York: Harper & Bros.

GLUCKMAN, MAX
1968 "Estrangement in the African Family," in Norman W. Bell and Ezra F. Vogel (eds.), *A Modern Introduction to the Family.* New York: Free Press, pp. 464–468.

GOLDENWEISER, ALEXANDER A.
1933 *History, Psychology, and Culture.* New York: Knopf.

GOODMAN, HENRY (ED.)
1949 *Selected Writings of Lafcadio Hearn.* New York: Citadel Press.

GOODY, ESTHER N.
1962 "Conjugal Separation and Divorce among the Gonja of Northern Ghana," in Meyer Fortes (ed.), *Marriage in Tribal Societies.* Cambridge, Eng.: Cambridge University Press, pp. 14–54.

GOUGH, E. KATHLEEN
1968 "Is the Family Universal—the Nayar Case," in Norman W. Bell and Ezra F. Vogel (eds.), *A Modern Introduction to the Family.* New York: Free Press, pp. 80–96.

GOULD, JULIUS, AND WILLIAM L. KOLB (EDS.)
1964 *A Dictionary of the Social Sciences.* New York: Free Press.

GREER, SCOTT A.
1965 *Social Organization.* New York: Random House.

HALL, EDWARD T.
1959 *The Silent Language.* Greenwich, Conn.: Fawcett.
1965 "Territorial Needs and Limits," *Natural History Magazine* 74: 12–19.

HAMILTON, EDITH
1945 *Mythology.* Boston: Little, Brown.

HAMILTON, MILTON W. (ED.)
1951 "Regulations for the Indian trade at Fort Stanwix, February, 1762," *Papers of Sir William Johnson.* Vol. 10. Albany: State University of New York Press, pp. 389–391.

HAMMOND, PETER B. (ED.)
1964a *Cultural and Social Anthropology.* New York: Macmillan.
1964b *Physical Anthropology and Archaeology.* New York: Macmillan.

HARLOW, HARRY F., AND MARGARET K. HARLOW
1961 "A Study of Animal Affection," *Natural History Magazine* 70 (10):48–55.

HART, C. W. M., AND ARNOLD R. PILLING
1964 *The Tiwi of Northern Australia.* New York: Holt, Rinehart and Winston.

HERSKOVITS, MELVILLE J.
1951 *Man and His Works.* New York: Knopf.

HOEBEL, E. ADAMSON
1960 *The Cheyennes.* New York: Holt, Rinehart and Winston.
1964 *The Law of Primitive Man.* Cambridge, Mass.: Harvard University Press.
1966 *Anthropology: The Study of Man.* New York: McGraw-Hill.

HOGBIN, IAN
1971 "Polynesian Ceremonial Gift Exchanges," in Alan Howard (ed.), *Polynesia.* Scranton, Penn.: Chandler, pp. 27–45.

HOIJER, HARRY (ED.)
1954a *Language in Culture.* American Anthropological Association Memoir No. 79. Vol. 56, No. 6, Part 2. Washington, D.C.: American Anthropological Association.
1954b "The Sapir-Whorf Hypothesis," in Harry Hoijer (ed.), *Language in Culture.* American Anthropological Association Memoir No. 79. Vol. 56, No. 6, Part 2. Washington, D.C.: American Anthropological Association, pp. 92–105.

HOLLOWAY, RALPH L., JR.
1967 "Tools and Teeth: Some Speculations Regarding Canine Reduction," *American Anthropologist* 69(1):63–67

HOLMBERG, ALLAN R.
1969 *Nomads of the Long Bow.* Garden City, N.Y.: Natural History Press.

HOLZER, HANS
1971 *The Truth about Witchcraft.* New York: Pocket Books.

HOMANS, GEORGE C.
1950 *The Human Group.* New York: Harcourt, Brace & World.

HOSTETLER, JOHN A., AND GERTRUDE ENDERS HUNTINGTON
1967 *The Hutterites in North America.* New York: Holt, Rinehart and Winston.

HOWARD, ALAN (ED.)
1971 *Polynesia.* Scranton, Penn.: Chandler.

HOWELL, F. CLARK
1965 *Early Man.* New York: Time-Life.

HOWELLS, WILLIAM
1962 *The Heathens.* Garden City, N.Y.: Doubleday.

HSU, FRANCIS L. K.
1961 *Psychological Anthropology.* Homewood, Ill.: Dorsey Press.

HULSE, FREDERICK S.
1971 *The Human Species.* 2nd ed. New York: Random House.

JAMESON, JOHN FRANKLIN
1909 *Narratives of New Netherlands 1609–1664.* New York: Scribner.

JENNESS, DIAMOND
  1959 *The People of the Twilight.* Chicago: University of Chicago Press.
JENNINGS, JESSE, AND EDWARD NORBECK (EDS.)
  1964 *Prehistoric Man in the New World.* Chicago: University of Chicago Press.
KAPLAN, BERT
  1961 *Studying Personality Cross-Culturally.* Evanston, Ill.: Row, Peterson.
KEESING, FELIX N.
  1964 *Cultural Anthropology.* New York: Holt, Rinehart and Winston.
KIPLING, RUDYARD
  1936 *All the Mowgli Stories.* New York: Doubleday, Doran.
KLUCKHOHN, CLYDE, AND DOROTHEA LEIGHTON
  1946 *The Navaho.* Cambridge, Mass.: Harvard University Press.
KROEBER, A. L.
  1917 "The Superorganic," *American Anthropologist* 19:163–213.
KRONENBERGER, LOUIS (ED.)
  1951 *Alexander Pope, Selected Works.* New York: Modern Library.
LABARRE, WESTON
  1964 "Animism," in Julius Gould and William L. Kolb (eds.), *A Dictionary of the Social Sciences.* New York: Free Press, pp. 26–29.
LAHONTAN, BARON DE
  1931 *Dialogues curieux et mémoires de l'Amerique septentrionale publiés par Gilbert Chinard.* Baltimore: John Hopkins Press.
LANGNESS, L. L., AND J. C. WESCHLER (EDS.)
  1971 *Melanesia.* Scranton, Penn.: Chandler.
LANTIS, MARGARET
  1952 "Eskimo Herdsman: Introduction of Reindeer Herding to the Natives of Alaska," in Edward Spicer (ed.), *Human Problems in Technological Change.* New York: Russell Sage Foundation, pp. 127–148.
LASWELL, FRED
  n.d. Barney Google and Snuffy Smith. King Features.
LEACH, MARIA (ED.)
  1949 *Dictionary of Folklore, Mythology and Legend.* 2 vols. New York: Funk & Wagnalls.
LEE, RICHARD B.
  1968 "What Hunters Do for a Living, or, How to Make Out on Scarce Resources," in Richard B. Lee and Irven DeVore (eds.), *Man the Hunter.* Chicago: Aldine, pp. 30–48
LEE, RICHARD B., AND IRVEN DEVORE (EDS.)
  1968 *Man the Hunter.* Chicago: Aldine.
LE GROS CLARK, SIR WILFRED E.
  1967 *Man-Apes or Ape-Men?* New York: Holt, Rinehart and Winston.
LE JEUNE, PAUL
  1897 "The Relation of 1634," in R. G. Thwaites (ed.), *Jesuit Relations & Allied Documents.* Vols. 6 and 7. Cleveland: Burrows Bros.

LENNEBERG, ERIC H., AND JOHN M. ROBERTS
  1961 "The Language of Experience: A Study in Methodology," in Sol Saporta (ed.), *Psycholinguistics: A Book of Readings*. New York: Holt, Rinehart and Winston, pp. 493–502.

LESSA, WILLIAM A., AND EVON Z. VOGT (EDS.)
  1965 *Reader in Comparative Religion*. 2nd ed. New York: Harper & Row.

LEVINE, ROBERT A., AND BARBARA B. LEVINE
  1966 *Nyansongo: a Gusii Community in Kenya*. New York: Wiley.

LÉVI-STRAUSS, CLAUDE
  1960 "The Family," in Harry Shapiro (ed.), *Man, Culture, and Society*. New York: Oxford University Press, pp. 261–285.

LINTON, RALPH
  1936 *The Study of Man*. New York: Appleton-Century-Crofts.
  1937 "One Hundred Percent American," *American Mercury* 40:427–429.
  1949 *Most of the World*. Edited by Ralph Linton. New York: Columbia University Press.

LIVERMORE, MARY A.
  1890 *My Story of the War*. Hartford, Conn.: A. D. Worthington.

LORENZ, KONRAD
  1963 *On Aggression*. New York: Harcourt Brace Jovanovich.

MADSEN, WILLIAM
  1964 *The Mexican-Americans of South Texas*. New York: Holt, Rinehart and Winston.

MALINOWSKI, BRONISLAW
  1929 *The Sexual Life of Savages*. New York: Liveright.
  1953 *Sex and Repression in Savage Society*. 4th impression. London: Routledge and Kegan Paul.
  1966 *Crime and Custom in Savage Society*. Totowa, N.J.: Littlefield, Adams.

MARTIN, PAUL S., GEORGE QUIMBY, AND DONALD COLLIER
  1947 *Indians before Columbus*. Chicago: University of Chicago Press.

MCCLELLAND, DAVID C.
  1961 *The Achieving Society*. New York: Van Nostrand.

MEAD, MARGARET
  1950 *Sex and Temperament in Three Primitive Societies*. New York: New American Library.
  1956 *New Lives for Old*. New York: Dell.

MINTURN, LEIGH, AND WILLIAM LAMBERT
  1968 "Motherhood and Child Rearing," in Norman W. Bell and Ezra F. Vogel (eds.), *A Modern Introduction to the Family*. New York: Free Press, pp. 551–557.

MOONEY, JAMES
  1965 *The Ghost Dance Religion*. Chicago: University of Chicago Press.

MUNSELL, JOEL
  1850 *The Annals of Albany*. Albany: published by the author.

MURDOCK, GEORGE PETER
  1949 *Social Structure*. New York: Macmillan.

1950 *Outline of Cultural Materials.* 3rd ed. New Haven, Conn.: Human Relations Area Files.

1968 "The Current Status of the World's Hunting and Gathering Peoples," in Richard B. Lee and Irven DeVore (eds.), *Man the Hunter.* Chicago: Aldine, pp. 13–20.

NETTING, ROBERT McC.
1968 *Hill Farmers of Nigeria.* Seattle: University of Washington Press.

NEW YORK STOCK EXCHANGE
1969 *Fact Book.* New York: New York Stock Exchange.

OLIVER, DOUGLAS L.
1971 "Horticulture and Hsubandry in Solomon Island Society," in L. L. Langness and J. C. Weschler (eds.), *Melanesia.* Scranton, Penn.: Chandler, pp. 52–67.

OPLER, MORRIS E.
1945 "Themes as Dynamic Forces in Culture," *American Journal of Sociology* 51:198–206.

ORCHARD, WILLIAM C.
1929 *Beads and Beadwork of the American Indian.* New York: Heye Foundation.

OSWALT, WENDELL H.
1966 *This Land Was Theirs.* New York: Wiley.

OTTENBERG, SIMON
1968 *Double Descent in an African Society.* Seattle: University of Washington Press.

OTTO, HERBERT A.
1970 *The Family in Search of a Future.* New York: Appleton-Century-Crofts.

PIERCE, JOE E.
1964 *Life in a Turkish Village.* New York: Holt, Rinehart and Winston.

POPE, ALEXANDER
1951 "Essay on Man," in Louis Kronenberger (ed.), *Alexander Pope, Selected Works.* New York: Modern Library, pp. 97–137.

POSPISIL, LEOPOLD
1964 *The Kapauku Papuans.* New York: Holt, Rinehart and Winston.

1967 "The Attributes of Law," in Paul Bohannan (ed.), *Law and Warfare.* Garden City, N.Y.: Natural History Press, pp. 25–41.

POWDERMAKER, HORTENSE
1933 *Life in Lesu.* New York: Norton.

PRICE-WILLIAMS, DOUGLASS R.
1968 "Ethnopsychology I: Comparative Psychological Processes," in James Clifton (ed.), *Introduction to Cultural Anthropology.* Boston: Houghton Mifflin, pp. 304–315.

PRUITT, IDA
1945 *A Daughter of Han: The Autobiography of a Chinese Working Woman.* New Haven, Conn.: Yale University Press.

QUINN, DAVID BEERS
1955 *The Roanoke Voyages 1584–1590.* 2 vols. London: Hakluyt Society.

RADCLIFFE-BROWN, A. R., AND DARYLL FORDE
1964 *African Systems of Kinship and Marriage.* New York: Oxford University Press.

RAGUENEAU, PAUL
1898 Relation of What Occurred in the Country of the Hurons . . . in the Years 1647 & 1648, in R. G. Thwaites (ed.), *The Jesuit Relations & Allied Documents.* Vol. 33. Cleveland: Burrows Bros.

RAPOPORT, ROBERT
1954 "Changing Navajo Religious Values," *Papers of the Peabody Museum.* Vol. 41. Cambridge, Mass.: Harvard University Press.

REDFIELD, ROBERT
1941 *The Folk Culture of Yucatan.* Chicago: University of Chicago Press.
1960 *The Little Community and Peasant Society and Culture.* Chicago: University of Chicago Press.

RICHARDS, A. J.
1964 "Some Types of Family Structure Amongst the Central Bantu," in A. R. Radcliffe-Brown and Daryll Forde (eds.), *African Systems of Kinship and Marriage.* New York: Oxford University Press, pp. 207–251.

RICHARDS, CARA E.
1957 "The Role of Iroquois Women." Ph.D thesis, Cornell University, Ithaca, N.Y.
n.d. "Present State of Social Anthropologic Research in the Diet Patterns, Sanitary Practices and General Activities of 9 Selected Project District Families," in Kurt Deuschle and Hugh S. Fulmer (eds.), "Progress Report Concerning the Period April 1957–March 1, 1959," pp. 53–61.
1963 "Modern Residence Patterns among the Navajo." El Palacio, Spring–Summer, pp. 25–33.
1969 "Presumed Behavior: Modification of the Ideal-Real Dichotomy," *American Anthropologist* 71(6):1115–1116.

RICHARDSON, F. L. W., JR., WITH JAMES BATAL
1949 "The Near East," in Ralph Linton (ed.), *Most of the World.* New York: Columbia University Press, pp. 461–547.

ROPER, MARILYN KEYES
1969 "A Survey of the Evidence for Intra-Human Killing in the Pleistocene," *Current Anthropology* 10(4, part 2):427–450, 456–459.

SAHLINS, MARSHALL D.
1964 "The Segmentary Lineage: An Organization of Predatory Expansion," in Peter B. Hammond (ed.), *Cultural and Social Anthropology.* New York: Macmillan, pp. 181–200.

SAPORTA, SOL (ED.)
1961 *Psycholinguistics: A Book of Readings.* New York: Holt, Rinehart and Winston.

SCHACHTER, STANLEY, AND L. WHEELER
1962 "Epinephrine, Chlorpromazine, and Amusement," *Journal of Abnormal and Social Psychology* 65:121–128.

SCHAPERA, I.
1941 *Married Life in an African Tribe.* New York: Sheridan House.

SCHNEIDER, DAVID M.
  1968 American Kinship: A Cultural Account. Englewood Cliffs,
    N.J.: Prentice-Hall.
SCHULTZ, JAMES WILLARD
  1964 My Life as an Indian. Greenwich, Conn.: Fawcett.
SCHUR, EDWIN M.
  1965 Crimes Without Victims. Englewood Cliffs, N.J.: Prentice-
    Hall.
SCIENCE NEWS
  1966 "Study Shows Biochemical Link: Tolerance for Pain and Sen-
    sory Deprivation," 90:425, November 19, 1966.
SEGALL, M. H., D. J. CAMPBELL, *et al.*
  1963 "Cultural Differences of Perception of Geometric Illusions,"
    Science 139:769–771.
SELEKMAN, BENJAMIN M.
  1947 Labor Relations and Human Relations. New York: McGraw-
    Hill.
SERVAN-SCHREIBER, J. J.
  1968 The American Challenge. New York: Atheneum.
SERVICE, ELMAN R.
  1971 Profiles in Ethnology. Rev. ed. New York: Harper & Row.
SHAPIRO, HARRY L.
  1960 Man, Culture, and Society. New York: Oxford University
    Press.
SIMMONS, LEO W. (ED.)
  1966 Sun Chief: The Autobiography of a Hopi Indian. New Haven,
    Conn.: Yale University Press.
SLOAN, ALFRED P.
  1941 Adventures of a White-Collar Man. In collaboration with Boy-
    den Sparkes. New York: Doubleday, Doran.
SPENCER, ROBERT F., JESSE D. JENNINGS, *et al.*
  1965 The Native Americans. New York: Harper & Row.
SPICER, EDWARD (ED.)
  1952 Human Problems in Technological Change. New York: Rus-
    sell Sage Foundation.
SPIRO, MELFORD E.
  1961 "Social Systems, Personality, and Functional Analysis," in Bert
    Kaplan (ed.), *Studying Personality Cross-Culturally.* Evanston,
    Ill.: Row, Peterson, pp. 93–127.
  1968 "Is the Family Universal—the Israeli Case," in Norman W. Bell
    and Ezra F. Vogel (eds.), *A Modern Introduction to the Family.*
    New York: Free Press, pp. 68–79.
STEPHENS, WILLIAM N.
  1964 The Family in Cross-Cultural Perspective. New York: Holt,
    Rinehart and Winston.
STEWARD, JULIAN H.
  1968 "Causal Factors and Processes in the Evolution of Pre-Farming
    Societies," in Richard B. Lee and Irven DeVore (eds.), *Man the
    Hunter.* Chicago: Aldine, pp. 321–334.
STEWARD, JULIAN H., AND LOUIS C. FARON
  1959 Native Peoples of South America. New York: McGraw-Hill.

SUGIMOTO, ETSU INAGAKI
    1934 *A Daughter of the Samurai.* Garden City, N.Y.: Doubleday, Doran.
SUMNER, WILLIAM GRAHAM
    1911 *Folkways.* Boston: Ginn.
SWARTZ, MARC J., VICTOR J. TURNER, *et al.*
    1966 *Political Anthropology.* Chicago: Aldine.
TALBOT, FRANCIS X., S. J.
    1956 *Saint among the Hurons: The Life of Jean de Brébeuf.* Garden City, N.Y.: Doubleday.
TAYLOR, GEORGE ROGERS
    1962 "The Transportation Revolution," *Economic History of the U.S.* Vol. 4. New York: Holt, Rinehart and Winston.
THWAITES, RUBEN G.
    1896–1901 *The Jesuit Relations & Allied Documents.* 73 vols. Cleveland: Burrows Bros.
TITIEV, MISCHA
    1963 *The Science of Man.* Rev. ed. New York: Holt, Rinehart and Winston.
TOFFLER, ALVIN
    1970 *Future Shock.* New York: Random House.
TURNBULL, COLIN M.
    1962 *The Forest People.* New York: Doubleday.
TYLOR, EDWARD B.
    1965 "Animism," in William A. Lessa and Evon Z. Vogt (eds.), *Reader in Comparative Religion.* 2nd ed. New York: Harper & Row, pp. 10–21.
VAN GENNEP, ARNOLD
    1960 *The Rites of Passage.* Chicago: University of Chicago Press.
WALKER, WINTON
    1959 *A History of the Christian Church.* New York: Scribner.
WAX, MURRAY
    1968 "Religion and Magic," in James Clifton (ed.), *Introduction to Cultural Anthropology.* Boston: Houghton Mifflin, pp. 224–242.
WEIDENREICH, FRANZ
    1939 "Six Lectures on Sinanthropus Pekinensis," *Bulletin of The Geological Society of China,* No. 19.
WESTERMARCK, EDWARD
    1921 *The History of Human Marriage.* London: Macmillan.
WHITING, JOHN W. M.
    1961 "Socialization Process and Personality," in Francis L. K. Hsu (ed.), *Psychological Anthropology.* Homewood, Ill.: Dorsey Press, pp. 355–380.
WILLIAMS, ROBIN M., JR.
    1964 *Strangers Next Door.* Englewood Cliffs, N.J.: Prentice-Hall.
WISSLER, CLARK
    1922 *The American Indian.* New York: Oxford Press.
WOLF, ARTHUR P.
    1966 "Childhood Association, Sexual Attraction and the Incest Taboo: A Chinese Case," *American Anthropologist* 68(4):883–898.

WOOLLEY, C. LEONARD
   1965   Ur of the Chaldees.   New York: Norton.
WYNNE-EDWARDS, V. C.
   1962   Animal Dispersion in Relation to Social Behavior.   London:
      Oliver and Boyd.
YANG, MARTIN C.
   1945   A Chinese Village.   New York: Columbia University Press.
YOUNG, FRANK W.
   1962   "The Function of Male Initiation Ceremonies: A Cross-Cultural
      Test of an Alternative Hypothesis," *American Journal of Soci-
      ology* 67: 379–396.
ZINSSER, HANS
   1935   Rats, Lice, and History.   Boston: Little, Brown.

Index

abandoning sick or aged, 24, 153
abortion, 26, 143
accumulation of goods, 38, 39, 54, 56, 57, 108
achieved status, *see* status
activity patterns, 13, 22–25, 54, 62, 65, 70, 76; farming, 54, 70; hunting, 13, 22–25
ad-hocracy, 116–117
affiliation, 226–228, 232–235, 238–241, 247–248
affinal, 118, 246; *see also* in-laws
afterlife, 73, 263, 273
age, 154, 177, 226
aggression, 17, 175–179
agriculture, 32, 39, 44–53, 68–70, 116, 210, 291; and animal domestication, 68; and civilization, 59; and cooperation, 52–53; and deferred gratification, 72; and future, 72; and horticulture, 68; and population, 58; and pottery, 60; and slavery, 57; and time, 72; and transhumance, 62; commercial, 77; decline in, 53; decision making in, 70; incipient, 39; methods in, 32, 66, 68; seed funnel in, 68; subsistence, 51
American Revolution, 162
animals: attitudes toward, 62, 126, 181–182; domestic, 29, 44, 60, 61, 62, 63, 65, 66, 68, 73, 76; game, 27, 33, 37, 39, 124–126, 252, 275; grazing, 61; treatment of, 31, 125–126, 181, 182
animatism, 257, 258
animism, 257, 258
antelope, 27, 33, 124–126
anthropologist, 182, 291, 298
anthropology: applied, 283–286, 293, 301; branches of, 97, 281–283, 287, 295–296; cognitive, 295, 296, 301; con-

troversy in, 297–299; definition of, 281–282; medical, 295–296; theoretical, 97, 283–284, 286–292, 293–295; training for, 182, 299–300
anxiety, 148, 151, 274–278
archeology, 281, 282, 287
Arndt, John P., 141, 157
art, 168, 249, 270, 271, 273, 282, 283, 288; cave, 36, 270, 271, 273
artifact, xiv, 28, 111, 184, 282
ascribed status, *see* status
athletes, 186
atlatl, 20, 32; *see also* weapons
attitudes, 70, 171; toward animals, 62, 126, 181–182; toward death, 9, 10, 12, 24, 26, 92; toward land, 55, 56, 199; toward life, 24, 26; toward nature, 51, 70, 71; toward romantic love, 244–245; toward sex, 215, 216, 217, 242; toward time, 72, 73; toward violence, 85, 252; toward women, 5, 85, 177, 206, 207, 210
Australopithecus: *africanus*, 15; *robustus*, 15
authority, 140, 141, 144, 147, 157, 158, 161, 228
avoidance, 153, 246
avunculocal, *see* residence patterns

BaMbuti, 122–130, 131, 132, 134, 150, 156, 158, 160, 182; *see also* Pygmies
band, 133
barbarians, 65, 251
barter, 109, 110
basic: assumption, 173, 174; maintenance system, 175, 176, 195; personality, 175; postulates, 211, 292, 293
beads: as money, 109; as riches, 85; gifts of, 85–88